AF291394

For my father Dave Illingworth,
a watchmaker who loved the sea

THE WATCH MAN
BALNAKIEL

SHONA ILLINGWORTH

Texts by

MARTIN A. CONWAY

CATERINA ALBANO

JILL BENNETT

STEVEN BODE

CONTENTS

FOREWORD

This publication revolves around two key works by the artist Shona Illingworth. Made one after the other between 2006 and 2009, the video and sound installations *The Watch Man* and *Balnakiel* are highly personal but extraordinarily resonant studies of memory, history and place that examine the damage that is done to the psyche by the experience of war and the equally pervasive and insidious marks that have been left on the physical landscape by the presence of the military. These two companion pieces have also been informed by a rich exchange between the artist and the cognitive neuro-psychologist Professor Martin A. Conway. Developed over a number of years, this ongoing dialogue has illuminated both the deep-seated influence and the complex and dynamic processes of memory, highlighting the spatiality of memory as well as its temporal dimension.

The nature and extent of this mutually instructive collaboration manifests itself in a series of texts by Conway that appear throughout the publication, and which are accompanied by some of the numerous 'memory drawings' that have been an important component in the creative exchange between artist and scientist. These are joined by sound drawings, photography, written material and diagrams by the artist, which further enlarge and reveal the process of her investigations. The depth of ideas opened up by this distinctive field of enquiry is further elaborated in a trio of specially commissioned essays, which draw out the intellectual and emotional range of this powerful body of work.

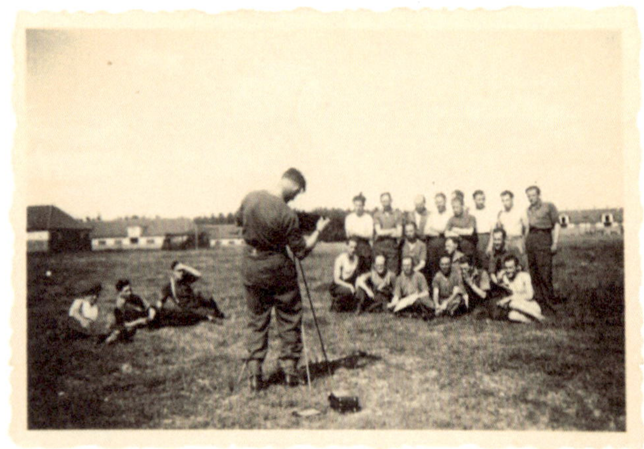

Fallingbostel April 1945
Photograph from the personal collection of the artist

THE WATCH MAN

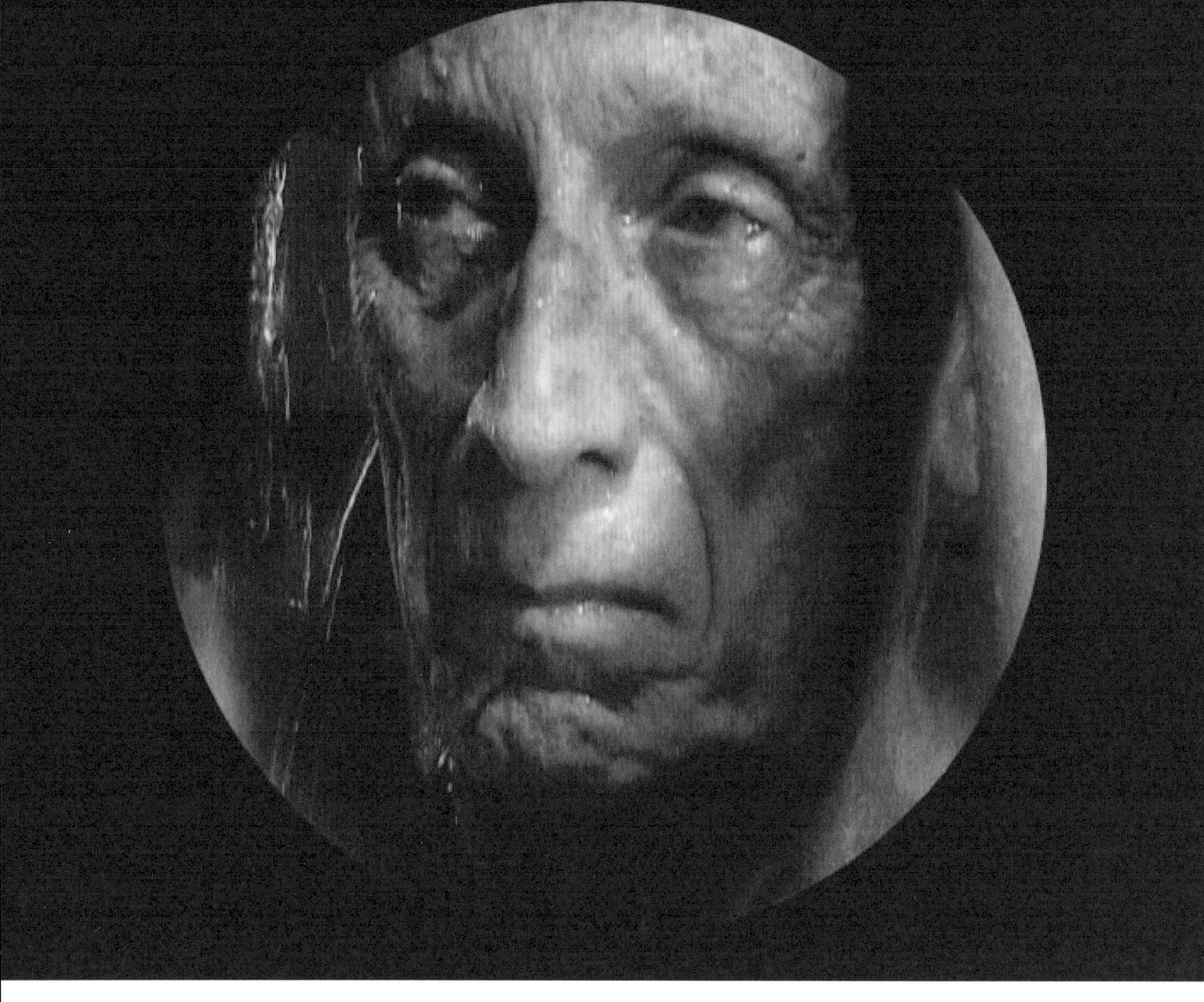

Digital video stills, sound transcript and
voice transcripts from *The Watch Man*, 2007

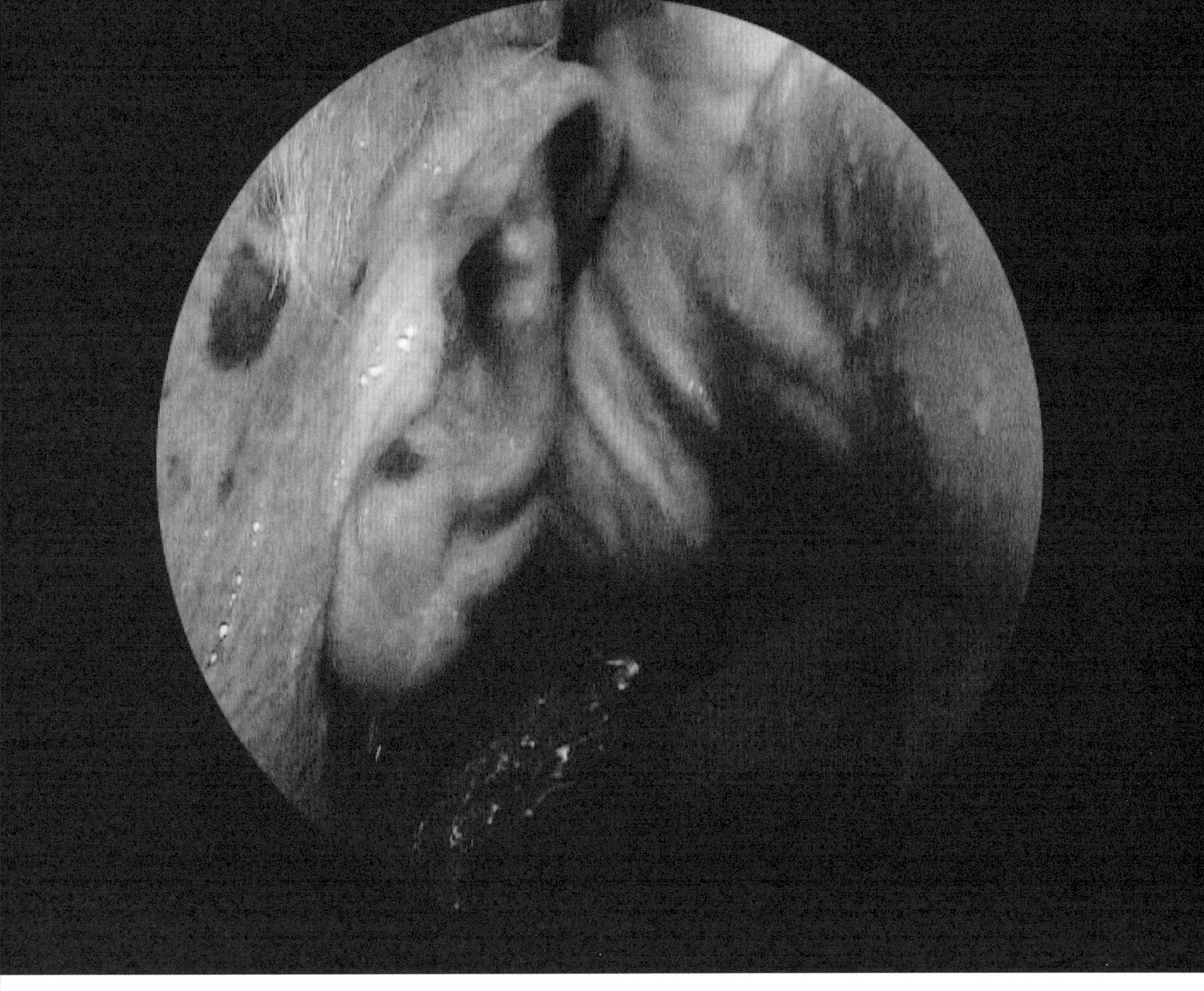

there were bodies in the woods for goodness sake

Sky - deep soft deep tone -
round edged pushing warm
note dummm dummm
dummm harder note echo
repeat under low frequency
click sharp cutting metallic
click tick tock clocks cogs
eye loupe and wheel close -
gentle flick of finger
spinning metal slipping
catching clicking bright
sound out of synch clocks
ticking riding over -
"The people did not want

The people did not
want to know – they
did not want to hear

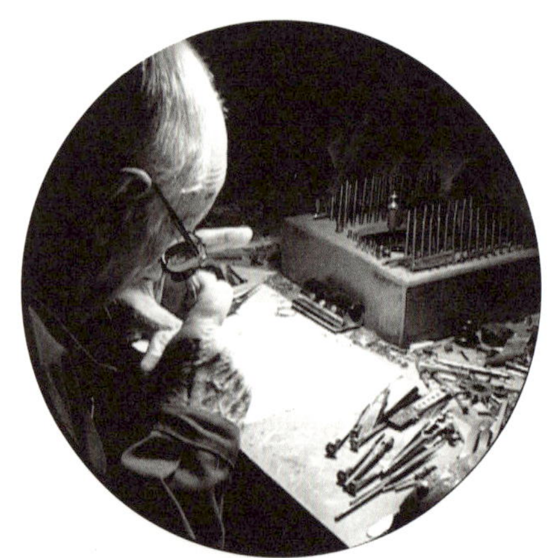

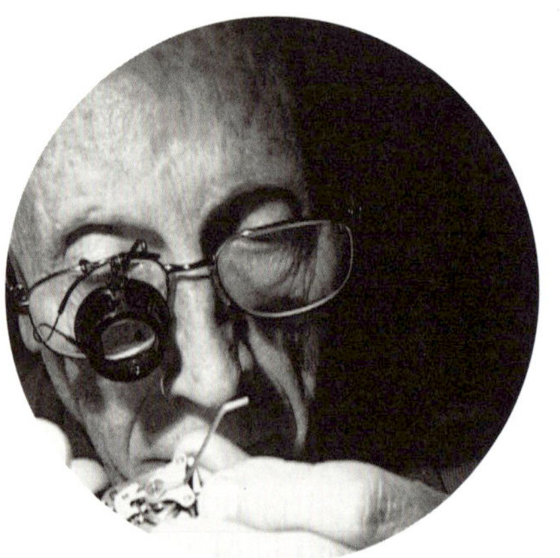

to know - They did not
want to hear". "You're
shunned - You're a survivor
damn you!" - clicking fast
rhythmical close, high thin
bright click chick clicking
over slipping metal over
deep soft low tone measuring
counting space rhythm undertow
- slightly out of synch - red
eye ruby magnified drawing
into centre hole, dark through
lenses .. eye vision moving in
- quiet high pitched whir -

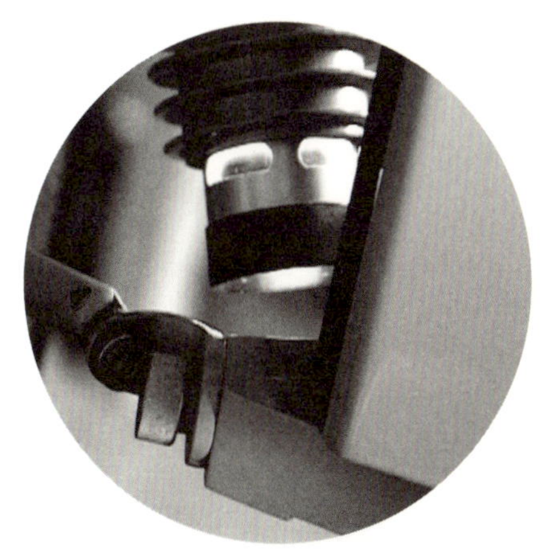

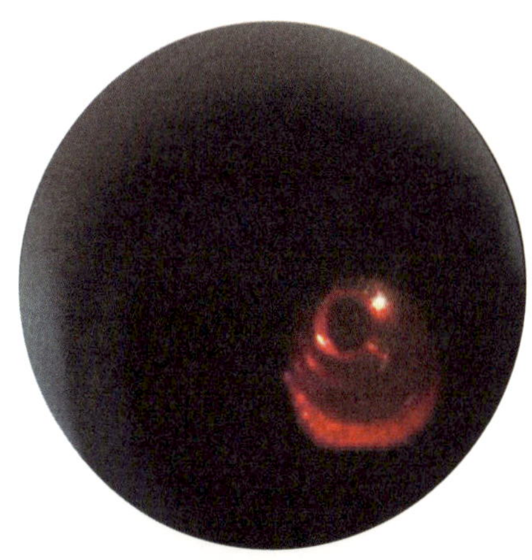

- spinning blade getting
closer louder faster _
clicking clocks stopped _
quiet deep low sound pacing
time dummm dummm
dummm - shattered gold-
fractured fragment bright
yellow gold constellation
on dark - drawing in,
reverberating - high spin
whir, deeper softer vibration
rising as eye moves across
ruby and gold - circling -
ruby becomes branches
criss-crossing orange sky -
scarred iris - blades spinning

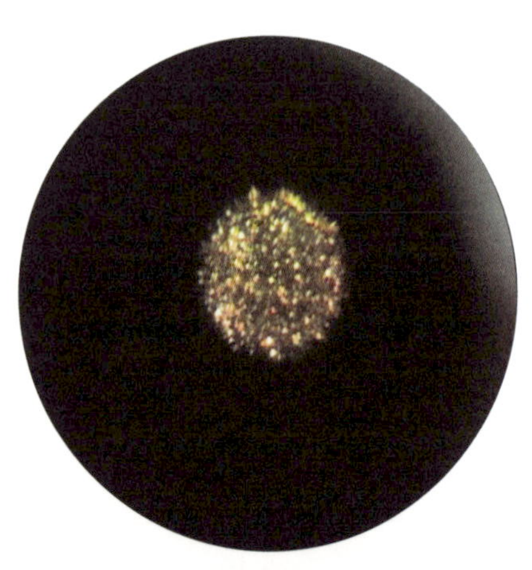

cutting sound in the air –
draw back – deep rumble –
sound felt behind the teeth
tongue pressing – drawing
back – blades cutting
high thin sound echo loop
thick in air – reverberating
in layers – pulling in
different directions –
cutting splicing the space
flat note pressing – one
tone behind the others –
an echo tone – draw back
dark pendulum – a shock
sound deep and low –

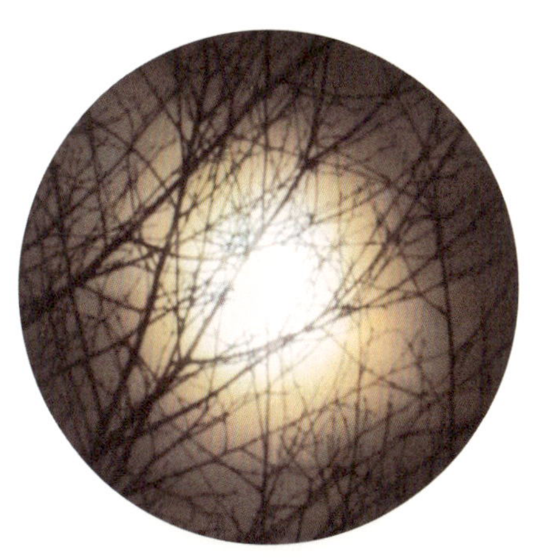 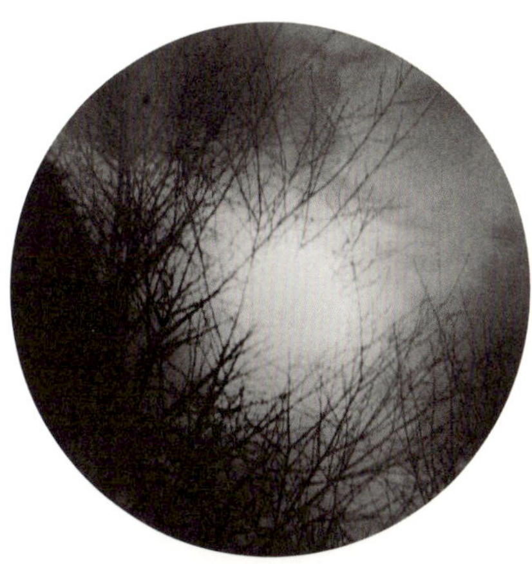 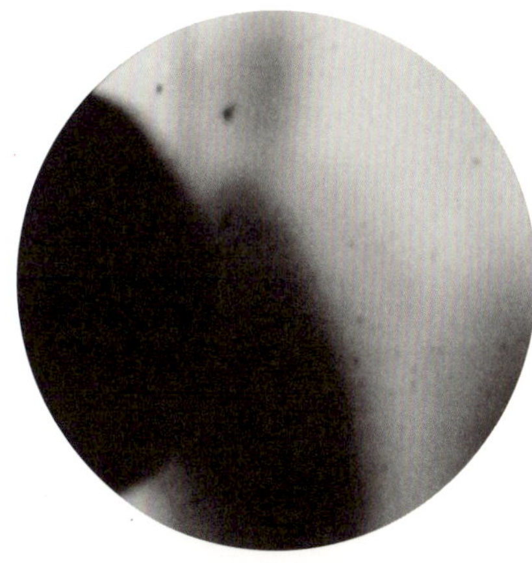

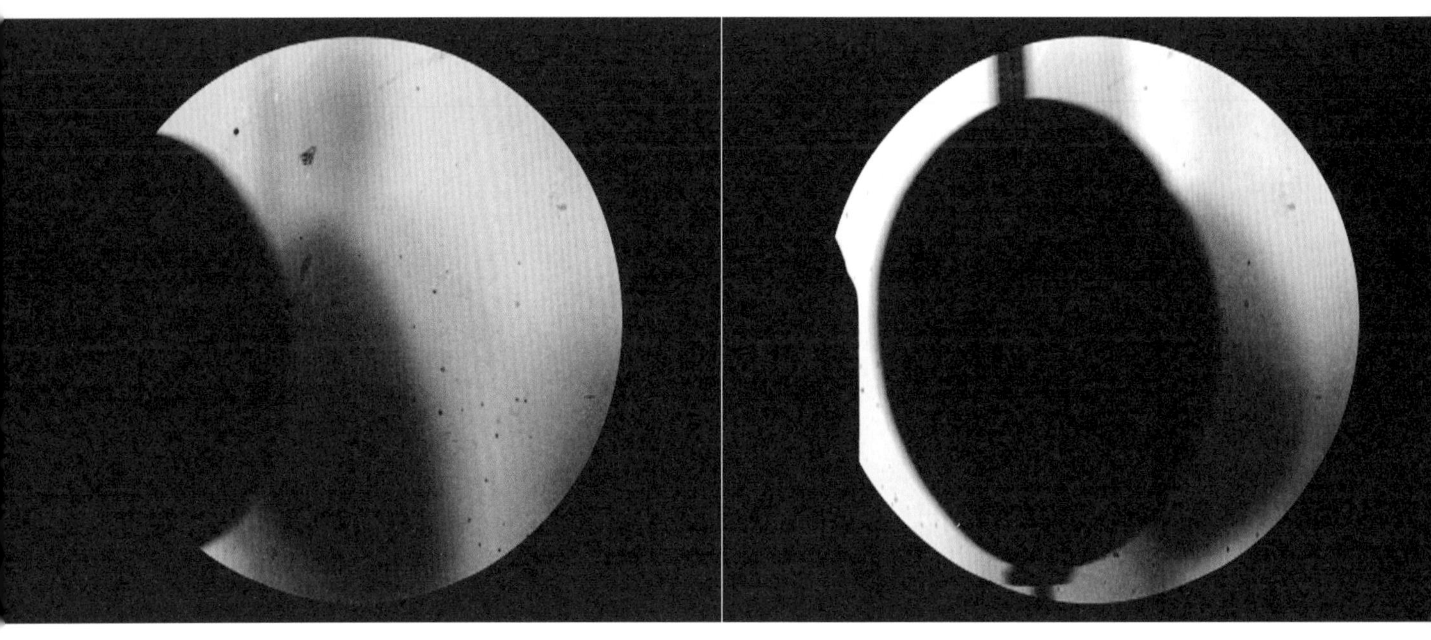

Over and over and over I would get this horrible –

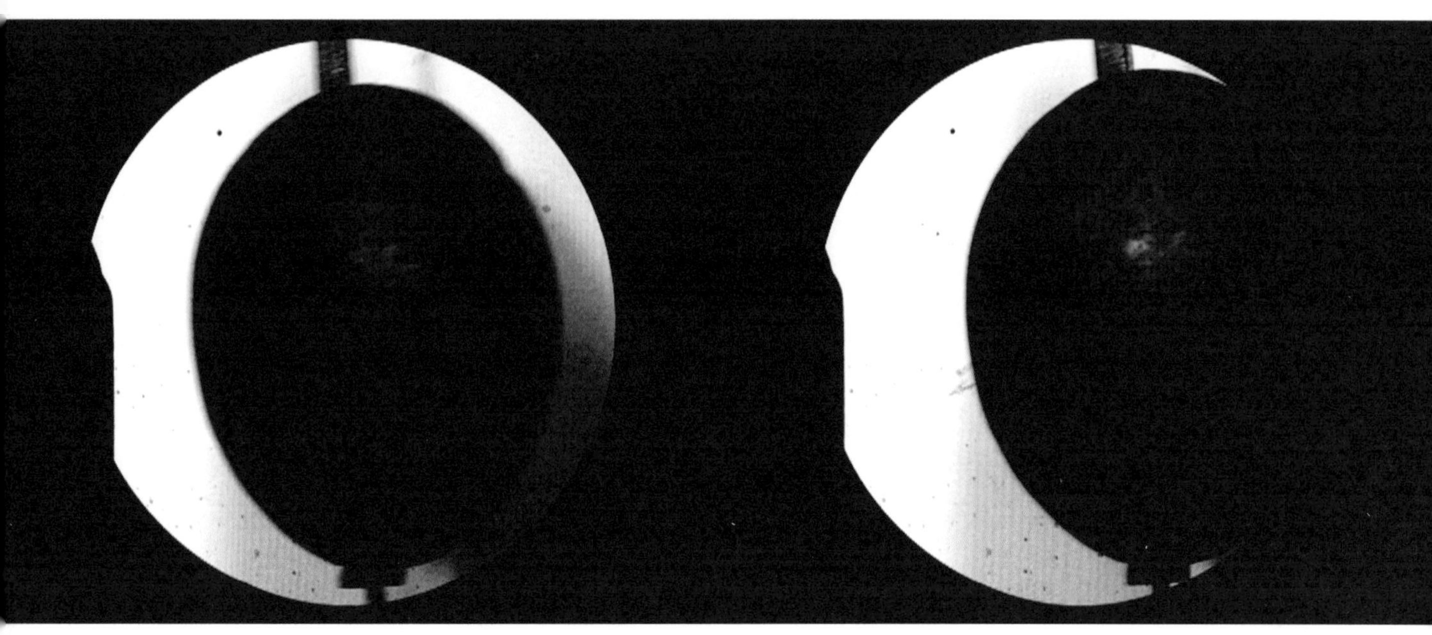

absolutely horrible – suffocating –

frightening in so much as it's unstoppable

"and it's - you think you're
gonna die sort of "feeling"
whirring blades fade away -
dark - shadow sphere swings -
deep low echo note swings -
thock - an underwater echo -
thock - deep soft deep tone
fills head and expands softly
against the temples, back
of the neck, in the chest -
dummm dummm dummm
metal spinning whirring,
metal on metal spinning
friction crackling over metal
spin - pushing forward -

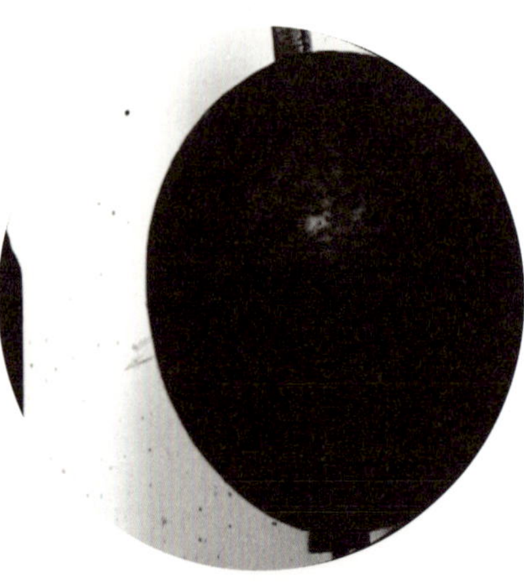

getting louder - low soft
deep tone, pacing rhythm,
swing pendulum shadow
casts dark curtain of bright
white spots - constellation
of reflected light passing
across a dark plane - pouring
running draining water, dripping
sharp hard splashing running
rivulets - hard echo sound -
over soft deep tone pacing
water - curling sound push
forward fall back push forward
fall back - hard bright drip, soft

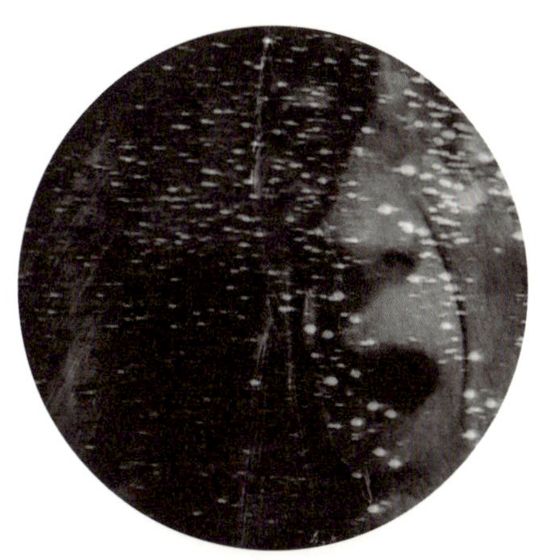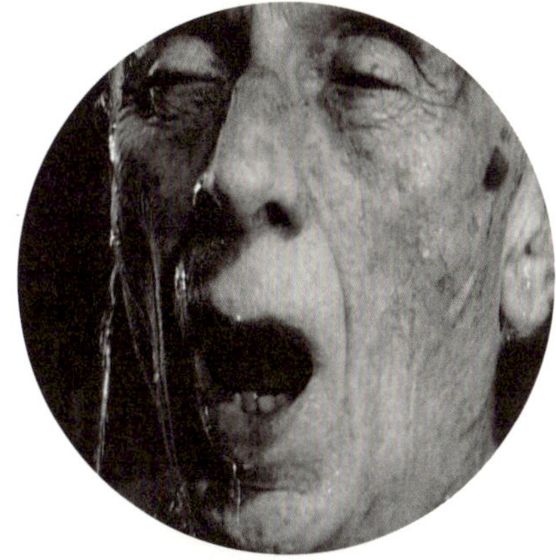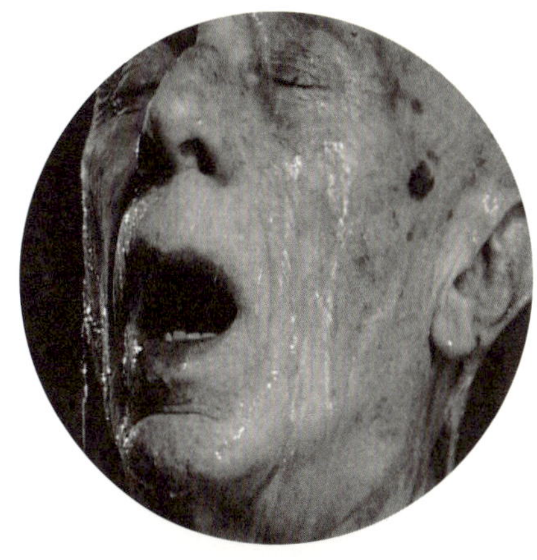

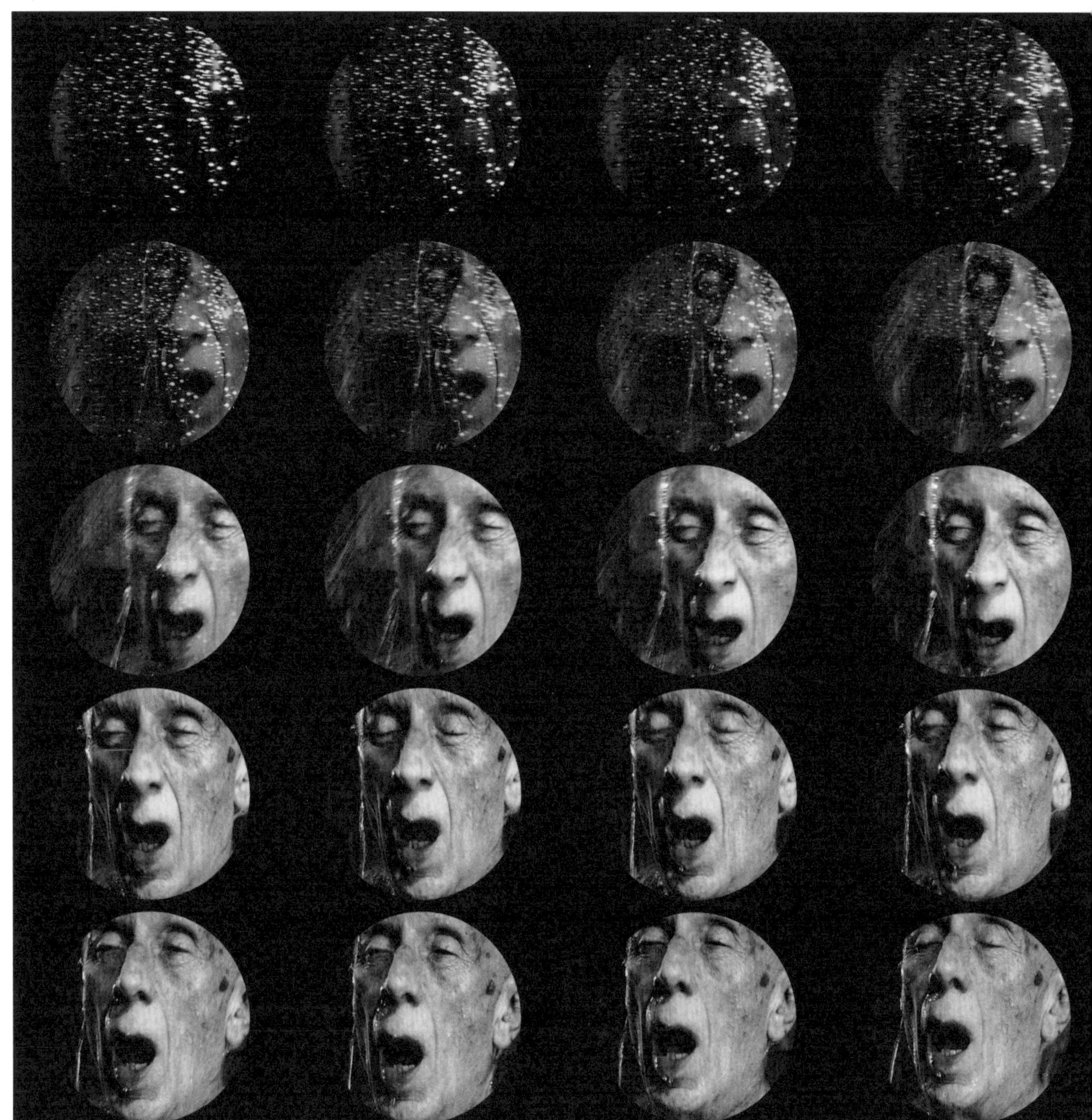

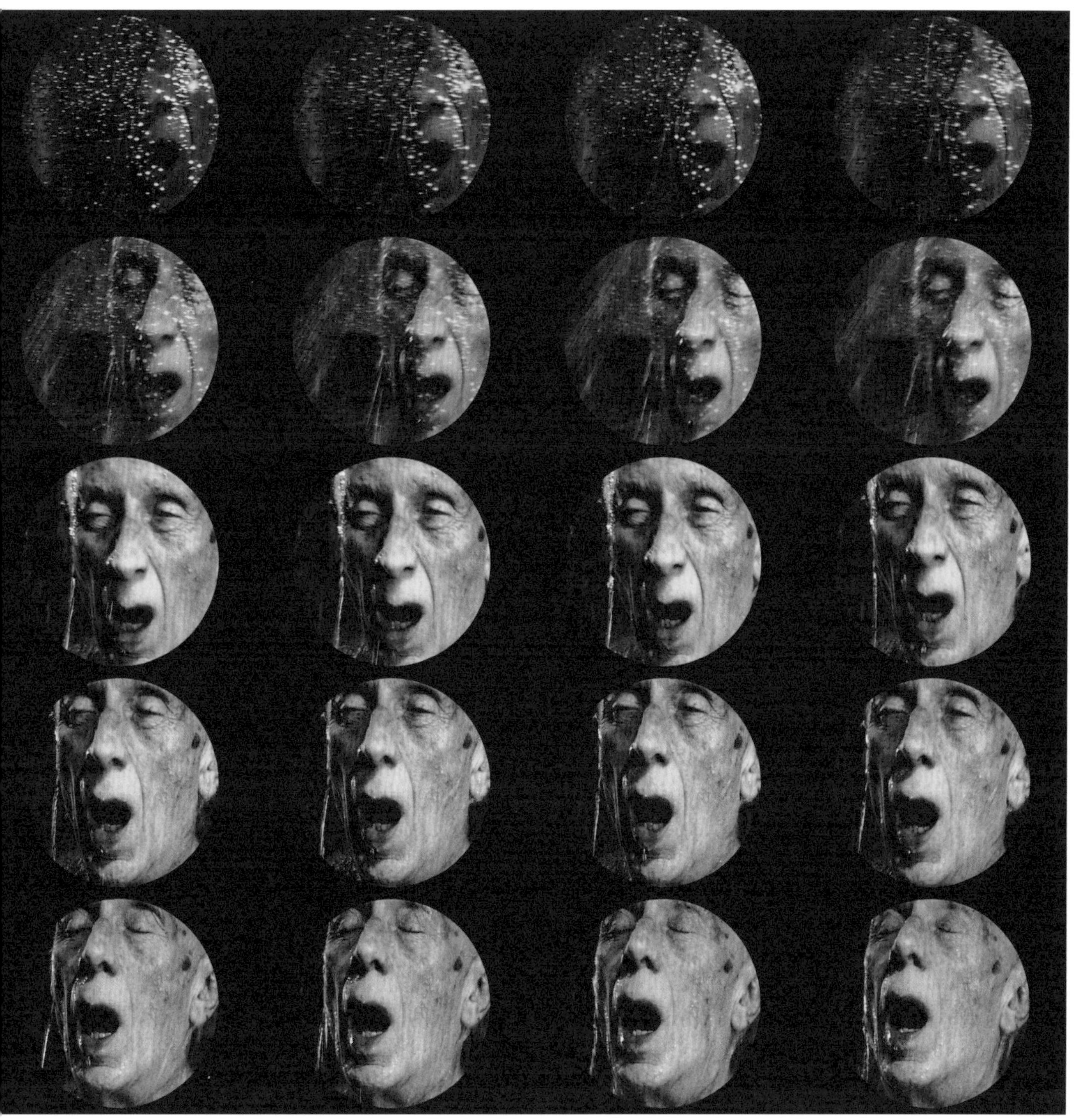

running flow, curling
gurgling draining - water
on skin on lips on hair
on lashes - louder bright
higher water sound pouring
dripping splashing round
head - turning ears - skin
on water on skin - gentle
lapping flowing - harder
coiling dripping - water on
water - hard echo chamber -
rush of water - sudden
urgent hard hammering
sound - intense driving heart

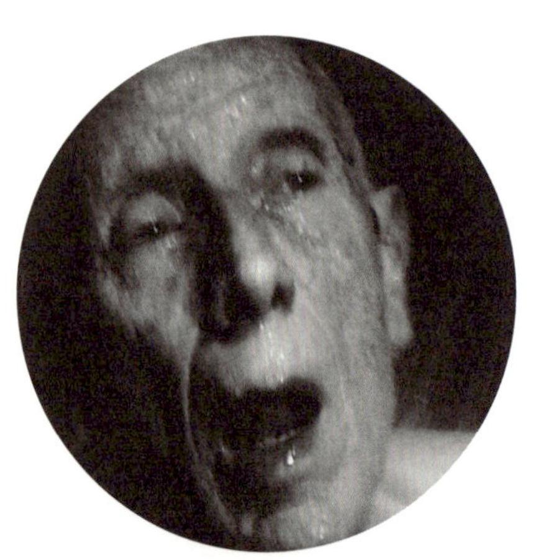

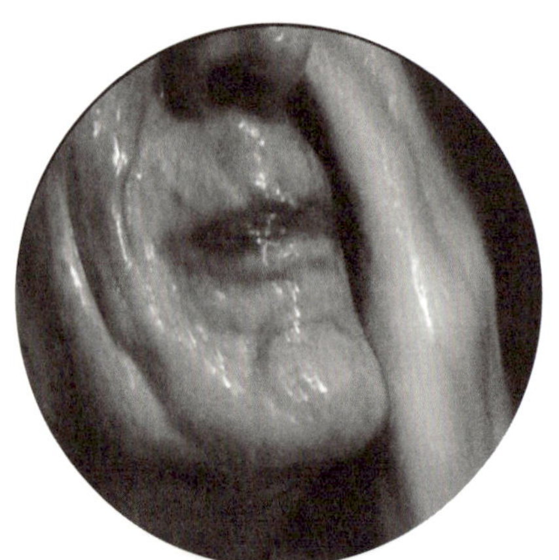

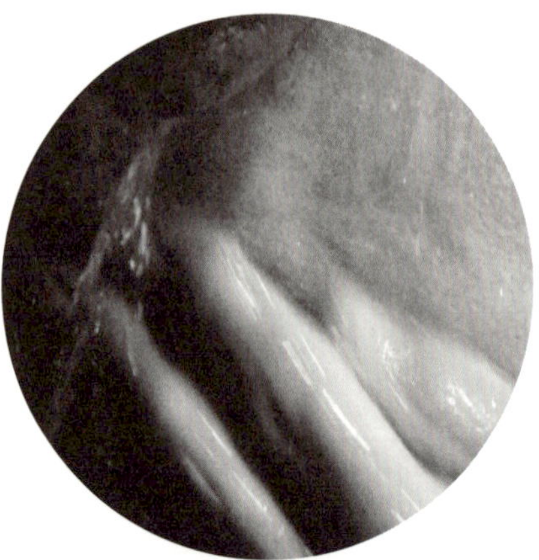

beat rhythm - closed eye
to open ear - sound passing
inside to out - outside to in -
water coursing down chest
wall - glistening rivulets -
move in - hammering louder
louder - water running -
hard bright high sound -
deep hammering driving
through it - close into chest
wall - water streaming down
face - dripping, running
hammering - rush of air -
thin fine rain in trees -
hammering sound -

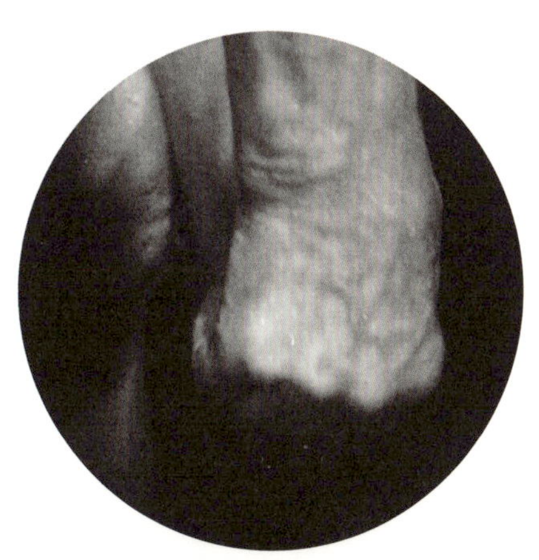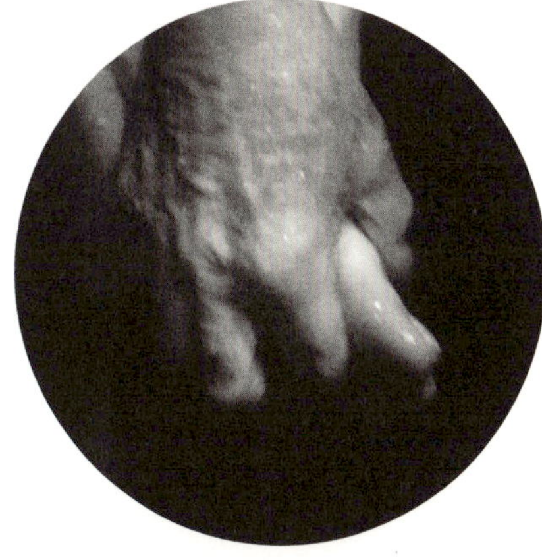

"There were bodies in the woods there for goodness sake" - air rushing wind - water running on skin - insistent hammering air - agitating rushing louder - rain filled air caught in branches - big space - rain drops hitting the ground - earth - wind filled rain pushing, rain static crackle, cut under with relentless hammering inside the chest wall - dark pendulum

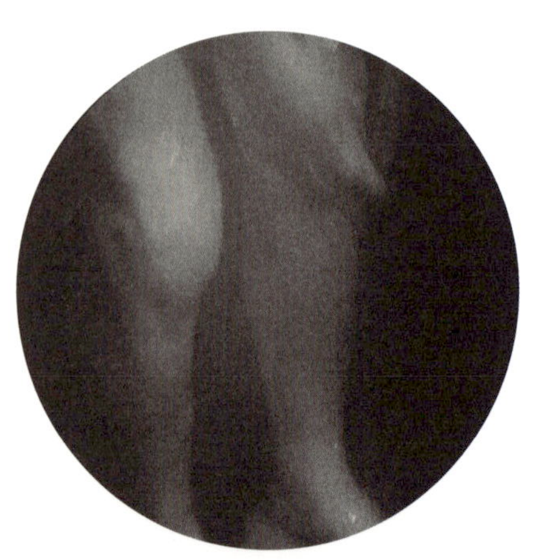

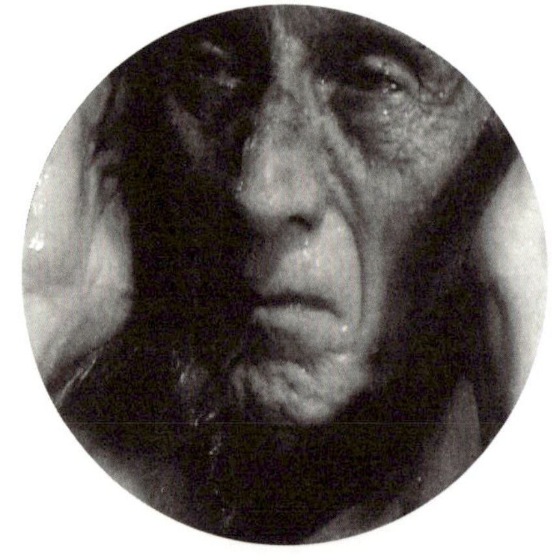

shadow swings eclipsing
light sphere - "As you
approached it there was
this very shallow - valley -
flat valley not terribly wide" -
metal on metal spinning,
cutting high pitched sound
into air - "Somewhere down
to the left there was smoke
rising" - spinning cutting
hard metal lathe spin piercing
air, fast rhythm cutting over
fading low hammering -
hot smoke to ear, lathe
spinning over ground, metal

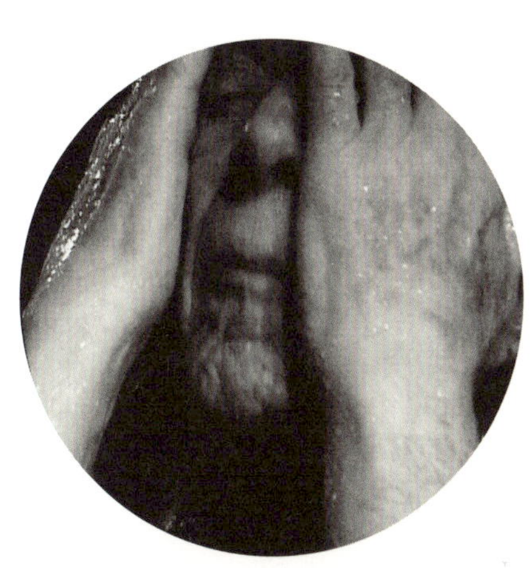

As you approached it
there was this very
shallow – valley –
flat valley not terribly
wide.

Wheel cutting like blades —
faint whir rising louder
and louder over spinning
metal whir racing, deeper
thrum rising as large blades
cut air turbulence,
reverberating whir hum,
deeper resonant rumble —
over cut and paced with
tock tick — tock tick — tock tick
tock tick — ching, metal clock
tock tick — fast paced urgent.
cutting air copter blade whir
louder and louder — high

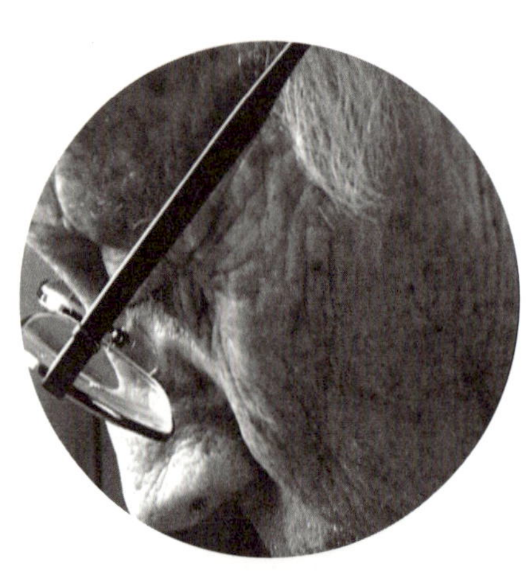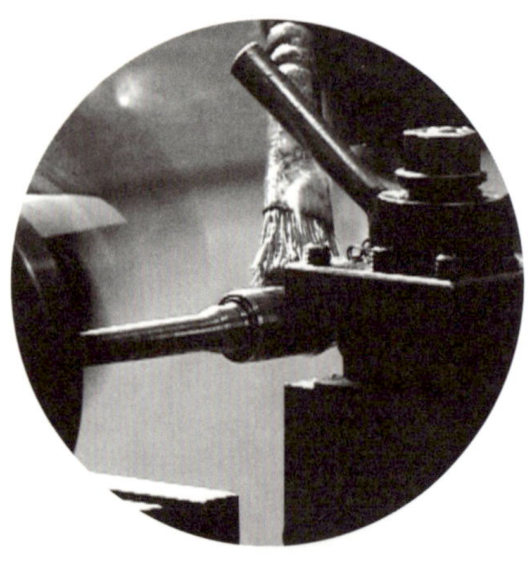

pitched thick reverberation
of ching ching metal echo
of clock ticking - hand
brushes over empty clock
face - copter blade whir
thickens - hammering
starts again - loud - ruby
set with tweezers magnified
through thick glass lens -
tock tick - tock tick -
hammering fades - quiet -
quiet escapement whir -
spinning metal cogs and
wheels cut into rhythm
of high thick cutting copter blade

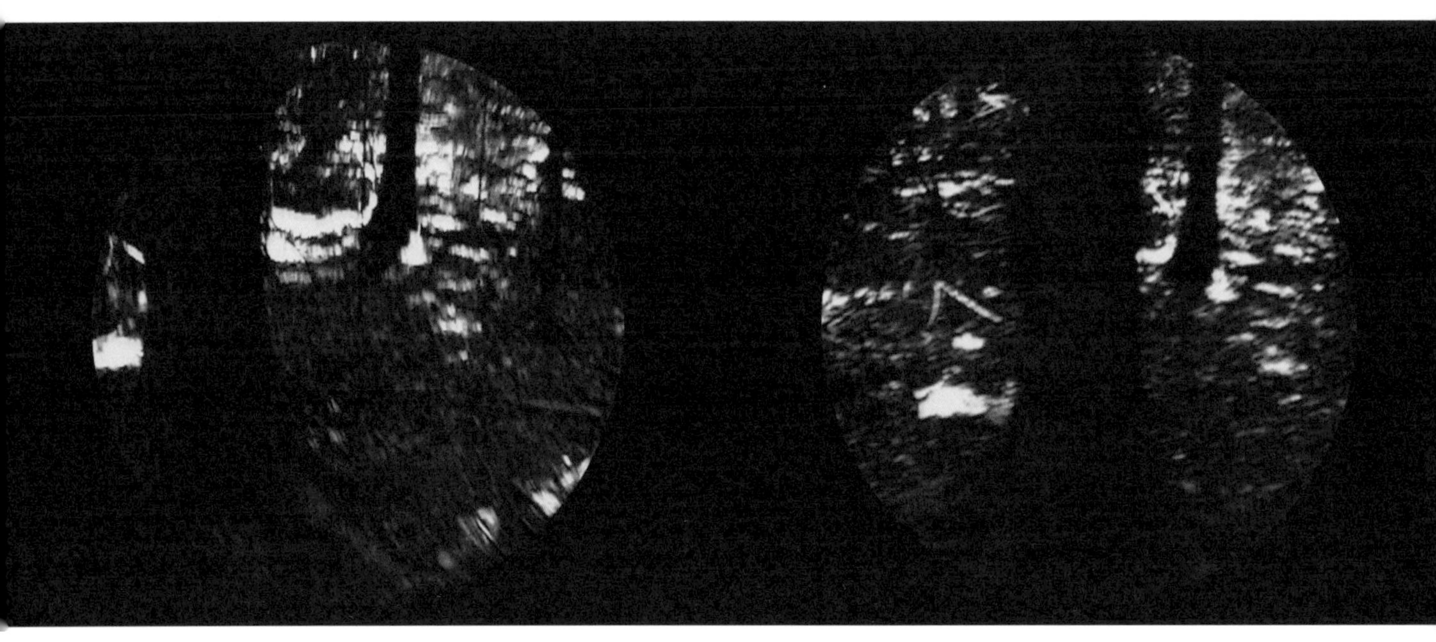

They'd already dug one –

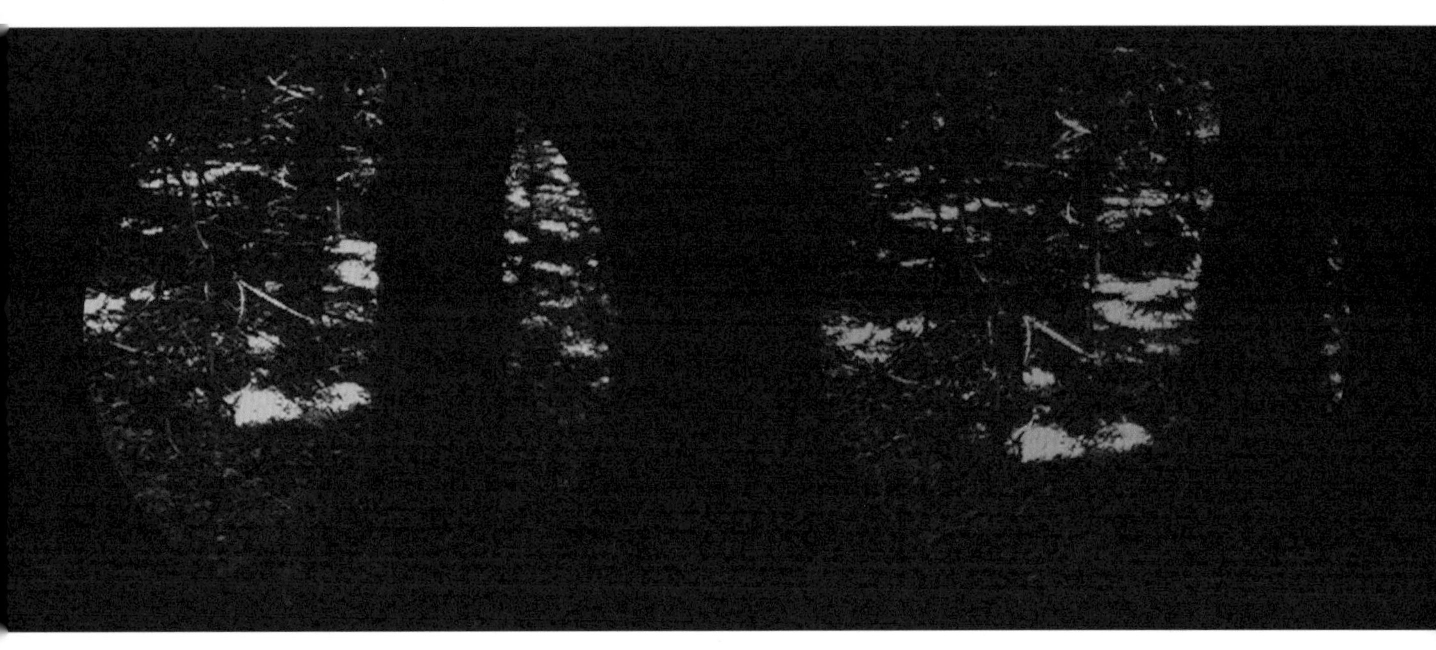

they'd filled it with corpses and they'd covered it over with soil

Whir quieter now – tock tick –
tock tick – tock tick –
lighter metal on metal
bright – fast pacing – hard
hammering builds up –
then quiet – sweep of white
tissue – quieter now – bright
metal ticking of clock, whir
hammering and lathe –
hammering, ticking metal
teeth cut drop wheel into
place, escapement spin –
bright delicate whir stopped

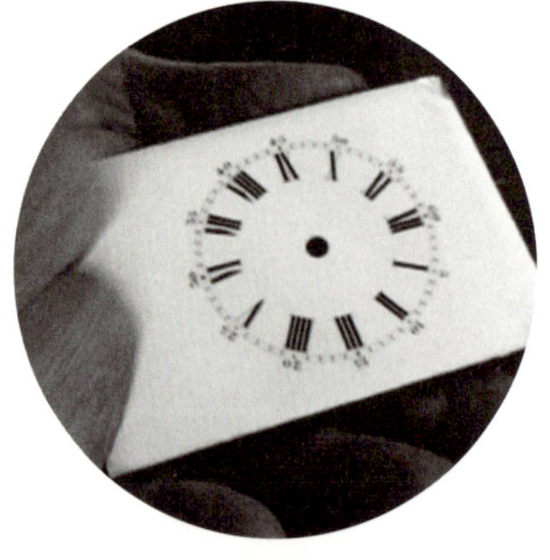

by hand, clock ticking fast
- dark pendulum shadow -
deep low thock sound
rumbles to softer echo
in thick air - pendulum
dark shadow sphere passes
across frame - clock
chimes twice - clock tick
slow and shadow passes
back - sound of metal
instrument dragging on
surface - intake of breath -
deep low sound and
pendulum passes -

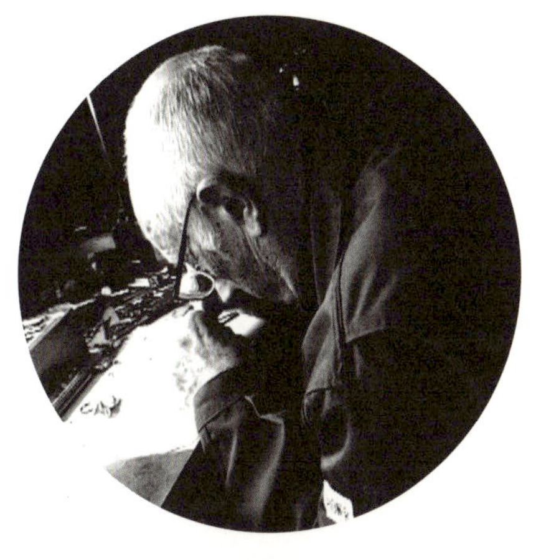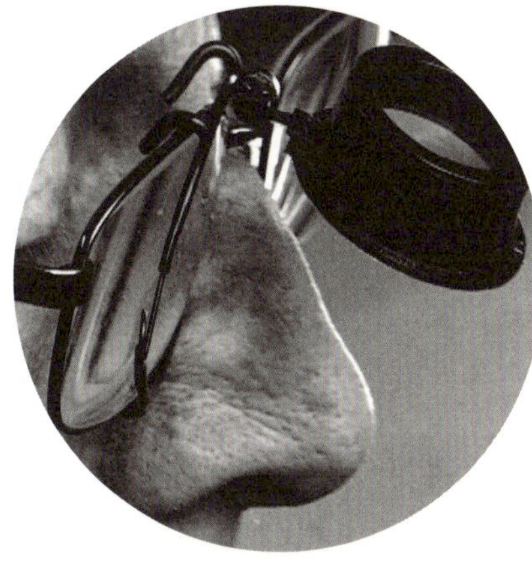

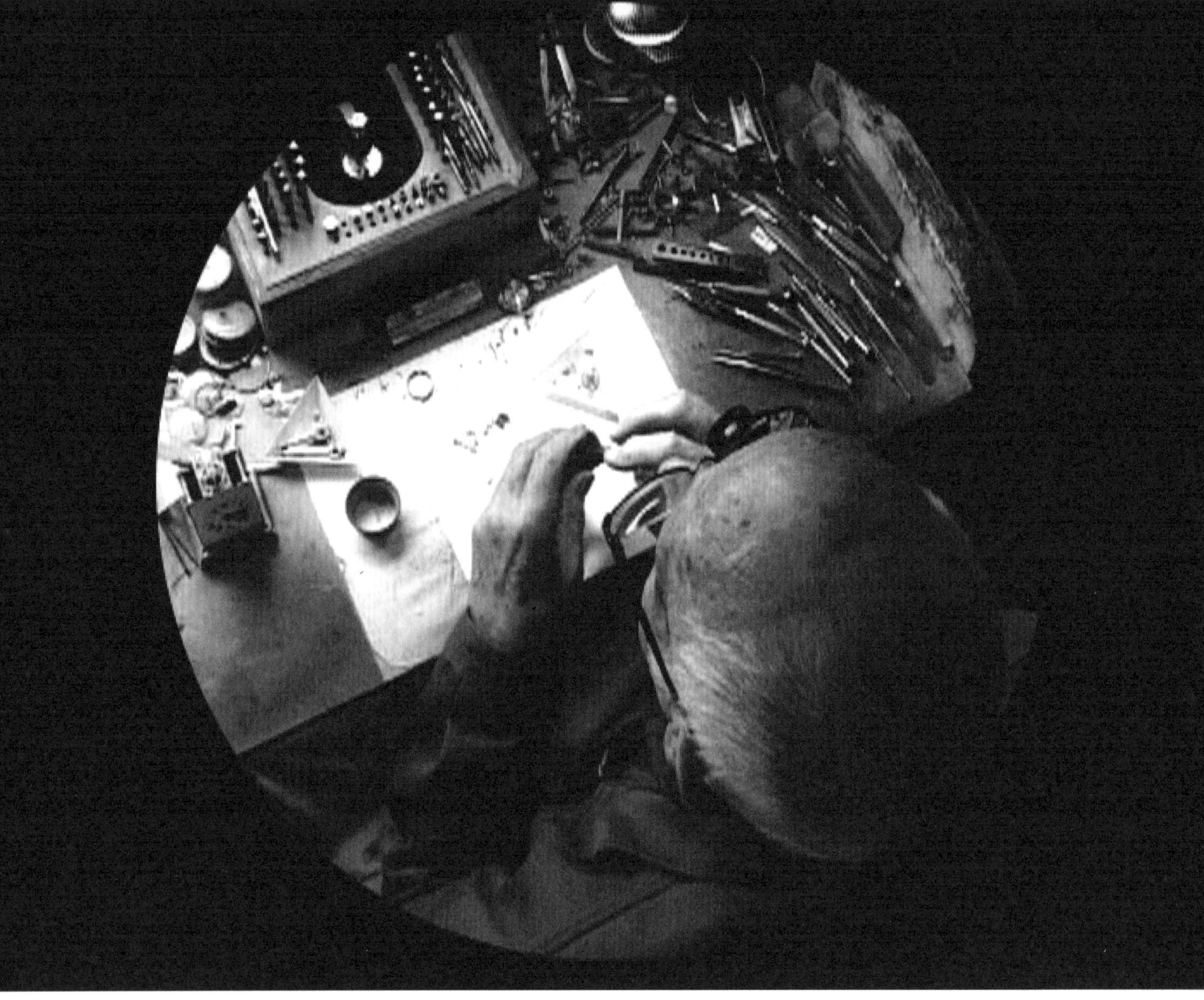

They'd already dug one quite huge grave

– just, just a huge, a huge cavity

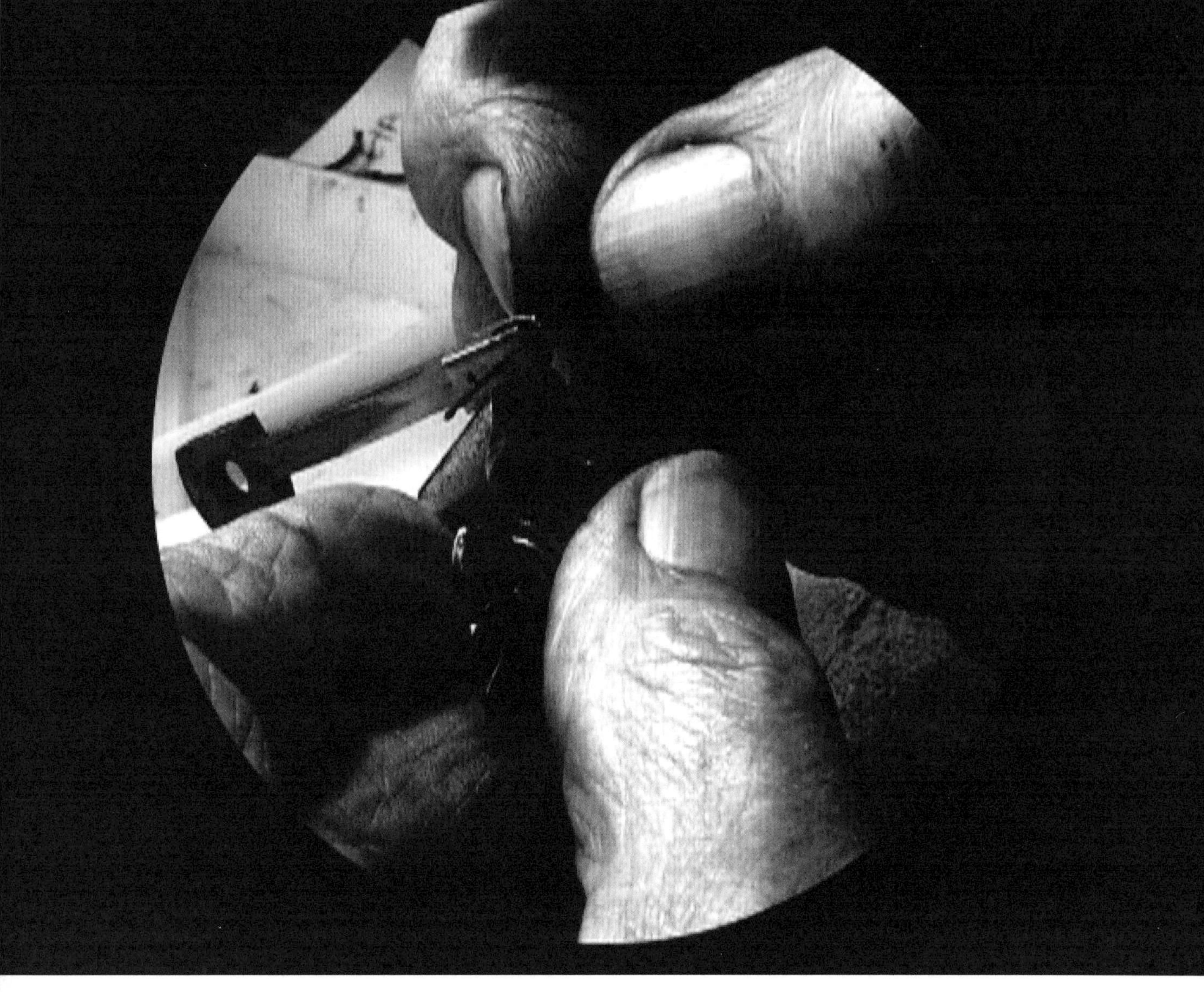

The next one – they were still actually bringing corpses

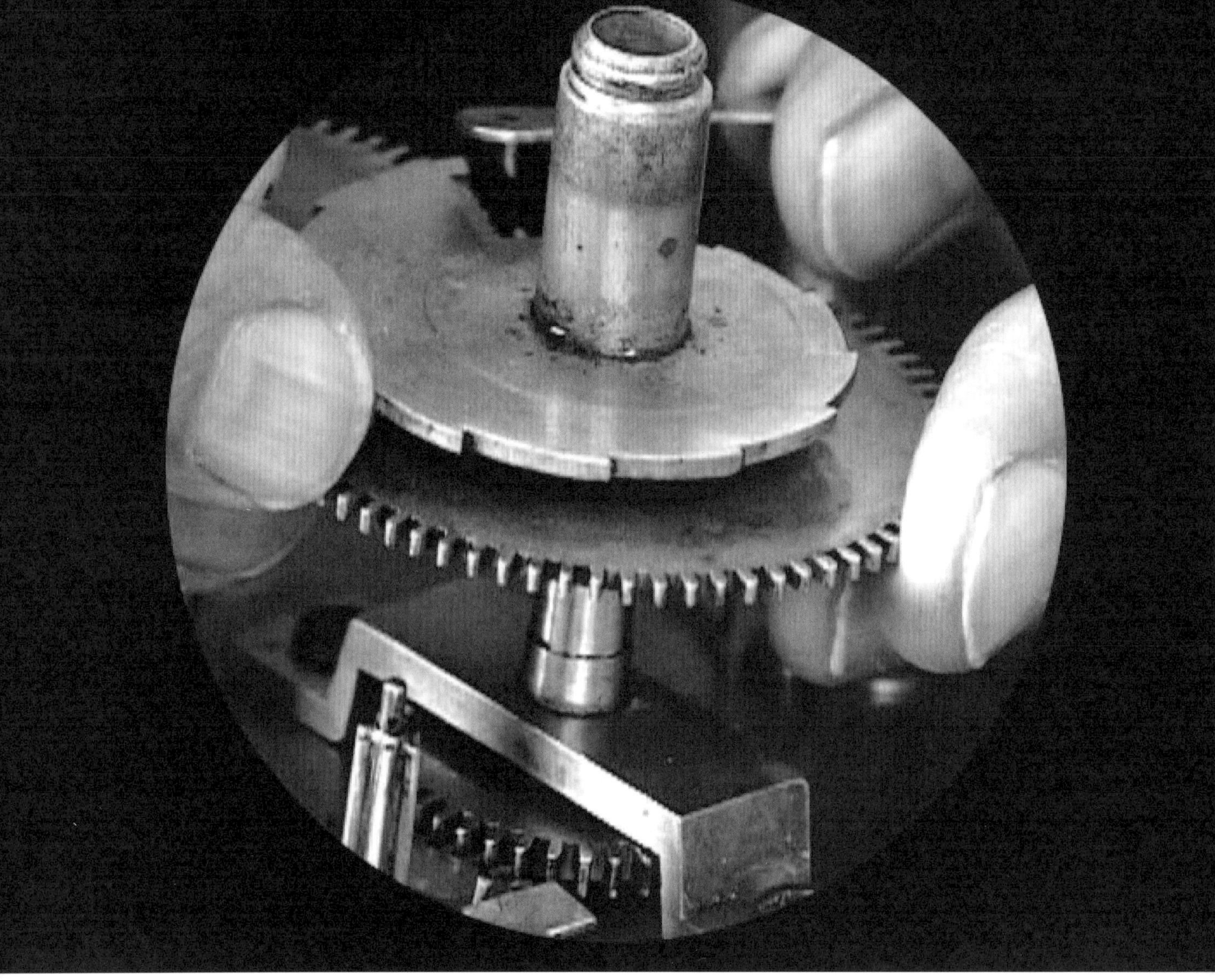

They were all skeletons,

they didn't really look like people, human beings at all,

they were just bone

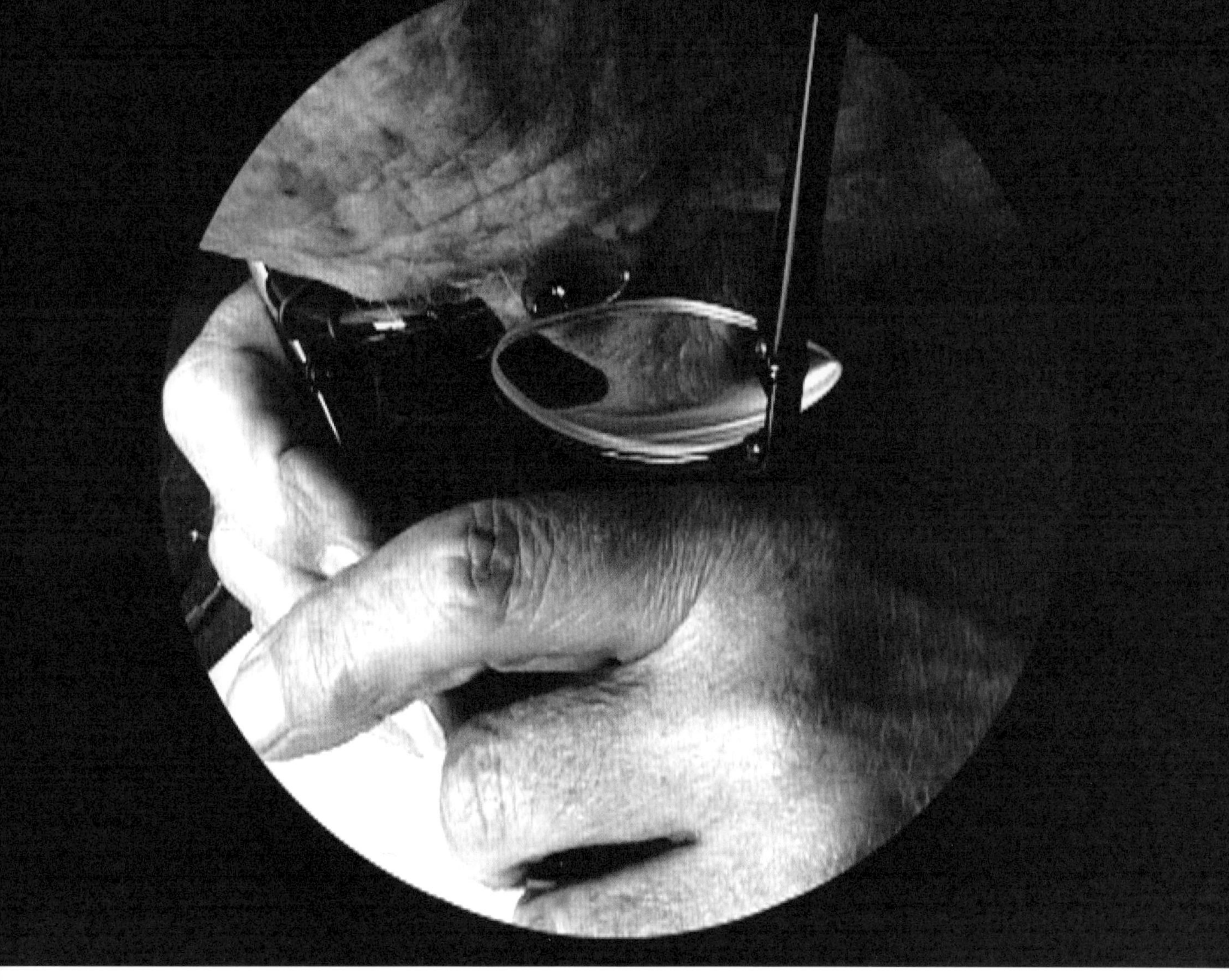

Four o'clock, just a minute past four

breath, breathing through nose
clock chiming - a gold bright
warm clear ringing sound -
fast - even paced now over
deep soft deep tone marking
pacing time moving - chiming
marks another rhythm, fading
out - pendulum swings with
deep resonant warm tone and
then low hard round edged
thock and echo sound dummm
dummm dummm quiet, low,
gentle - deep echo chamber cut
through with sudden insistant
hammering hammering hammering
and bird sound - high tweeting

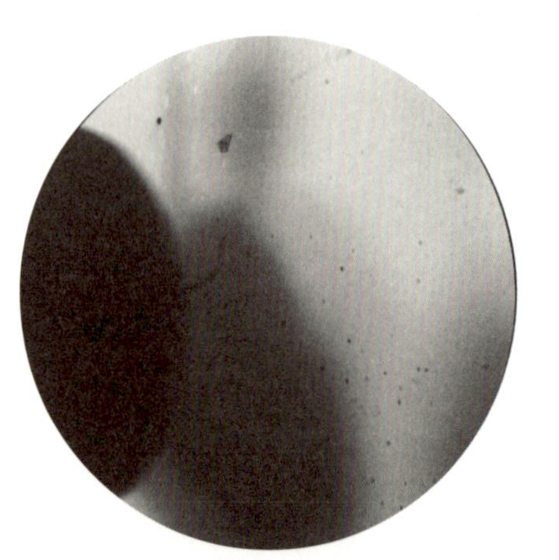
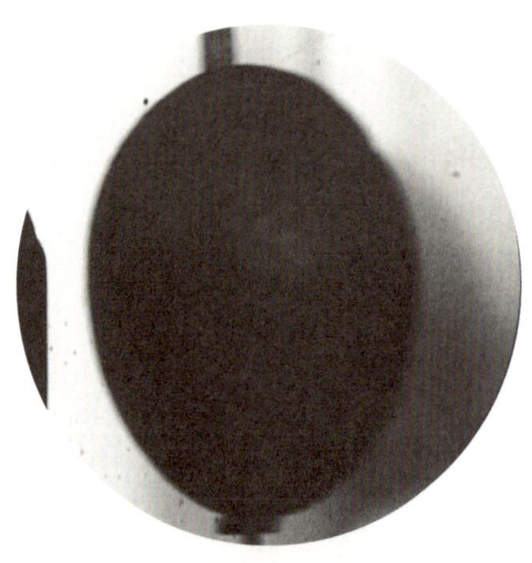
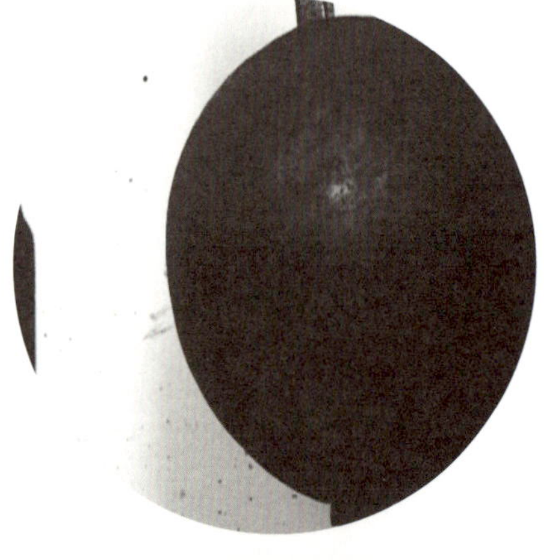

as pendulum shadow crosses
over face with eyes closed —
birds chattering tweeting,
high shrill voices over
continued fast paced hard
hammering — metal on metal
grinding spinning whining —
metal on metal echo — metal
on metal abrasion — low soft
deep sound, marking, pacing —
"All around were these people.
they were just figures. they
have to call them not people" —
they were just figures" —
"they were not walking — not
talking — they were simply very,
very slowly moving around " —

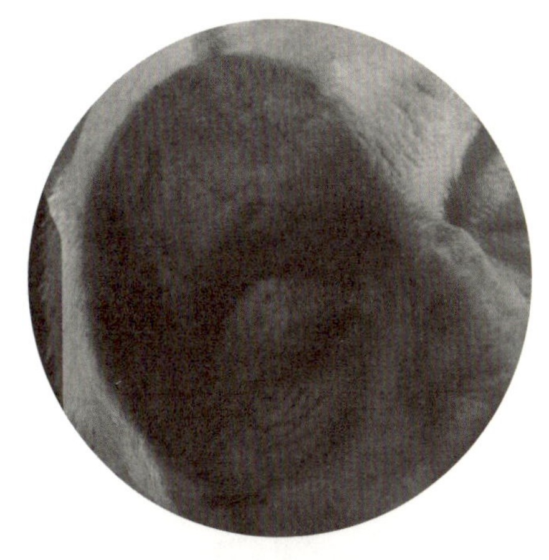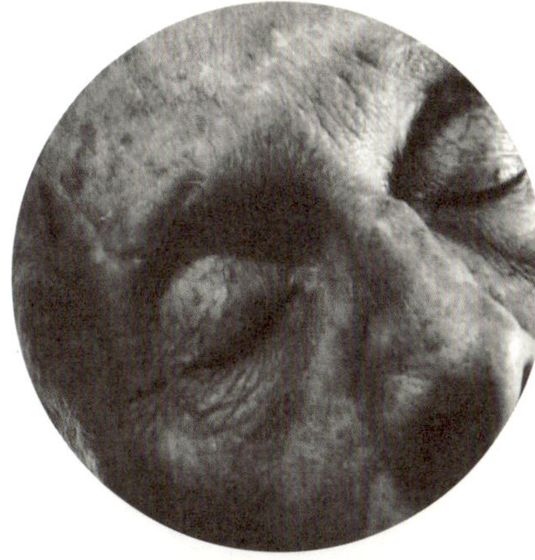

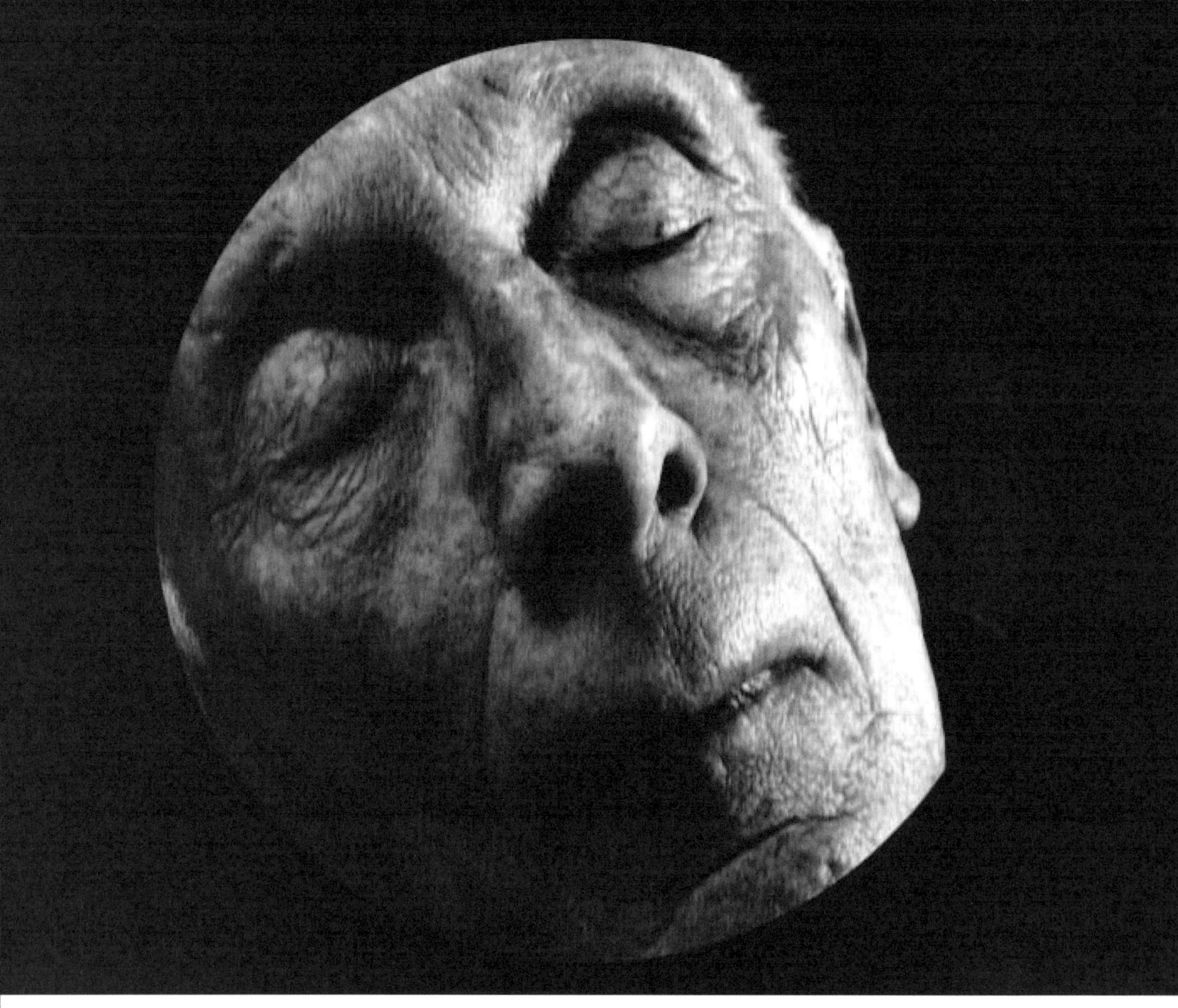

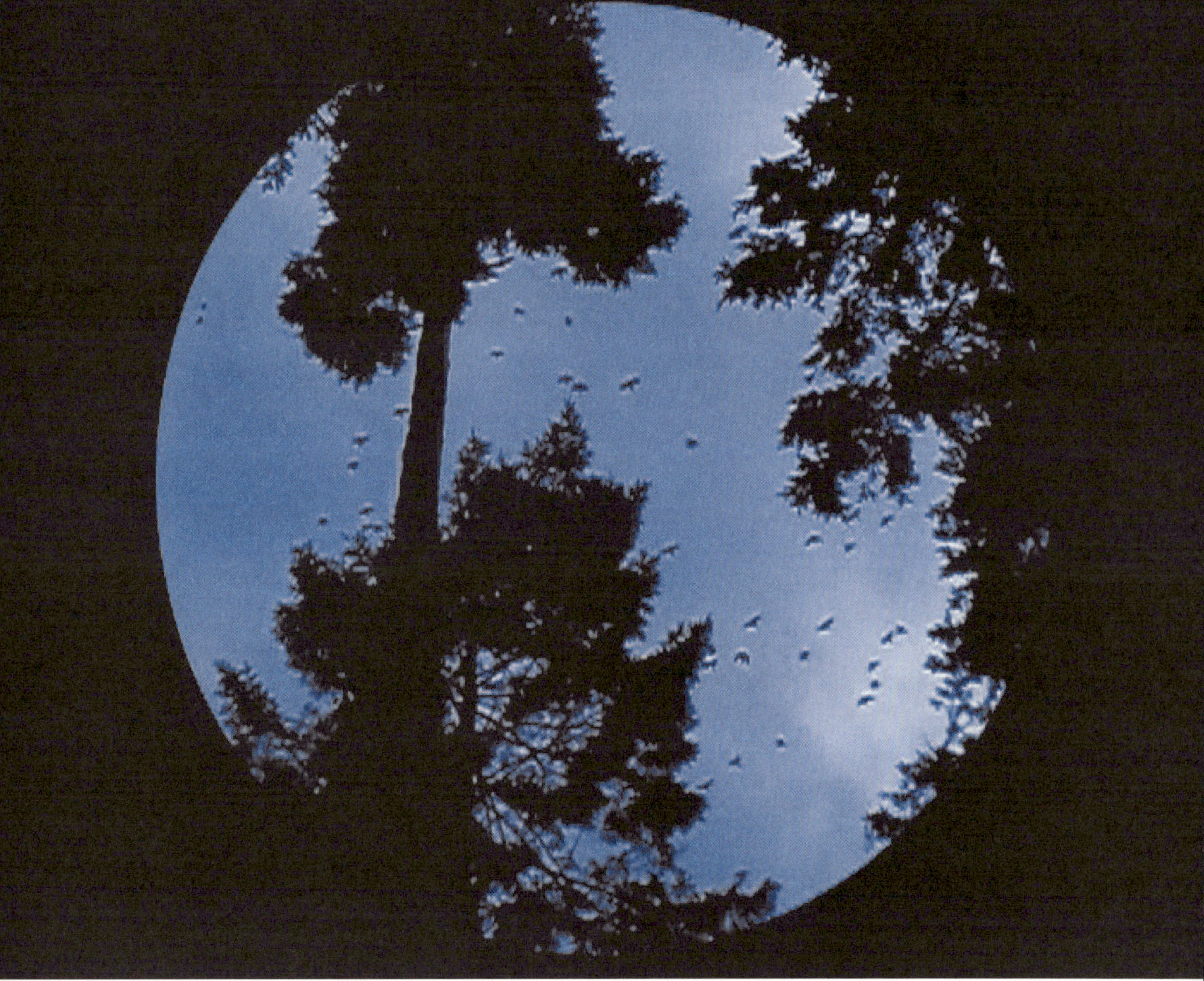

They had a blanket over them, grey army blanket over them,
so they were just this shrouded figure,
they were just shuffling, shuffling along

They were not looking anywhere, they were not looking, they
were not speaking, they were not reacting in any way

The smell permeates
everywhere, it was the
smell of decay

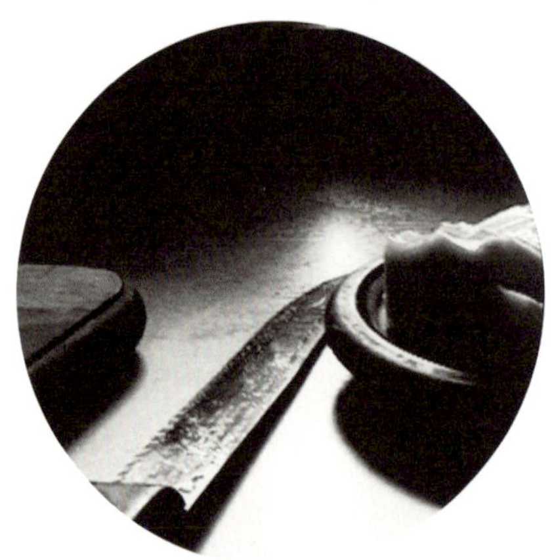

rushing swirling air –
metal on metal spinning
quiet, getting louder louder
– wind' fades softly caught
in sunlit web – metal whine
and clanking – move across
the pockmarked surface
of plates – fast ticking –
four swinging metal spheres
marking, pacing, backwards
and forewards – metal
whine fades – a second and
third clock – different pace,
slow tick tock tock – tick tock
tock – faster tick tick tick
tick – hand on radio –

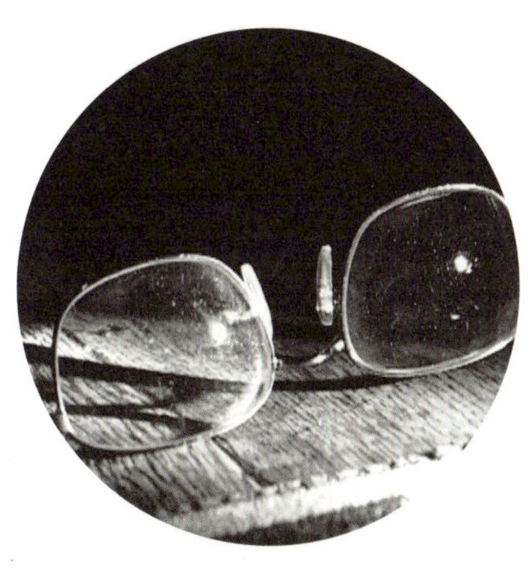 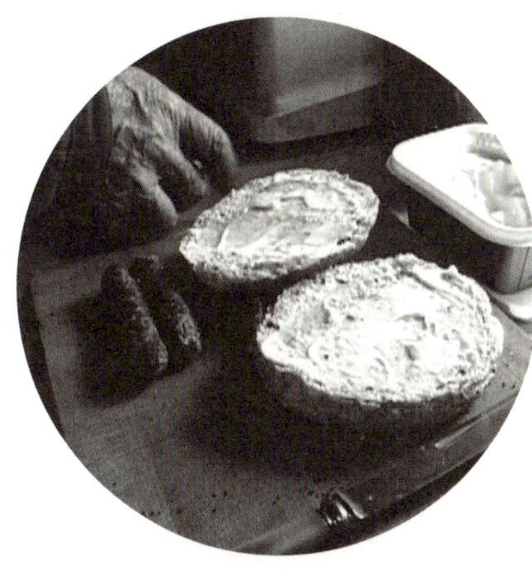

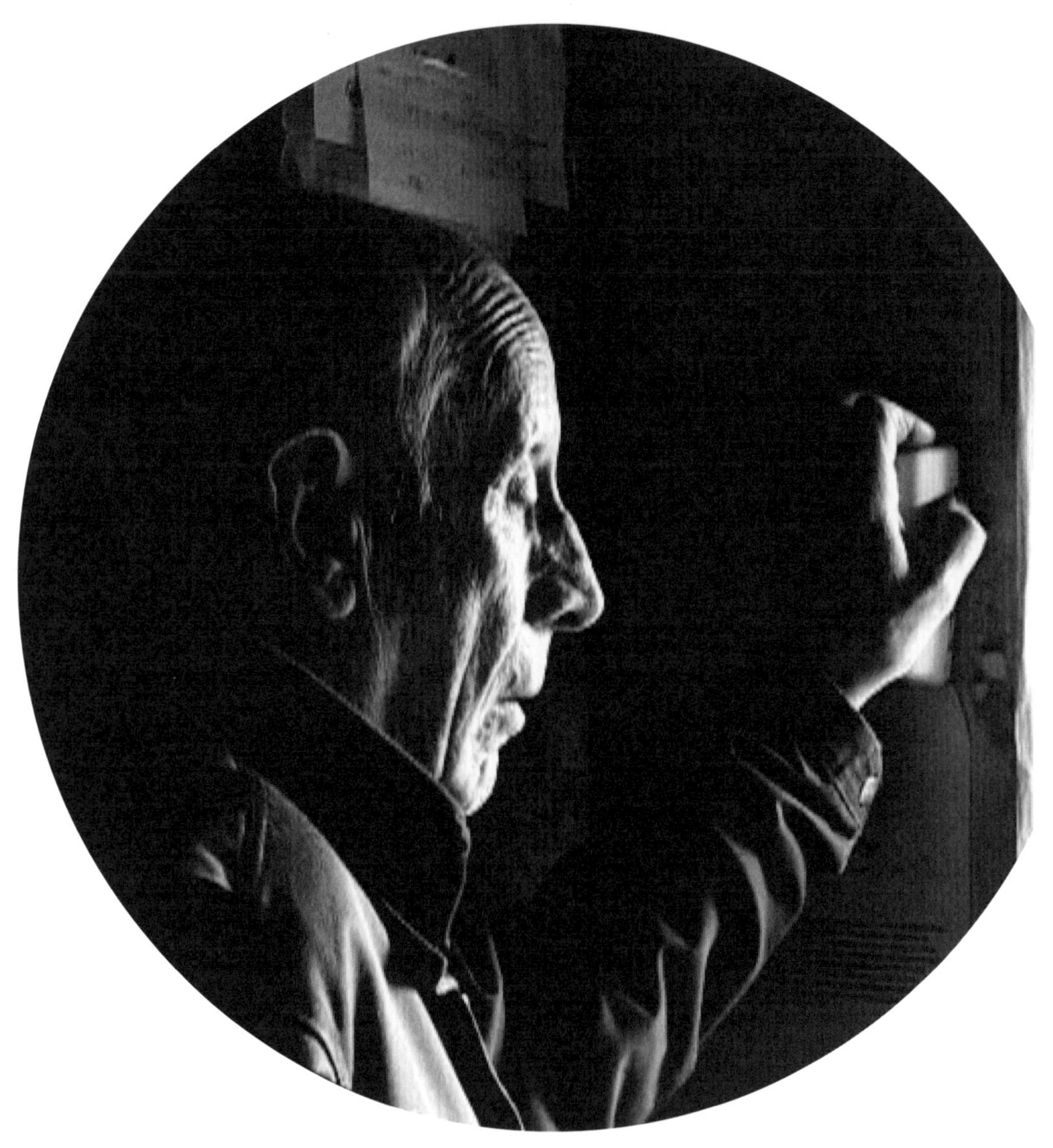

Still refuses to trust its own people,
tried to erase from history its violent response
to a democracy movement nearly twenty years ago

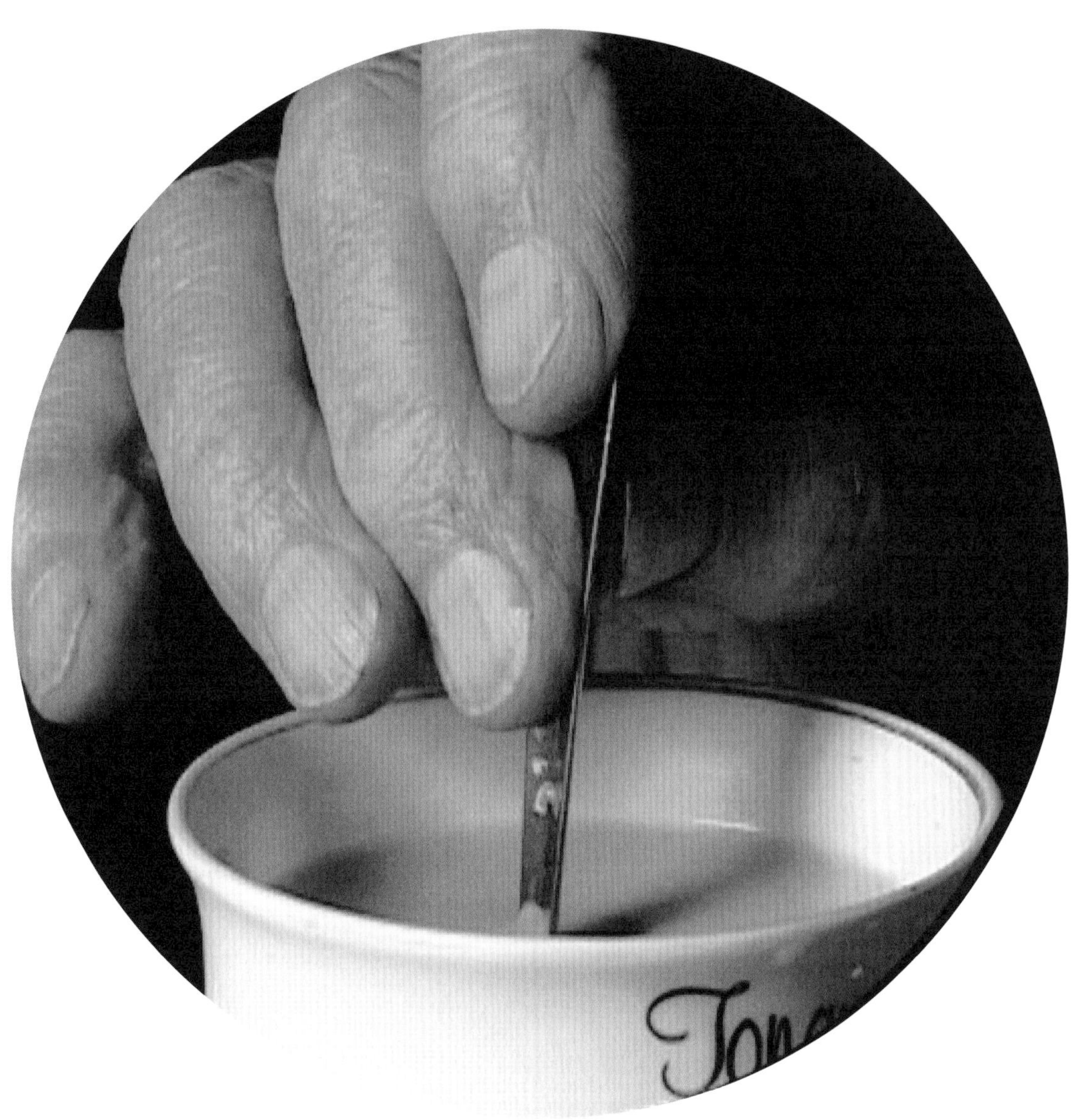

Extract from radio broadcast, BBC Radio 4

breath — teaspoon hits
the edge of a china cup
as sugar drops — tea
pouring from a spout —
tick tick tick tick — a
sigh as the teaspoon
stirs knocking the china
with a bright clear ching —
tick tick tick tick —
head turns as ticking
fades — eyes — quiet —

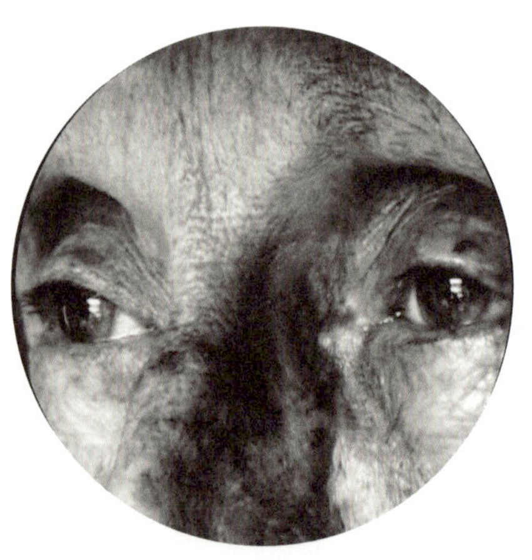

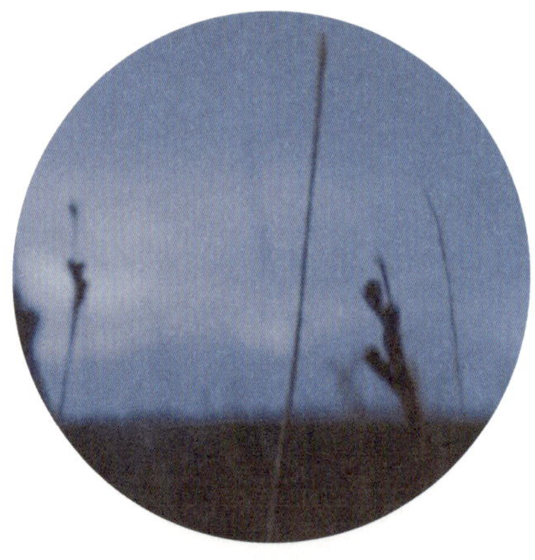

"I was the youngest in
the unit, we were
country boys" _

I was certainly,

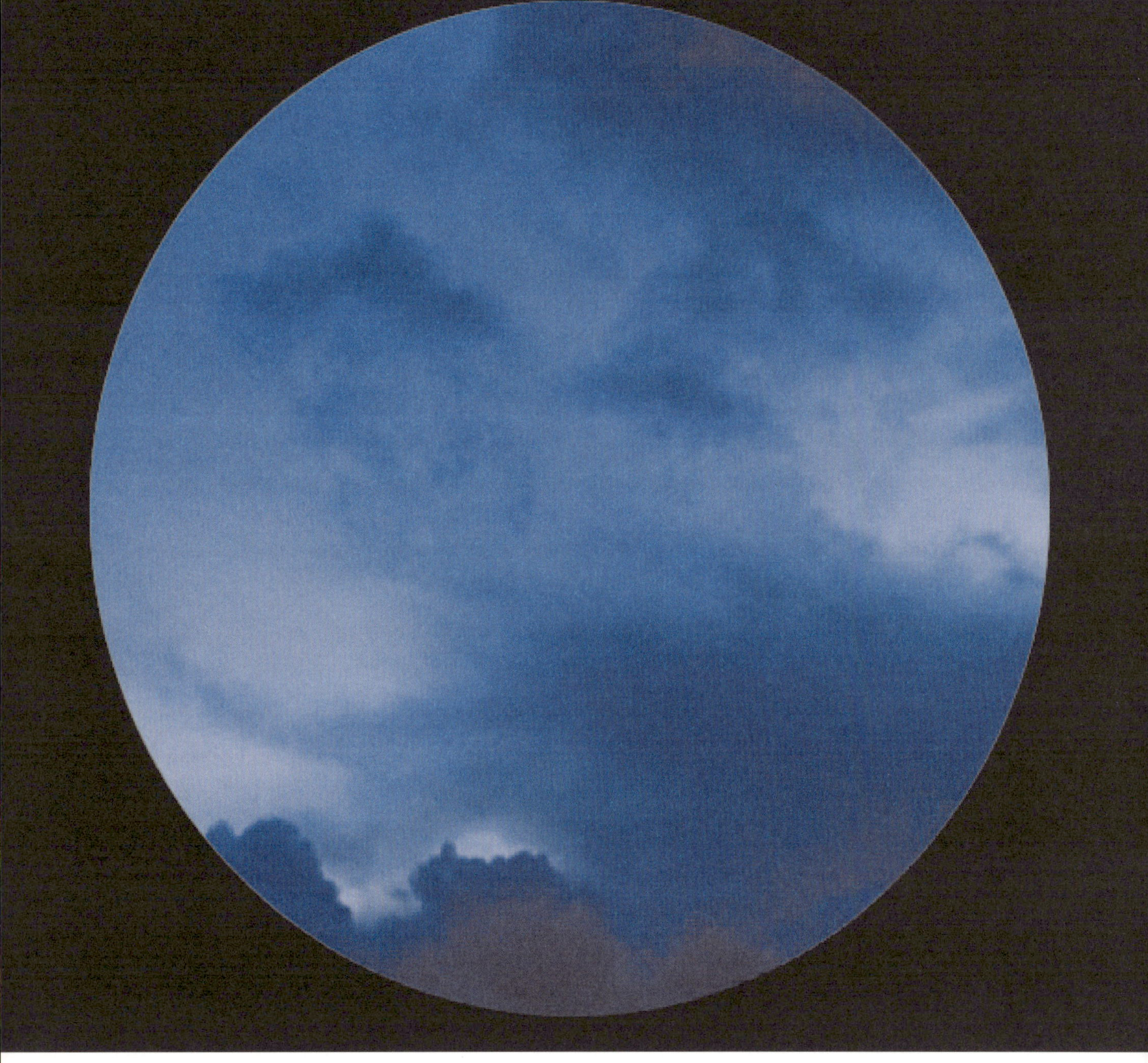

I was a seaside boy

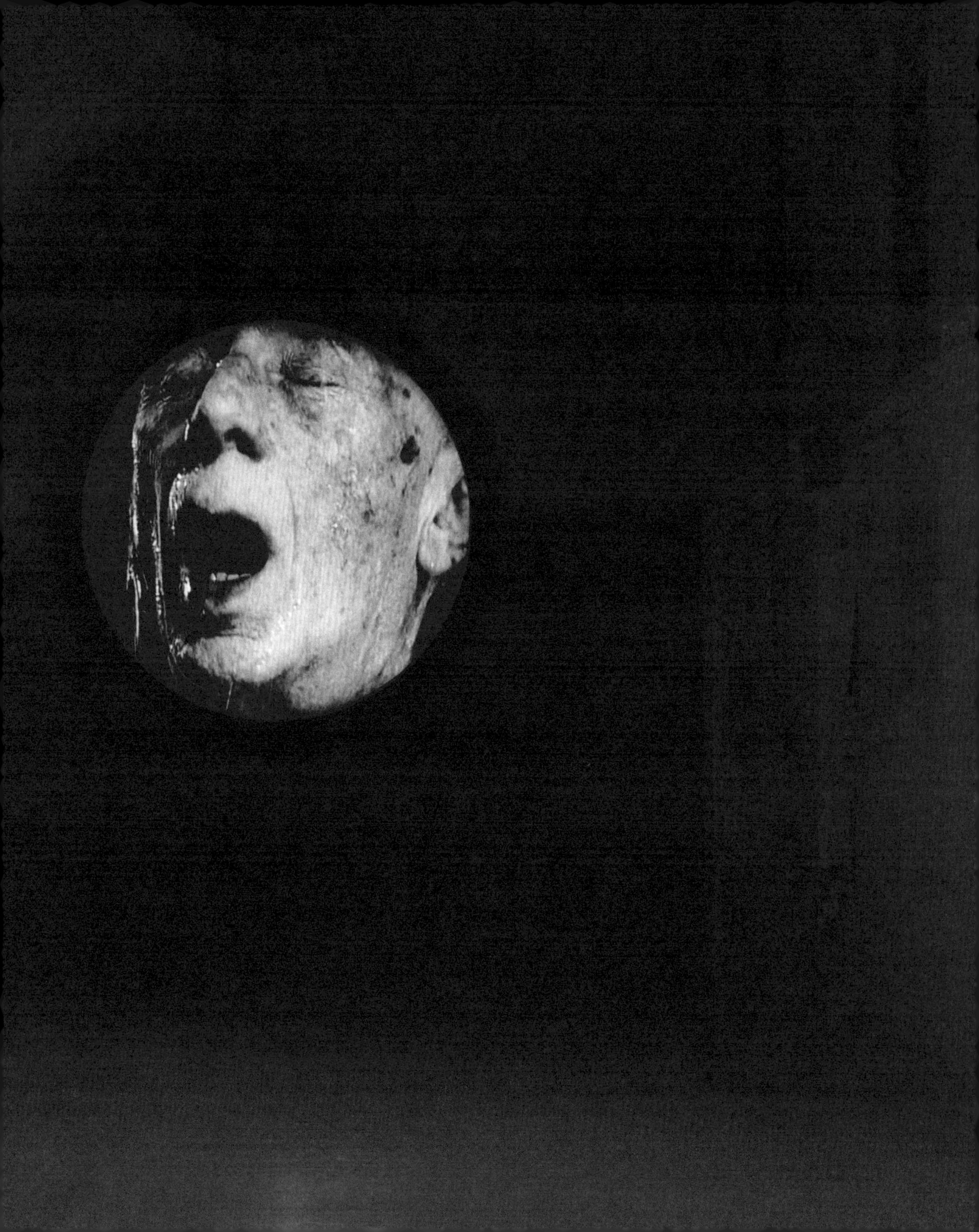

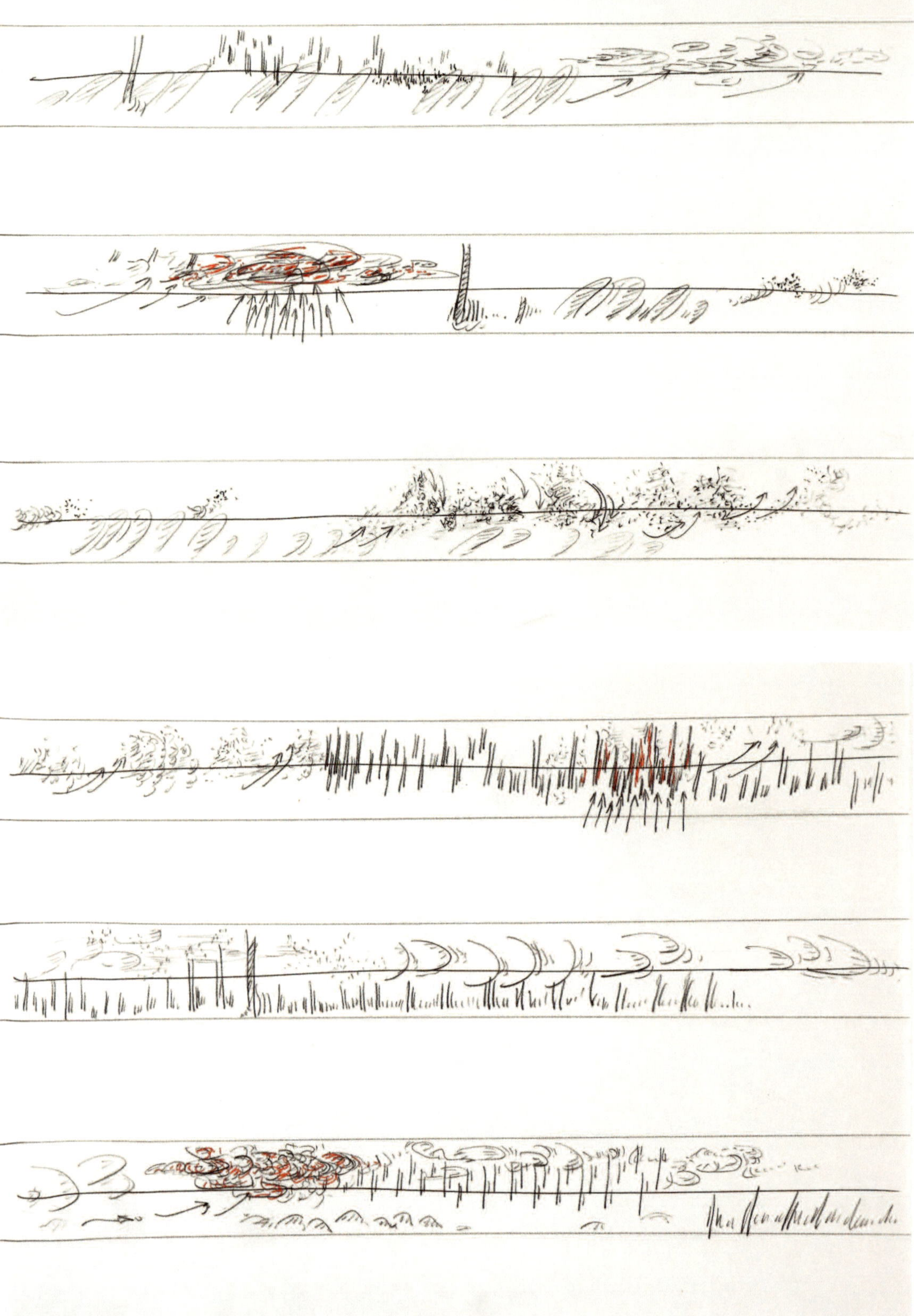

Previous page: *The Watch Man*, 2007. Installation view, Dilston Grove, London 2007. Photograph Simon Phipps. Duration 17 minutes – shown on a seamless and continuous loop. Video projected onto circular screen suspended over luminous red floor with immersive three-dimensional multi-channel sound.

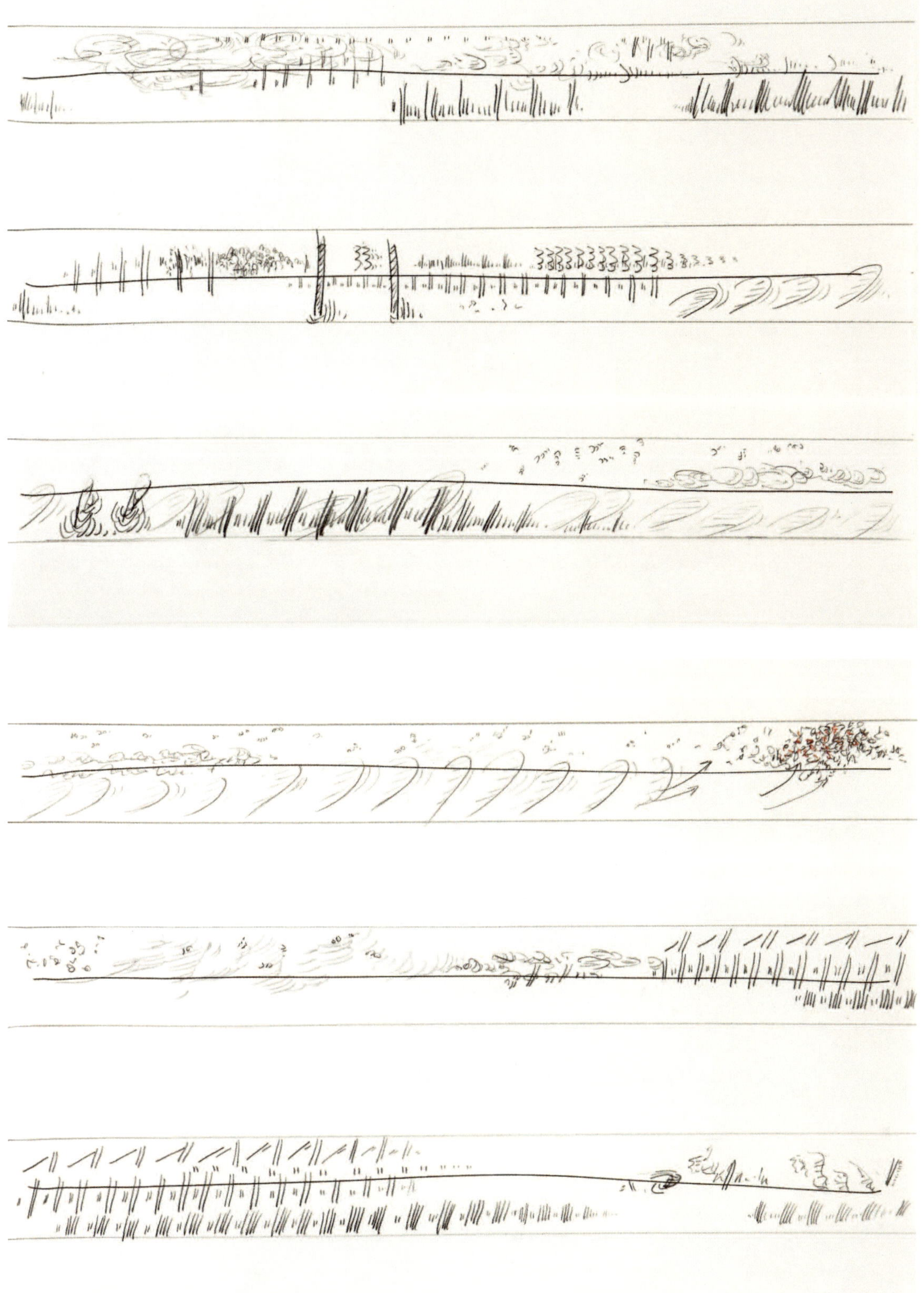

The Watch Man – Sound Drawings, 2007–2010. Graphite on paper. Each 415 mm × 290 mm. Linear sound drawings combining multi-channels of sound into one synchronised forward temporal order. Showing relative densities of sound, audio frequencies, volumetric layering, texture, tonal shifts and types of sound.

Traumatic events in which a person experiences the threat of death, possible major physical injury, threat to the integrity of the self and/or similar damage to other people, as well as the condition that is sometimes termed 'mental defeat', are intense and often give rise to the common clinical syndrome of Post-Traumatic Stress Disorder (PTSD)[1]. One of the major features of the disorder is persistent and intrusive memories which come to mind and emotionally destabilise the individual.

A traumatic event typically gives rise to three to five very vivid details of what are sometimes referred to as 'hot spots'[2]. It seems that virtually any detail can become a hot spot and then intrude into memory triggering negative emotions: guilt, high anxiety, fear and even intense sadness. These intrusive memories of details are often referred to as 'reliving', however this is probably somewhat misleading. The reason why, is that often a person with intrusive memories and PTSD will have hot spots that originate from their thoughts and feelings rather than from the actual event itself and these may also take the form of erroneous details and even false memories.[3]

It is clear that even when a person has recovered from PTSD, the vivid aspects of the memory are still retained and can be brought to mind intentionally by the individual. It seems that these vivid memories originating in traumatic experiences and often involving a period of PTSD, sometimes delayed for many years, can persist over a lifetime and influence an individual during that time. The video and sound installation, *The Watch Man*, is an exploration of the profound, life-persisting effects of trauma on one individual, a man who had witnessed the liberation of Bergen-Belsen as a young British soldier in 1945[4].

The memories derived from this experience are vivid, fragmentary and intrusive and have taken a lifetime to control. Although not often consciously represented, these memories nonetheless haunt the perimeter of consciousness constantly pressurising it for entry into consciousness or conscious representation. These memories carry information that is destabilising for the self and consequently when they gain conscious representation they are edited, changed and reconstituted into forms that are fragmentary, in an attempt to make them more bearable. But this process is only inconsistently effective and fragmentary images can arise that undermine the self and lead to an experience of mental defeat and associated negative emotions such as profound anxiety, guilt and an intense sense of a loss of control. Through an intimate focus on the experience of one individual, *The Watch Man* explores the wider effects of traumatic experience and of living with memories that need to be dealt with and controlled in ways that allow the self to continue with a meaningful existence.

1
American Psychiatric Association, 1994.

2
Grey, Holmes & Brewin, 2001.

3
see Conway, Meares & Standart, 2004, and Ehlers, Hackmann & Michael, 2004, for more accounts of intrusive re-experiencing in PTSD.

4
Although not suffering from clinical levels of PTSD 'The Watch Man' was nonetheless profoundly traumatised by the horror that he encountered.

This drawing tries to capture the idea that trauma memory details may become linked to other non-traumatic memory details. When the non-traumatic memory details, which could be as ordinary as the sound of water in a shower or light filtering through conifer trees, are retrieved they immediately activate the trauma memory, with which they are associated. In this case the traumatic memory detail then becomes intrusive and can evoke tremendously powerful negative emotions.

The diagram also tries to represent the idea that there may be some traumatic memory details which cannot be accessed. Nonetheless these inaccessible traumatic memory details may continue to influence processing and even remembering in indirect but significant ways, for instance by inducing negative emotions, which occur apparently for 'no reason'.

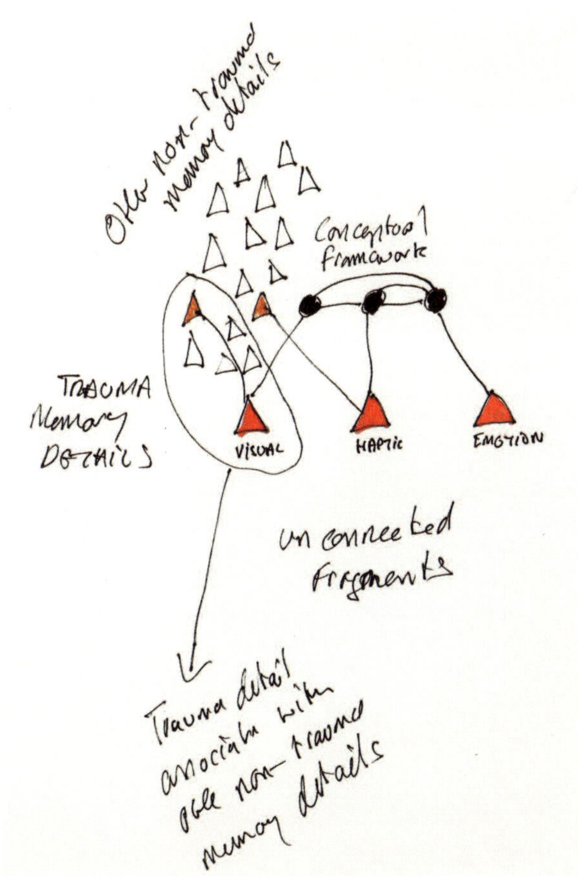

Memory Drawings – Trauma Memory Details, 2006. 415 mm × 290 mm (detail).
Made by Martin A. Conway in conversation with Shona Illingworth.

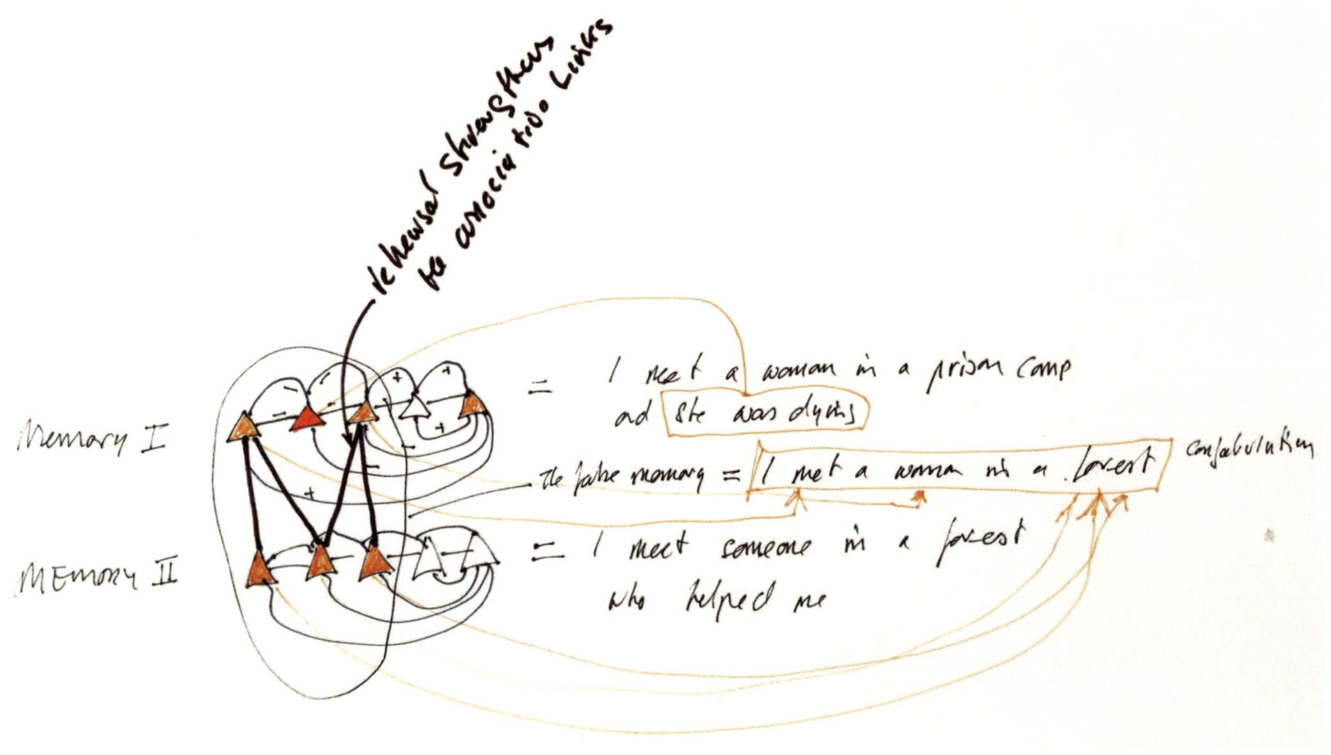

Memory Drawings – Confabulation, 2006. 415 mm × 297 mm. Made by Martin A. Conway in conversation with Shona Illingworth.

Confabulated memory, or at least a plausible confabulation, contains information from one's life which is true but which in the memory is configured in ways that are false.

Many factors contribute to the creation of a false memory but three which are particularly important are the process of rehearsal, source monitoring failure and imagination inflation. Rehearsal simply refers to the fact that a person thinks and/or talks a lot about a memory which initially they know to be either false or to contain incorrect details. In this drawing, 'The Watch Man' who met a woman in a prison camp who was dying, created a rather more neutral, even peaceful false memory of meeting a woman in a forest who helped him. This confabulation contains aspects of the original memory that are true but reconstructs them so they omit important information which is disturbing and destabilising to the self such as the fact that the woman was dying in horrific circumstances of maltreatment and malnutrition. The false memory became a sort of safe haven for 'The Watch Man' to go to in his memory. He himself was aware that the memory was false, nonetheless over the years of rehearsal, he gradually came to experience it as a true memory. In effect, he began to forget the source of his memory which was in fact imagination and not reality.

The distinction however between imagination and reality is much more complicated than we usually realise: much of 'reality' is imagined in any case. Moreover, what we remember is not reality but our experience of reality. When malleability is put in the service of memory for traumatic experiences, then it almost certainly serves powerful adaptive functions in allowing the individual to continue negotiating the difficulties of social life without being destabilised by emotions that would otherwise paralyse them.[1]

1
Conway, M. A. (2005).
Memory and The Self. *Journal of Memory and Language, 53 (4)*, 594–628.

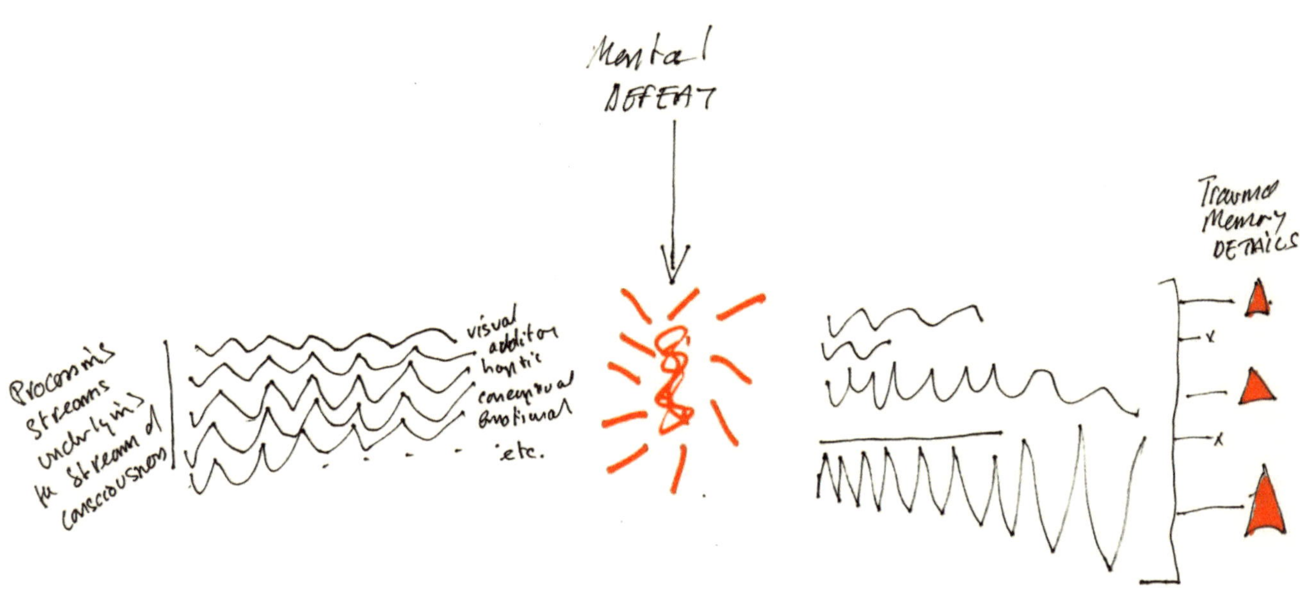

Memory Drawings – Mental Defeat, 2006. 415 mm × 290 mm (detail). Made by Martin A. Conway in conversation with Shona Illingworth.

Some researchers have suggested that the experience of mental defeat during a traumatic event is essential to the formation of fragmentary intrusive traumatic memories that will come to form the basis of the psychological illness of Post-Traumatic Stress Disorder (PTSD). In this drawing, it is assumed that processing streams which underlie consciousness are gathering information from various sensory domains, such as visual, auditory, haptic etc, and from the internal milieu of affects and cognition, and feeding these into central and control processing domains in regions such as the Thalamus and frontal networks. This information is then configured into an enduring representation of ongoing experience in long-term memory. Other networks in other parts of the brain will also be influencing this construction, particularly networks that deal with 'working memory'. Collectively this complex of interlocking networks distributed throughout the brain is known as the default network – which is where we go when we are 'not thinking'.

Mental defeat is the moment when the self can no longer deal with or process ongoing experience – for example when a traumatic event occurs that is beyond the ability of the self to either manage or adapt to.

The effects of this instance of intense anxiety is to break up the memory representation which is being created, almost like having an emotional bomb dropped into and fragmenting it. Those fragments then become the basis of a later traumatic memory; intense and vivid fragments with pockets of amnesia surrounding them represented and constructed in ways that don't necessarily reflect the temporal nature of the original experience. However, in those uncensored moments when we have sunk into the default network, memory images may arise that otherwise would have been prevented from attaining conscious representation.

The brain is never doing nothing. Even in sleep the brain is active and processing and in touch with the external world. In everyday life when attention fluctuates and we go offline and our mind wanders, and perhaps we daydream, the brain system that modulates this is the default network. So when the default network is active we remember the past perhaps as it was, perhaps as it could have been and we think about the future, perhaps as it will be and perhaps as we'd like it to be. The default network can be thought of as the remembering-imagining system. At any moment we all exist in an epoch of the remembering-imagining system as it moves through time in a window of consciousness with the past fading and the future manifesting, and our goals proceeding or not: the memory was kept out of mind or not. Within the remembering-imagining system it is not possible to imagine the future without remembering the past.

Next pages: *Forest* 2007. Black and white giclée print.
406 mm × 304 mm

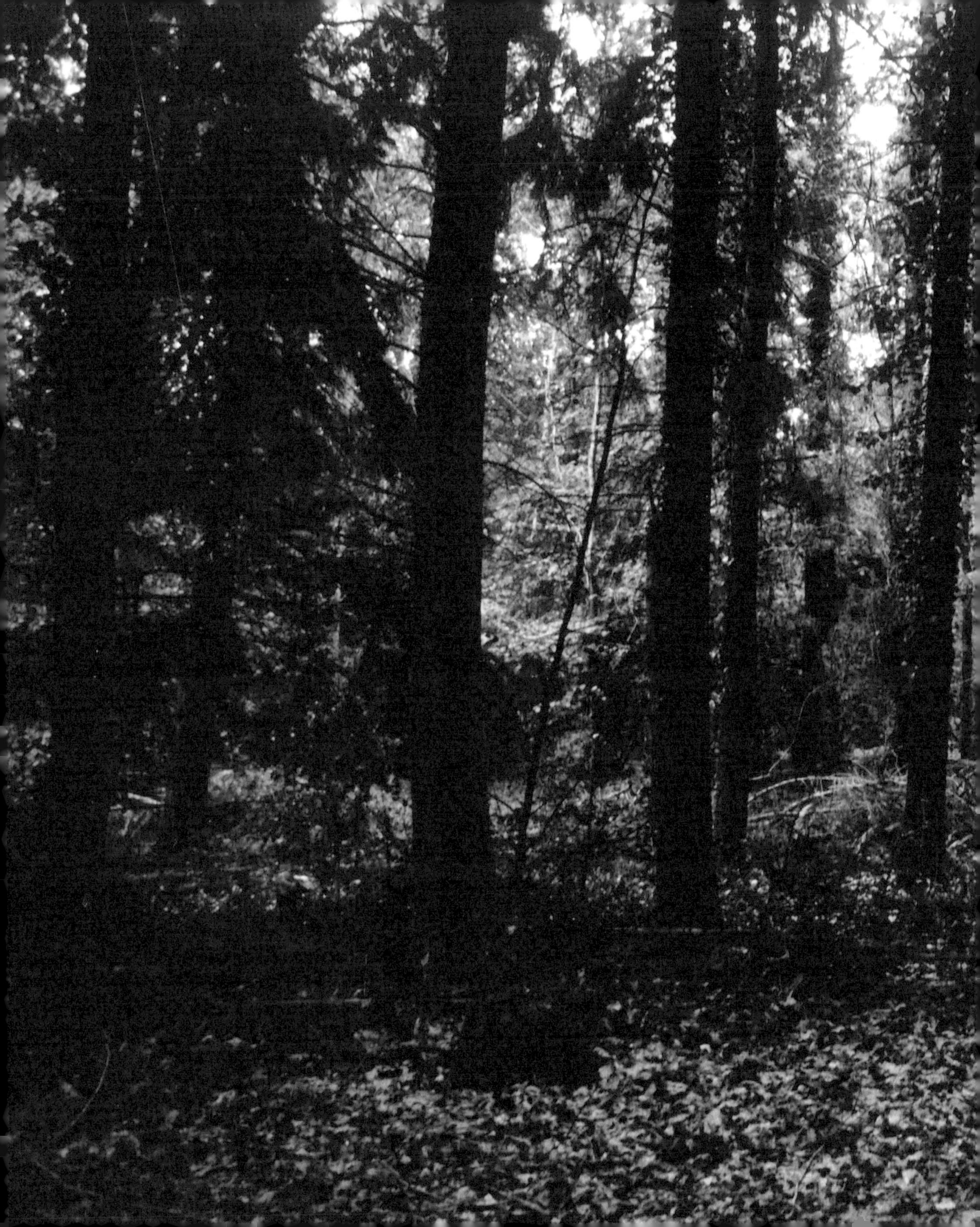

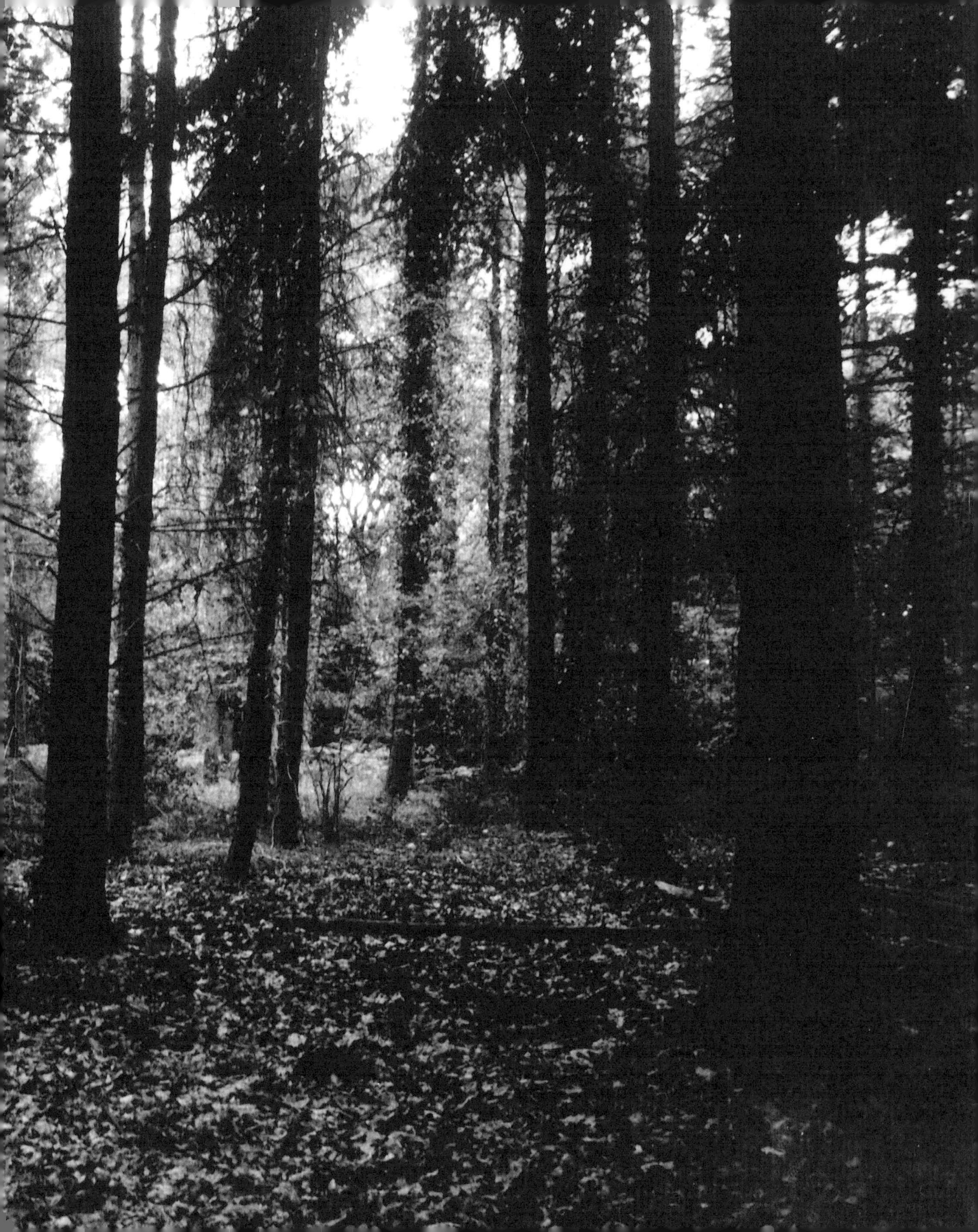

Steven Bode

SOMEONE HAS TO BE THERE

'Deeply lost in the night.

Just as one sometimes lowers one's head to reflect; thus to be utterly
lost in the night.

All around people are asleep.

It is just play-acting, an innocent self-deception, that they sleep in
houses, in safe beds, under a safe roof, stretched out or curled up
on mattresses, in sheets, under blankets; in reality they have flocked
together as they had once upon a time and again later in a deserted
region, a camp in the open, a countless number of men, an army,
a people, under a cold sky on cold earth, collapsed where once they
had stood, forehead pressed on the arm, face to the ground,
breathing quietly.

And you are watching, are one of the watchmen; you find the next
one by brandishing a burning stick from the brushwood pile beside you.

Why are you watching?

Someone has to watch, it is said.
Someone has to be there.'

Franz Kafka, *At Night*

'Alongside the 'war machine', there has always existed an ocular
(and later optical and electro-optical) 'watching machine' capable of
providing soldiers, and particularly commanders, with a visual perspective
on the military action under way. From the original watch tower
through the anchored balloon to the reconnaissance aircraft and remote-
sensing satellites, one and the same function has been indefinitely
repeated, the eye's function being the function of a weapon.'

Paul Virilio, *War and Cinema*

Within the precision-geared workings of the military machine, the look-out man has an indispensible function. The eyes of his unit (and, by extension, of his people), he scans the horizon for minuscule movements and changes, for anything out of the ordinary. The first to notice the other side advancing, and to feel the anxious *frisson* of danger and threat, he is also the first to put his head above the parapet. Like those special forces who operate covertly behind enemy lines, his is a vicarious, profoundly precarious existence – his habitual state of alertness only ever an instant from a fully-blown state of alert. A dutiful subject who is fixated, often haunted, by the presence of an invisible object, he patrols the edge of this psychological frontline, his absolute readiness masking an underlying existential uncertainty.

Shona Illingworth's video and sound installation *The Watch Man* is an intimate portrait of one such army veteran, sixty years after his formative experiences in the Second World War. Private David Illingworth (the artist's father) was never in the vanguard of the action, or singled out for special responsibility. Nonetheless, as a 19-year-old junior member of the Royal Electrical and Mechanical Engineers, he found himself exposed to one of the most harrowing episodes of that turbulent chapter of history. In April 1945, as the thud of battle reverberated several miles to the east, Illingworth was one of a small group of British soldiers delegated to investigate a hitherto obscure compound of buildings named Bergen–Belsen that had been abandoned, under unusual circumstances, by retreating German troops. Rumours had been circulating about the place for some time, but whatever had been shared in the upper echelons was unlikely to have been communicated to the ordinary soldiers who were tasked with their mission that day.

If the camp was eerily unguarded, Illingworth and his colleagues were totally unprepared for what they were about to see. A foretaste of what would await them was provided by an enveloping stench of disease and decay that announced itself long before their destination was reached. The source of this miasma became immediately evident when they crossed the perimeter of the camp, where untold numbers of emaciated bodies were strewn across the ground; some of them dumped unceremoniously, others simply left lying where they expired. Moving among them, a procession of wraith-like figures, shrouded in blankets, shuffled, as if sleepwalking through a nightmare from which they had long ceased to believe they would awake. Even worse was to follow in the forest fringes at the edges of the camp, where a multitude of carcasses and skeletons were piled up in crowded mass graves. Before the name of Bergen–Belsen became a watchword for man's inhumanity to man, the members of this small company of soldiers were among the first outside witnesses to a horror that would soon be revealed to an uncomprehending world.

Shona Illingworth's starkly evocative seventeen-minute work examines her father's struggle to come to terms with what he encountered on that day, and the tangle of memories and emotions that have stayed with him ever since. Palpably vivid and persistently disturbing, these images and feelings were a shadow from his past that he shared with very few people, and whose discomfiting effects he was extremely reluctant to admit. The hold that this incident continued to have on him is demonstrated all too clearly, however, in a series of deeply affecting recollections that punctuate his daughter's video – each of them presented within an ominous, unsettling soundscape that hints at an inner turmoil underlying his words. If the halting, emotional nature of this act of recall is especially poignant, other fragments of what he has been asked to remember are more obviously disconcerting - to us, and, at times, it would appear, even to him. One particularly powerful memory, involving a young female inmate (one of twins) who he later sees walking in a sunlit glade some distance from the camp, seems almost to unravel in the telling, as Illingworth starts to realise both the inherent unlike-liness of the event, and its possible conflation, in his mind, with a different person, at another time and place. For all its dubious provenance, it is exceptionally revealing that he has clasped this image to him, like a picture in a locket, for over six decades. As is often the case with the memories that haunt us, we may not always know how they have come into our possession, but the unconscious charge that they carry means that we are hugely unwilling to let them go.

The presence of these ghosts, and the memorial vigil this particular survivor has chosen to enact for them, lends *The Watch Man* much of its mournful resonance. Ticking away inside it, taking its cue from the various timepieces that appear at regular intervals, is a not-so-hidden sub-text of parallel, sometimes competing, significance. Throughout his life, David Illingworth had a passion for antique clocks and watches, applying his mechanic's deftness of hand and eye to fix and restore them. Moving backwards and forwards, following the rhythmic pattern of the pendulum that dolefully orchestrates the piece, the video shines a light on these contrasting faces: first, the watchman, eyes wide shut, haunted by an indelible image which, once seen, can never be erased; then, the watch man, eyes wide open, behind his magnifying glass, assembling and disassembling the delicate instruments he knows and loves. As we, in turn, watch him, in the camera's spotlight, yet transparently lost in the moment, we are left in little doubt that this repair work is not only engrossing and absorbing, but therapeutic, even liberating.

These recuperative actions, however small-scale and incremental, are also inescapably symbolic. In the sanctuary of his workshop, David Illingworth, we can hardly fail to note, devoted a large part of his life to the act of resetting the clock; or, to ratchet up the metaphor a little bit, making time start over again. While this meticulous, intricate labour would have had its material satisfactions, it most likely had a deeper set of psychological compensations. It is not uncommon, of course, for people to gravitate towards what they feel they can change for the better in the face of larger, irrational forces they feel unable to control. Away from the comforting torch-beam of light that is a recurring motif of *The Watch Man*, these demons lurk at the edges of the frame. The horror is out there, it seems to say: in the shape of the void; or an unspoken dread, whose name inspires fear but can never be uttered aloud. These thoughts are positively encouraged by the video's overwhelmingly Gothic mood – the dull gleam of the moon over a pall of murky, wintry trees transporting us, with a hint of a shiver, to that dead-time in the darkest hour of the night, when no one is safe, and only the watchers keep the shadows at bay. Counting down to its own zero-hour, it heightens the spirit of the uncanny that pervades the piece, making you think of the old folk tale of the clock in the hall that stops dead when its owner passes away; and prompting you to speculate about a point in David Illingworth's past when part of his psyche may have become comparably arrested. Psychologists contend that our experience of time either orbits or, alternatively, becomes snagged on such a pivotal event, or *punctum*. In the captivating sequence where Illingworth places a tiny ruby in the mechanism of a watch to better regulate its movement, we may be watching a pre-echo of the moment his daughter discovers the rosebud around which much of his mind still turns.

Shona Illingworth certainly comes across as her father's daughter in her fascination for the mechanics of memory. With similar diligence and sensitivity, she trains her camera-eye upon this nearest and dearest of subjects, emulating the circular optic through with which her father peers through the lens of his microscope. As close as you would expect of someone whose personal attachment stems as much from affinity as simple proximity, her understanding of him has been magnified further by a series of exchanges with the cognitive psychologist Martin A. Conway, an expert in the vicissitudes of memory, particularly trauma memory. This dialogue, while informing the video elements, is made most manifest in a series of 'memory drawings' that accompany the installation: quickfire diagrammatic sketches, generated in the heat of conversations with Conway, that materialise Illingworth's efforts to get to grips with the complex paths and formations that memory establishes in the brain. Aids to understanding, these otherwise functional illustrations have both a graphic impact and a beguilingly poetic quality. In reference to the case of her father, they can also be seen, perhaps, as an attempt to isolate, even at some level remotely defuse, the traumatic psychic material that has lodged within him; a minefield of memory that, as the drawings attest, lies mostly underground, slowburning and combustible. Primed and ready to sound an alarm, its incendiary nature gives the quotidian ticking of the clocks a much more sinister undertone.

Before they can unpack that trauma material, Conway must first lead Illingworth deeper into what, from his neuro-scientific perspective, actually makes the mind tick. A further set of memory drawings illuminates this labyrinth, comparing standard neuro-logical patterns and procedures with the defences the brain puts up when it encounters troubling, disabling thoughts. One of these processes is the phenomenon of confabulation, a strategy whereby two separate recollections are conjoined to create a stand-in for an original traumatic event that has been repressed. (David Illingworth's 'memory' of the girl in the forest is a striking example of this). Specialist step-by-step readings of her father's personal horrorscope, Illingworth and Conway's collaborative drawings demonstrate that, for such a precision instrument, the mind is intriguingly resourceful and adaptable, especially under duress. For all that inbuilt robustness, however, it is not infinitely shockproof. It should come as little surprise, then, when it becomes disordered, or misses a beat.

Like many ex-servicemen, David Illingworth took time to adjust to a new envi-ronment at home. The events of the last few weeks of the war were never mentioned – not only because he found them impossible to talk about but because he felt that people simply didn't want to hear. On his return, he established a small watchmaker's business; then, seeking a more creative outlet for his natural dexterity, enrolled in a ceramics course at a local art school. Some time after, an unexplained upheaval in his circumstances caused him to re-locate to Scotland, either in search of work, or simply to get away from it all. Whatever the reason, the wide-open spaces of the Scottish Highlands offered an ideal backdrop for a new life, and it was here that he met Shona Illingworth's mother, an artist and ceramicist. It may not have been coincidence that his next move was even further northward. Having heard about a former military base on the coast of Sutherland that was being offered as artists' workshops and residences, the Illingworths moved their young family to the newly founded 'craft village' of Balnakiel in 1968. For anyone seeking to escape the rat-race, or excited by the prospect of building an alternative society, its position at the outermost margins offered a perfect opportunity to begin again. At the furthermost edges of the land, and barely registering on the map, Balnakiel was not so much a wild place as a 'last place'. With its drab, utilitarian architecture lending its haphazard cluster of Nissen huts the air of an unusually bleak and forsaken prison camp, it is also the last place you would have expected David Illingworth to want to be.

The area around Balnakiel has long been a look-out station for the British military. Perched amid a curve of high cliffs only a few miles from Cape Wrath, it watches over the sea-lanes of the North Atlantic, of paramount strategic importance during the two World Wars. Following changes in the technologies of surveillance, an early warning radar base, to be maintained by a small unit of soldiers, was established at Balnakiel, near to the site of an earlier radio mast. Not long after, as the Cold War opened up a new front in military geopolitics, and as advances in remote sensing set a new benchmark for surveillance techniques, this once-crucial listening post lost much of its original *raison d'etre*. Increasingly out on a limb, the base was abandoned little more than ten years after it was completed, its barracks and outbuildings eventually becoming the shell of the new craft village. Which is not to say that the military quickly vacated the area. No longer a major gathering-point of frontline intelligence, this remote outpost was accorded an important new function as a proving-ground for future frontline operations. Much of Shona Illingworth's childhood echoed to the roar of Royal Navy helicopters taking off and landing next door to her home, and to the equally deafening boom of thousands of training runs in which junior bomber pilots practised dropping their first live loads. The firing range of Garvie Island is still used for this purpose to this day, by RAF crews going to Afghanistan or Libya, or as part of NATO war games or other international exercises.

It is something of a platitude to say that Balnakiel is geographically and meteorologically exposed. On any given day, it can be hit by several different extremes of weather, few of them balmy or serene. Yet while it bears the brunt of the merciless winds from the north and west, its real raw nerve is, arguably, to its rear, in the area to the south and east of the nearby village of Durness, where the land is conspicuously marked by the effects of the 19th century Highland Clearances. Ruined crofters' houses dot a quintessentially haunted landscape in which identikit forested plantings stand out in chequerboard relief against a barren moonscape of mountains and moors. In many ways, one could say that this landscape is doubly haunted – by the ghosts of those killed, or forcibly evicted, in the past; and also, as a collateral effect of the latest colonial army to occupy this desolate terrain, by the phantom presences of virtual targets in wars yet to come. As the wind fails to drown out the noise of the overflying planes, it seems even stranger that this is also the place – not quite at war but, at the same time, nowhere near at peace – that David Illingworth elected to live.

A natural companion piece to *The Watch Man*, Shona Illingworth's 35-minute video, *Balnakiel*, follows the earlier project's template in its rich, allusive interplay of image and sound. Shot on location where she spent so many of her early years, it downplays a biographical impulse in favour of an investigation into the area's distinctive spirit of place. Although an intermittent chorus of voices (many of them family and friends) provides an elliptical commentary, Illingworth often lets the powerful imprint of the landscape speak for itself; sometimes experienced at close quarters, sometimes laid out like a map. The opening sequence of the film, an aerial view of the village and its surrounds, is indicative of this approach – the slow-motion glide of the airborne camera instilling a feeling of wonder (and oneness with nature) whose dream-like thrill of disembodiment is deliberately confused with the anonymous, all-seeing gaze of a battlefield drone. Foregrounding the two competing perspectives that vie for prominence in this corner of the world, this eye-opening prelude (half paean, half reckoning) sets the tone for much of the rest of the work.

Around Balnakiel, the hills are alive with the sound of manoeuvres. Illingworth's video certainly brims with their omnipresent crackle and hum. Monopolising their own locked-off band of the airwave spectrum, pilots communicate with their on-the-ground commanders; their terse, coded language sizing up, and dividing up, the land below. Elsewhere, a gentle hubbub of other voices makes its presence (and its opinions) felt on a more domestic frequency – the patchwork testimony of a cross-section of villagers describing the day-to-day habits and anxieties of life under the flight-path; their plaintive refrain providing not so much a voiceover, as such, as a keening, resonant undertone. Meanwhile, the very air seems alive – with the elemental properties of ozone, of thunder, of natural electricity; all of them propagating the highly charged atmosphere that makes the place what it is. The RAF Tornadoes may gather out of nowhere like the violent storms that give them their name, but the local weather is eminently capable of unleashing its own displays of shock and awe.

The continuing face-off between an enclave of back-to-nature idealists and a hostile, domineering military produces its own set of rumbles and flashpoints. Born as much of ideological antipathy as mutual incomprehension, this undercurrent of resentment finds an echo in the equally uneasy coexistence between the 'incomers' of the craft village and the longstanding residents of Durness. Despite her deep affection for her childhood home, Illingworth has definite sympathies for the older inhabitants, and a genuine sensitivity for the long-suffering character of the locality. This troubled legacy, and its impact on the collective psyche, is explored in a number of one-to-one conversations with the residents; and, as before, mobilises Conway's insights into the influence of memory. If *The Watch Man* is, among other things, a study of the effects of trauma on an individual, *Balnakiel* considers how a shared experience of a similarly fraught history reverberates within a community. This shift from the individual to the group gives Illingworth and Conway's dialogue a new line of inquiry, and their resultant memory-drawings a slightly different complexion. As if these more speculative exchanges required them to rethink their terms of engagement, the drawings seem relatively open and on-the-fly. Maybe it is a mark of the military mind-set that permeates the area, but what they occasionally start to resemble are blackboard sketches of battlefield tactics – rehearsals for a rescue-and-recovery mission; coordinated movements to flush out an unseen antagonist.

A further analogy is suggested by the shots of the military control-tower in *Balnakiel*. The fulcrum of the video, it looms large within the footage in the same way that its distinctive architecture dominates the local scene. From this panoramic vantage-point, the Air Force ground controller guides his pilots to their targets – each strike executed within this field of 20–20 vision; each bomb detonated in little more than a blink of an eye. So much so, that it does not seem too much of a flight-of-fancy when Conway conjectures how the operational hub of the command-centre might loosely correspond to a specific area and function of the brain (called the 'central executive') that monitors and polices memory. Raining instant thunder from on high, this latter-day watchman in his high-tech panopticon seems omnipotent, imperious; the master of all he surveys. It is telling, however, that when the bomb finally drops, in the final seconds of the video, it explodes in eerie, ghostly silence. As we watch a new generation of pilots being put through their paces for a potential next instalment in the so-called War on Terror, *Balnakiel* and *The Watch Man* remind us how the source of this fear, and its concomitant feelings of apprehension and threat, is, like the original basis of a trauma, not so easy to pinpoint, let alone eradicate. Someone (or something) has to be behind it, we are assured. Someone has to be there. The greater truth is that we are always chasing phantoms: figments of ourselves that haunt us even as they elude us; fragments of the past that hover in the shadows even as we try and give them name and form.

Next page: *Echo Loop*, 2007. Series of Super-8 film stills of Balnakiel village, Garvie Island and Cape Wrath Range Control. 72 images in total, dimensions and composition variable

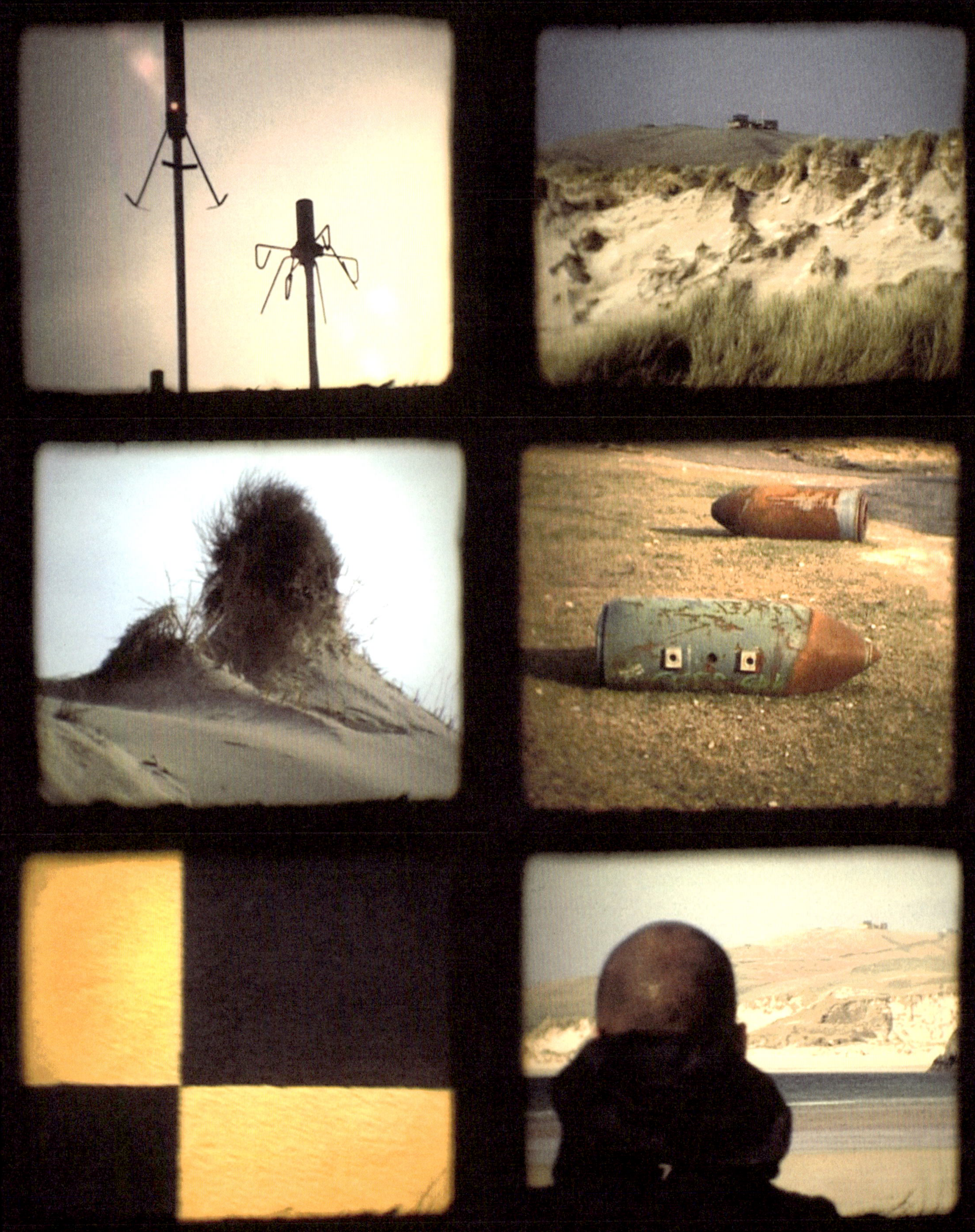

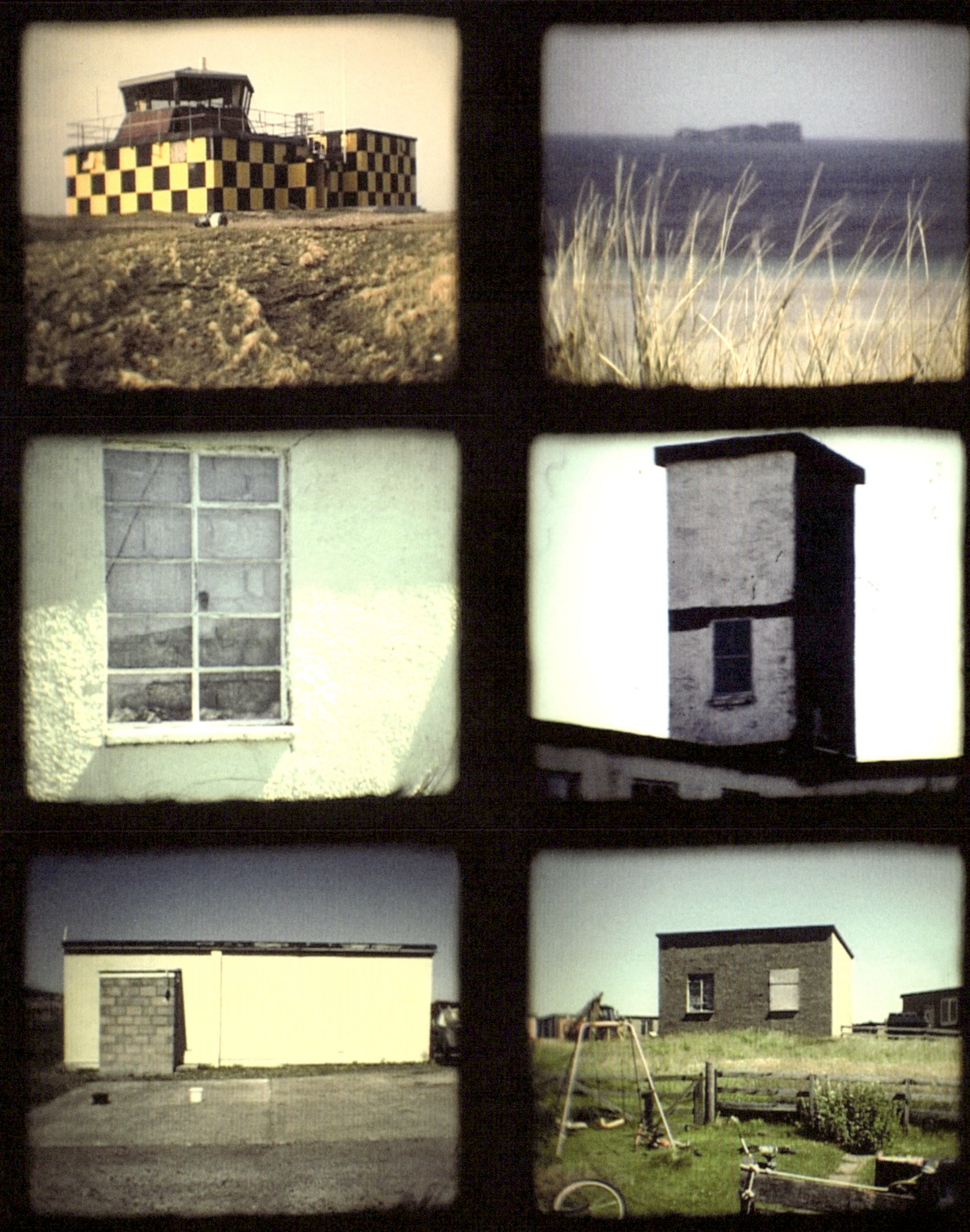

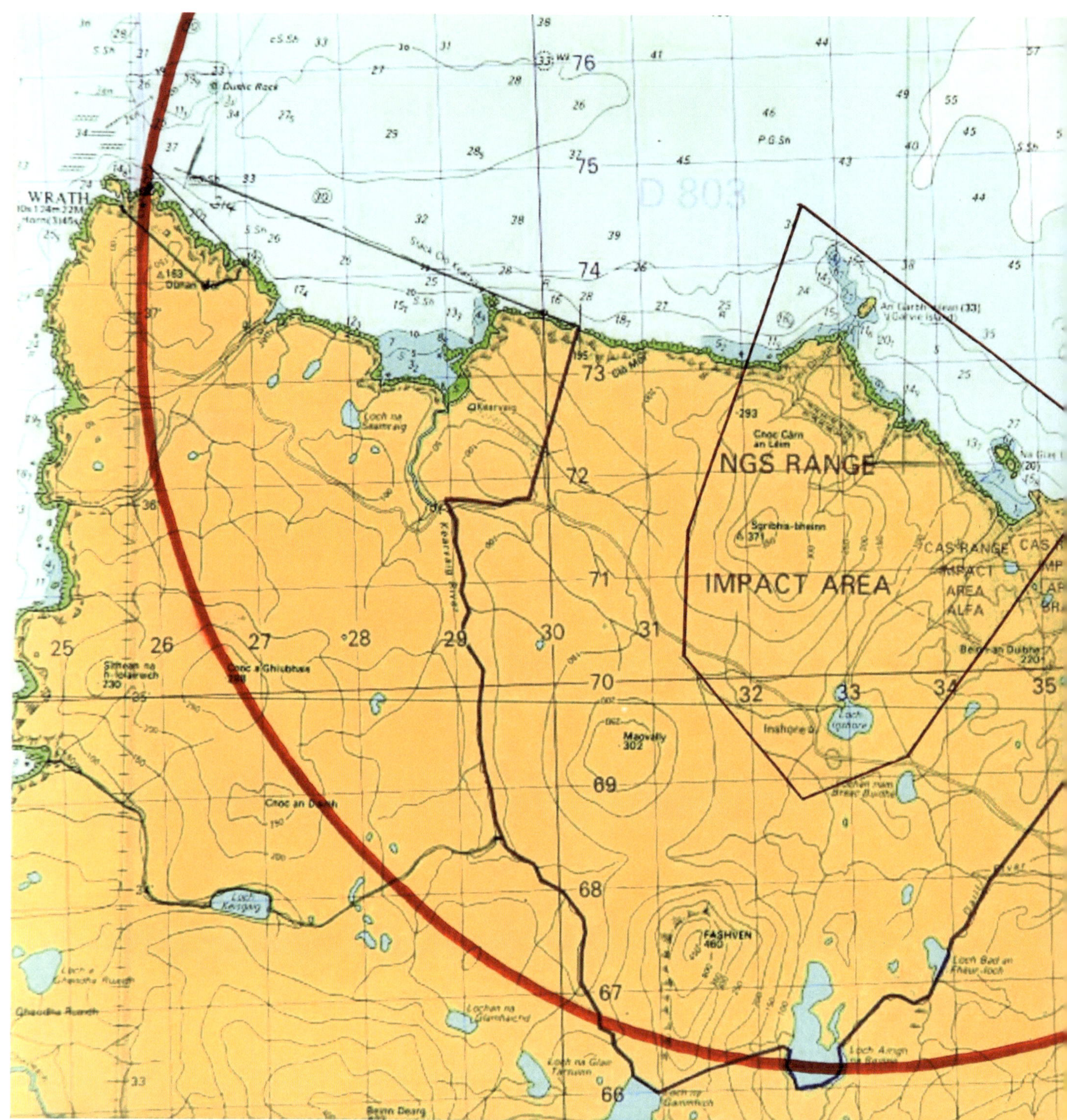

Impact Bravo Alpha: Cape Wrath Bombardment Range, 2009. 275 mm × 180 mm. Chart, pen and paper. Chart of Cape Wrath Bombardment Range, north west Highlands of Scotland detailing the perimeter of the Danger Zone and the locations of the Range Control Tower, Balnakiel and the Clearance village of Durness.

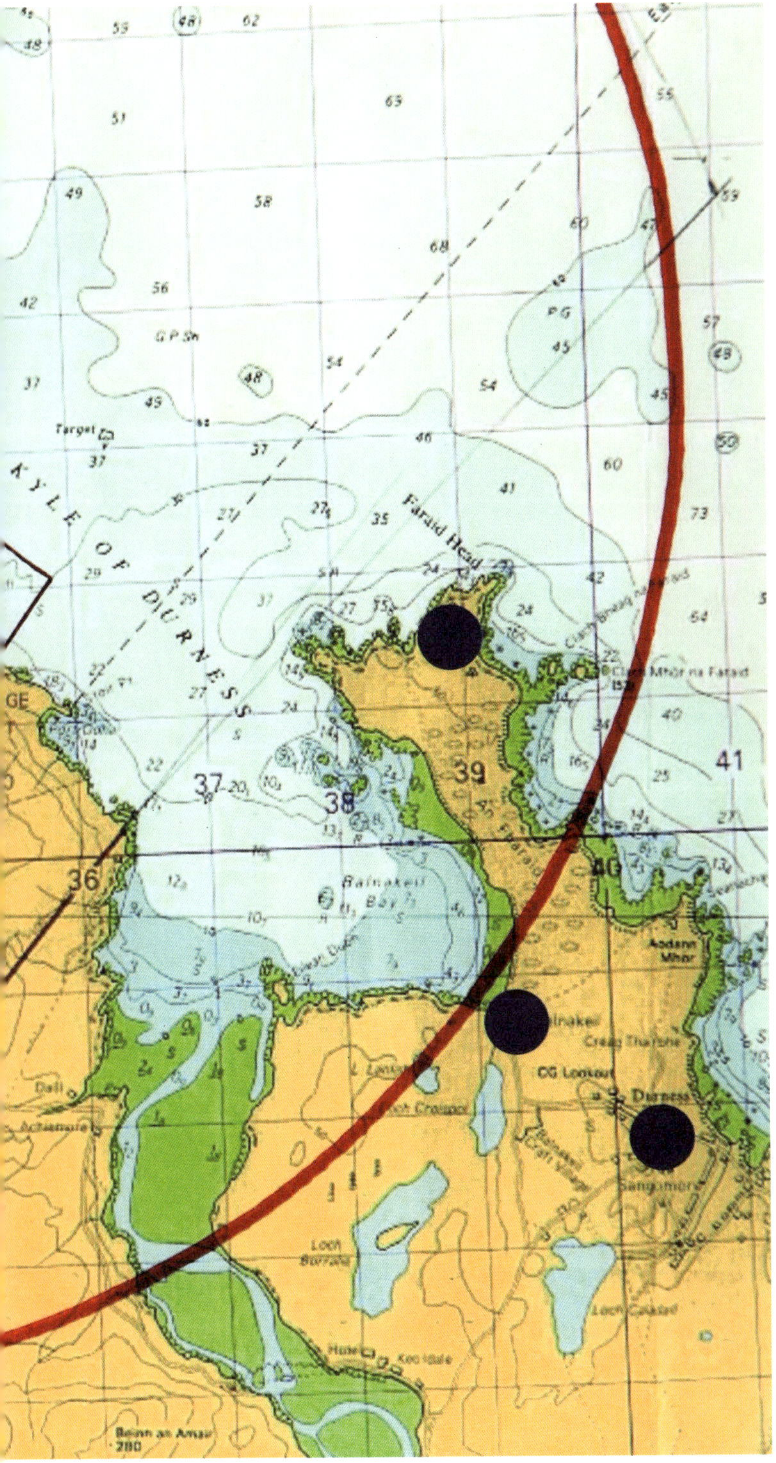

There are different ways to conceptualise space. We know that the hippocampus is important for representing routes. We can imagine that some sort of abstract representation of space, namely a mental model, which might be of your personal space, your space in the world as it were, would be partly determined by memory and partly by the environment. So if you can imagine it is some kind of memory environment interaction then it is going to be different for these different groups.

For the local people it is going to be an almost complete integration between memory and physical environment and physical space. Here the landscape is charged with affective cues facilitating their memory and subsequently allowing them to imagine a future in that landscape. For the local people the landscape works to create and preserve individual memories that link them into the history of their times in a space. For the incomers with their histories tied up in other landscapes, this landscape only gradually comes to be an affective cue. For the military it is serving the purpose of creating a mental schema where there are no individual memories. A schema, which can then be transposed to a site of conflict or war in another part of the world. The military are disconnected from that specific landscape but not that 'type' of landscape and when they transfer to a site of conflict elsewhere, the disconnection which allows routine action continues.

BALNAKIEL
SURVEY

This publication refers to the location of the film *Balnakiel* using a spelling taken from the Gaelic name for the place, Baile na Cille. This is an adaption from the Gaelic that most Gaelic speakers would have used. The spelling of the name of this location has undergone many transitions over the years. The current spelling, Balnakeil, is the one now used on Ordnance Survey maps of the area.

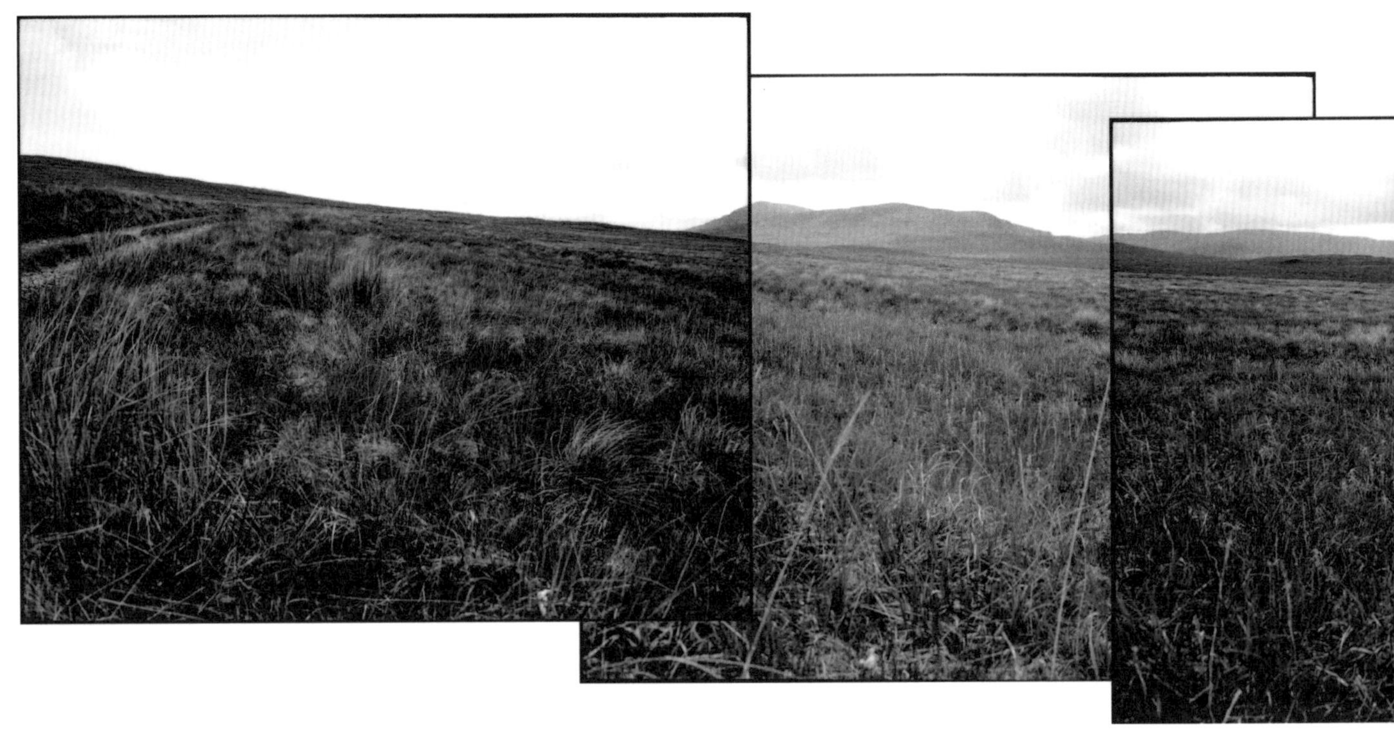

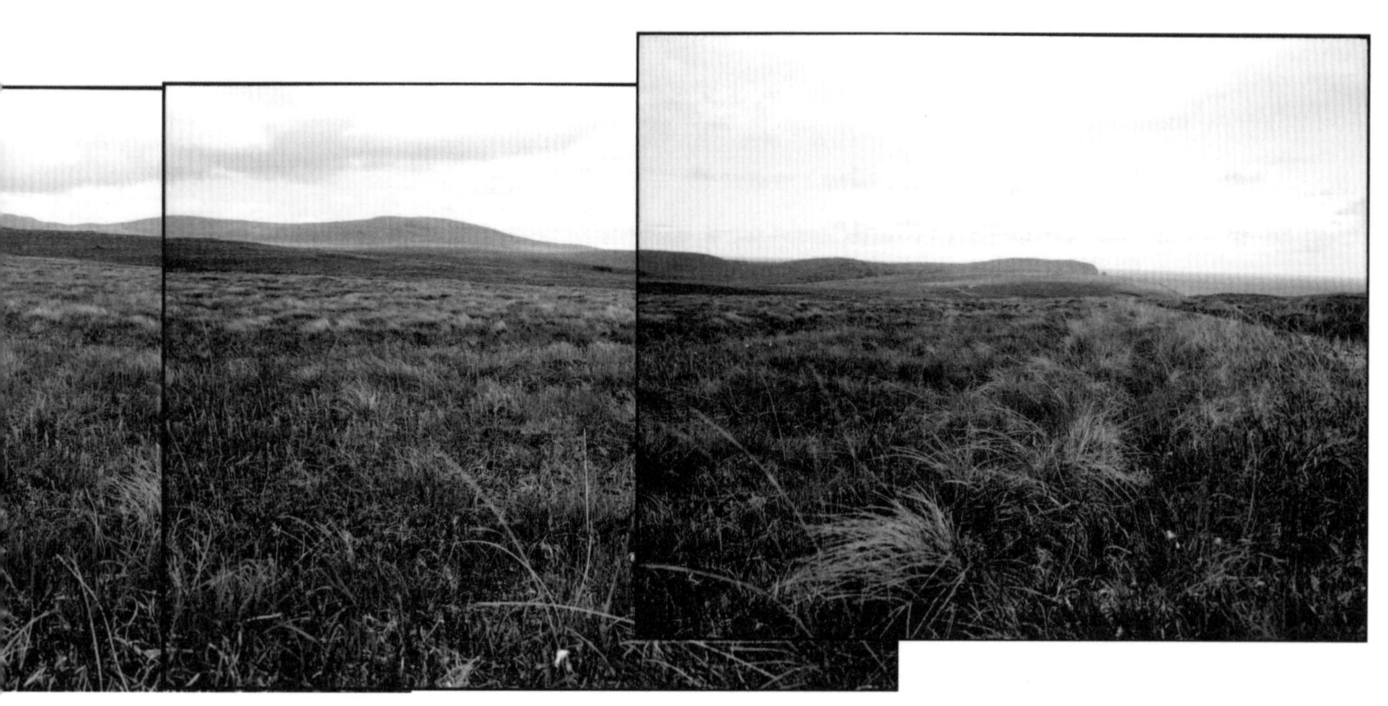

Operation Joint Warrior – Cape Wrath Bombardment Range, 2010. Five black and white giclée prints. Each 762 mm × 508 mm. Cape Wrath Bombardment Range and military training ground for sea-based, airborne and terrestrial exercises, used as preparatory training for active service combat operations or, as more commonly termed, war and conflict. Operation Joint Warrior is codename for military training exercises on Cape Wrath Bombardment Range involving the armed forces of NATO member states, including the UK, the US, Canada and France.

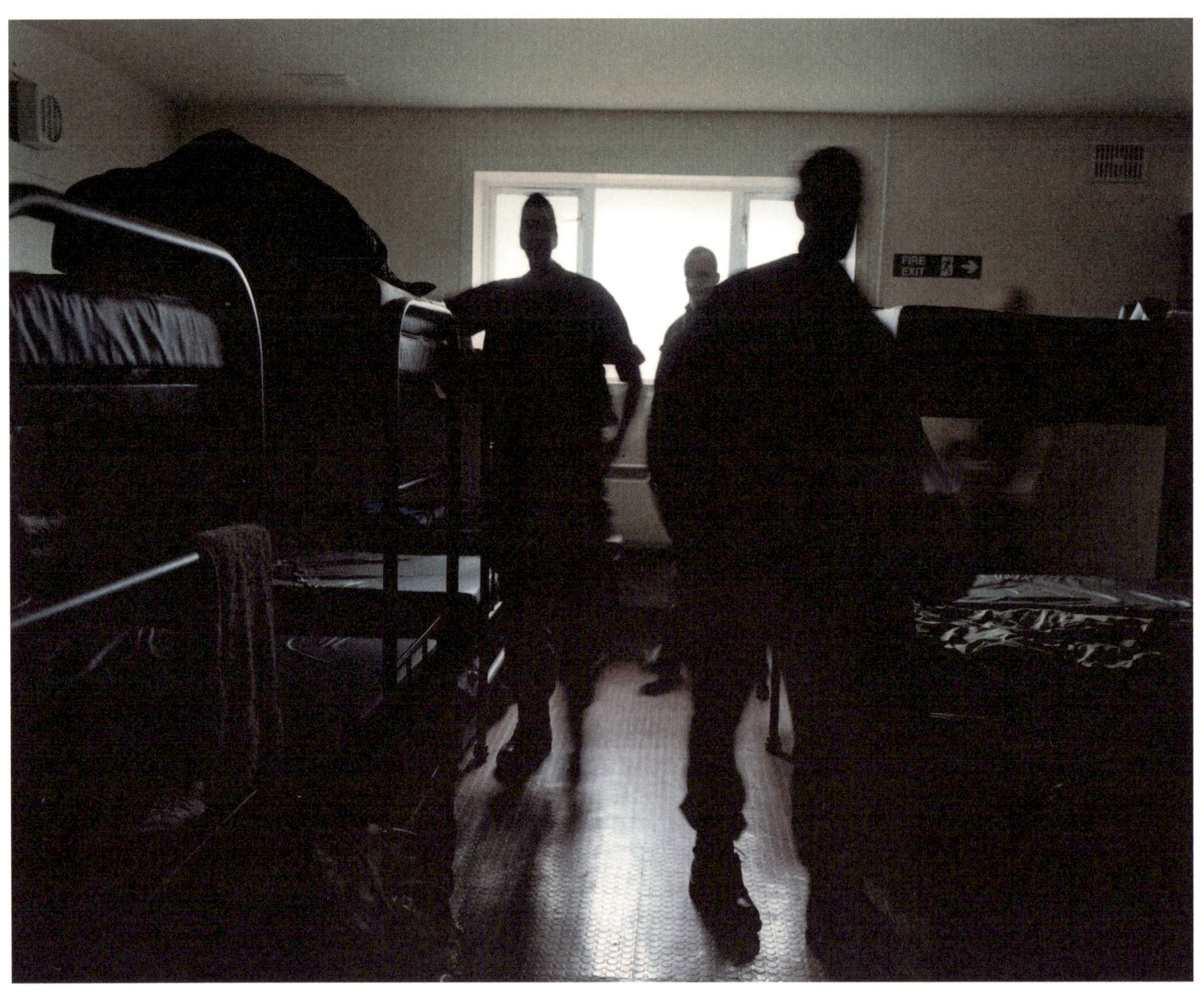

FIRE
EXIT

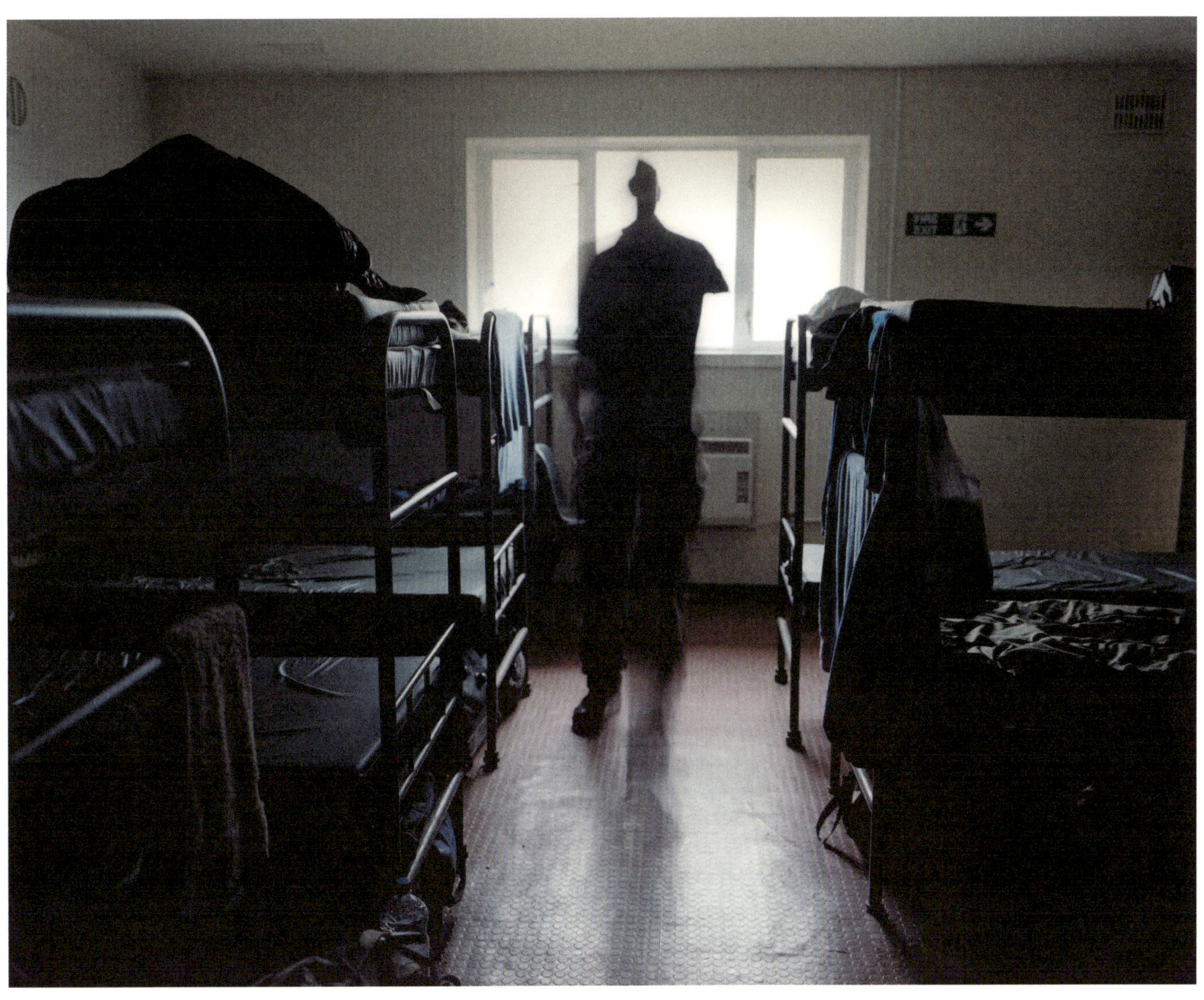

In The Closing Shadow of a Falling Bomb, 2010. From a series of ten giclée prints. Each 508 mm × 406 mm. Officers and soldiers of 29 Commando RA and officers and marines of 2 and 4 ANGLICO Marine Corps, Bunk room, Range Control, Cape Wrath Bombardment Range. The camera shutter remained open for the period of time from the aerial release of a bomb to it striking its target.

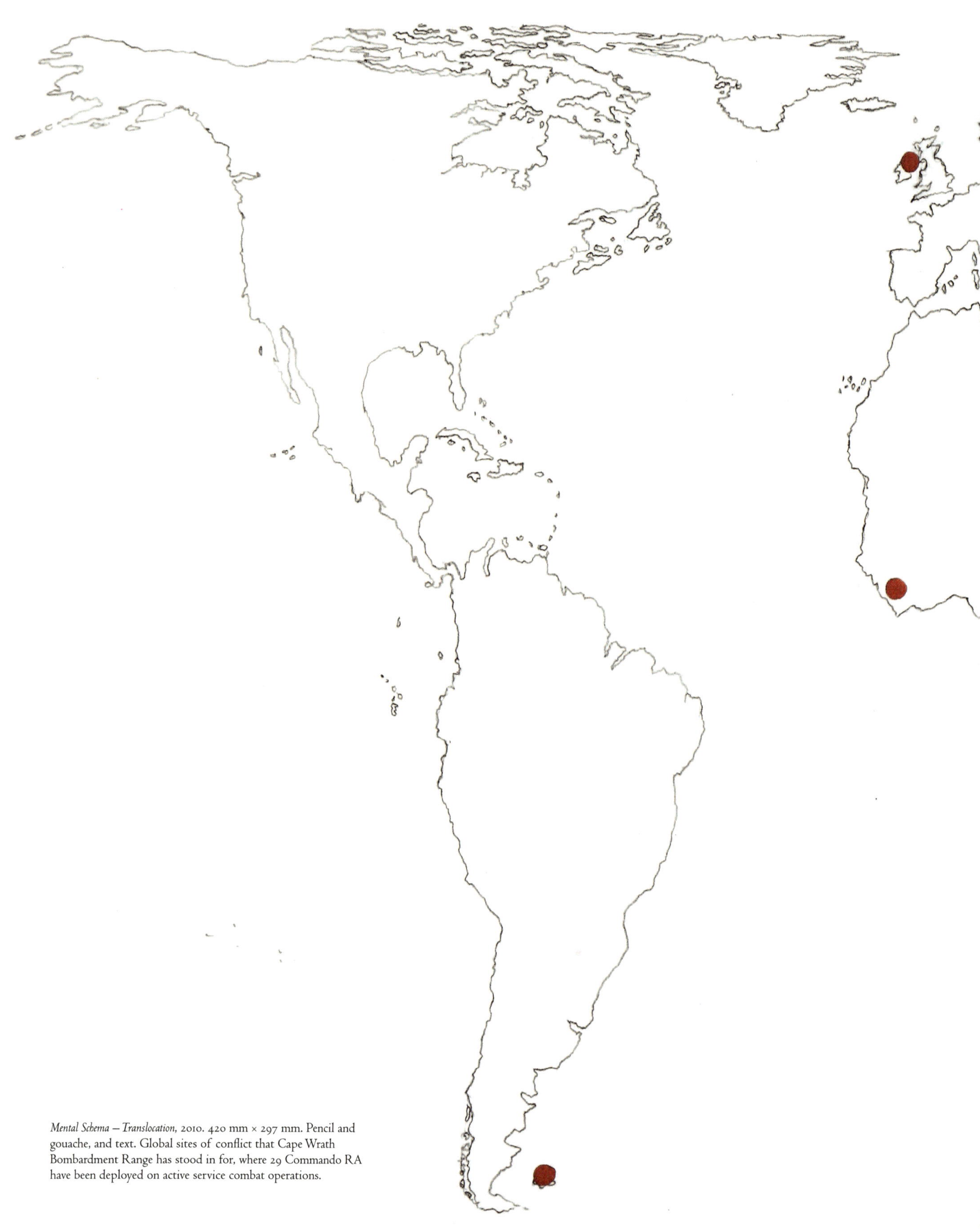

Mental Schema — Translocation, 2010. 420 mm × 297 mm. Pencil and gouache, and text. Global sites of conflict that Cape Wrath Bombardment Range has stood in for, where 29 Commando RA have been deployed on active service combat operations.

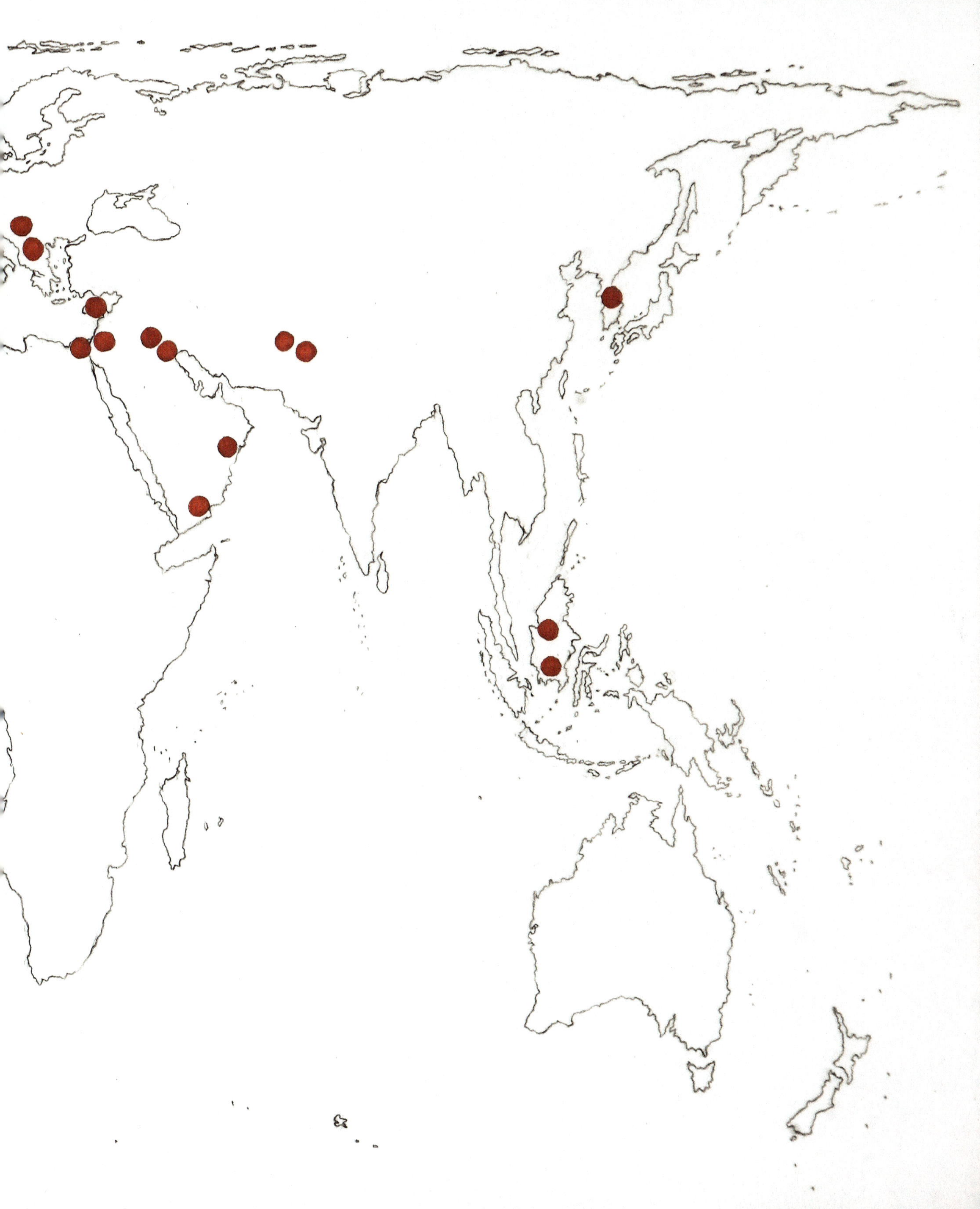

June 1946–January 1947
The Quetta and Murree hills, in what is now the border region
between Pakistan and Afghanistan

1947
Rafah, Southern Gaza Strip, in and around the border area with
Egypt

1955
Gun positions in seventeen locations in the Malayan jungle,
these include a position in a clearing near the Malaysian village
Hulu Langat 25 miles east of Kuala Lumpur

April 1951
Imjin River, the natural division between North and South Korea

1956
Karaolos Camp Famagusta, Boghaz and up into the Troodos
Mountains, Cyprus

1964
The Radfan Hills, Aden, Republic of Yemen

1956
Port Said in Sinai, and the Suez Canal, Egypt

1963
Jungle area in the Balai Ringin region of Borneo

1972
Desert area around Salalah and the Jebel Eesali, Dhofar, Oman

1975
South Armagh, Northern Ireland

1982
San Carlos Bay, Mount Harriet and Port Stanley,
Falkland Islands

1992
Kuwaiti desert border into Iraq and positions around the city
of Basra

1996
Mount Igman overlooking Sarajevo, Bosnia

June 1999
Macedonian border to the Kosovan capital Pristina

August 2000
Jungle camps and mangrove swamps of Rokel Creek outside
Freetown, Sierra Leone

March 2003
The Iraqi desert particularly around the Shatt-Al-Basrah
waterway to the west of Basra, Iraq

2009
The Kajaki Dam in Helmand province, Southern Afghanistan

Mental Schema – Translocation, 2010. Dimensions and media
variable. Since the Second World War, Cape Wrath
Bombardment Range has provided the training ground
and effective surrogate terrain for the preparations for war
and conflict around the globe. A selection of those sites of
conflict are listed above: in all of which 29 Commando RA
have seen action.

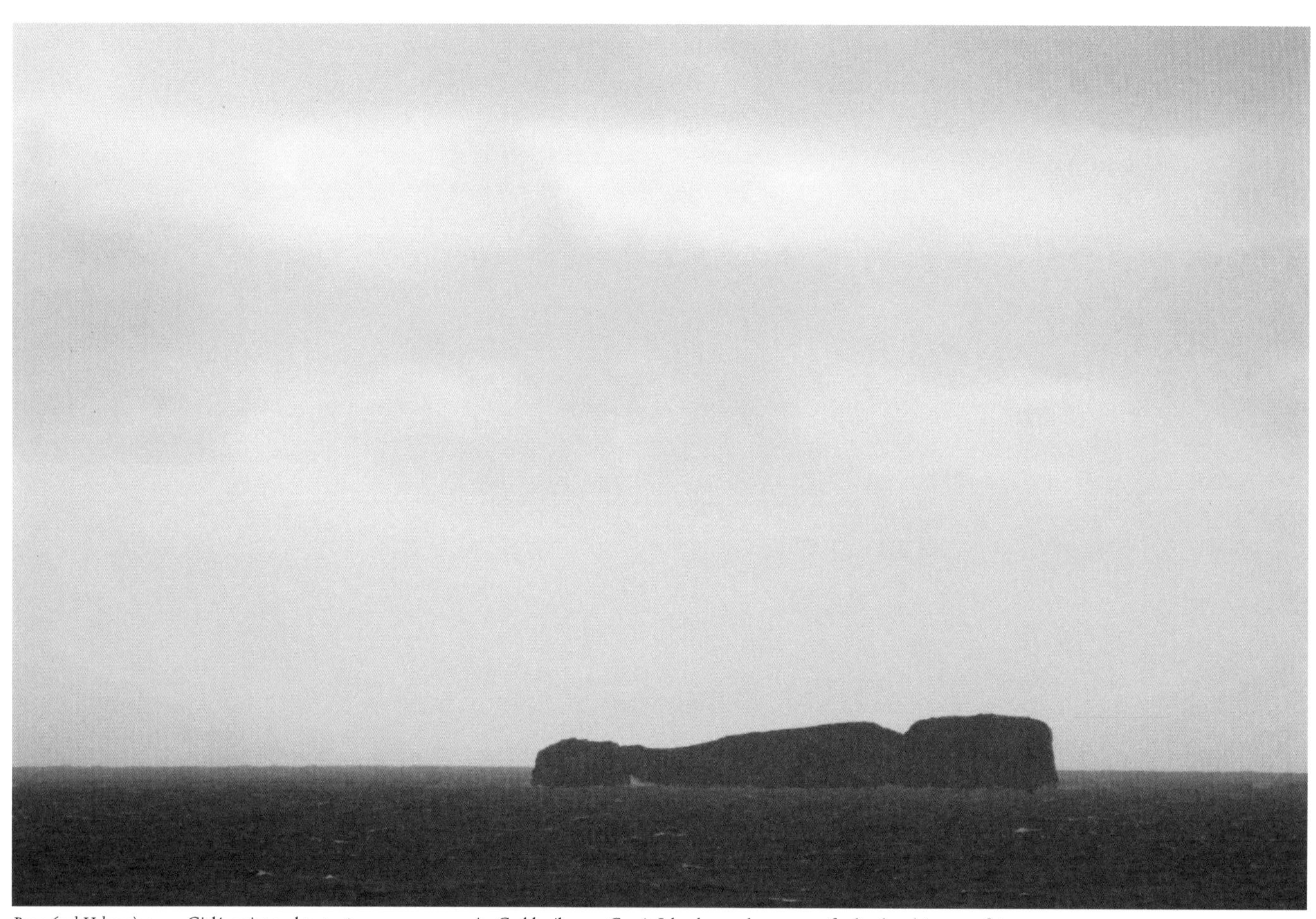

Prone (and Holocene), 2009. Giclée print and text. 360 mm × 240 mm. An Garbh-eilean or Garvie Island – used as a target for live bombing runs firing live 1000lb bombs. Located close to shore within the Cape Wrath Bombardment Range.

**Early Holocene Period
c. 9,700 BCE–8,000
Open landscape dominated by crowberry heath and juniper
Climate warms and birch and hazel woods established by
7,500 BCE
Pollen grains contain sporopollenin, an extremely decay-
resistant compound, which aids pollen preservation in
lake and peat sediments for tens of thousands of years
In these tundra environments pollen from crowberry shrubs
is adapted to be transported by wind over long distances**

Notes from conversations on Cape Wrath Bombardment Range with Dr Anson W. Mackay,
Reader in Environmental Change, ECRC, Dept. Geography, University College London, London.

that's what I always felt when you went
outside at Balnakiel... you were aware
of the sound of your climate
like the vibration... almost the world
turning
you were aware of this huge passage
of time under your feet...

there is something slightly oppressive
about the place, maybe it's not, maybe
it's just overwhelming, maybe it's just
so sensorially overwhelming to be here
nothing inside has a chance to get
out...

rock and bog and mountain and granite
and hard, hard country
and then you come to Durness and
there is this rich, rich verdant green
grass and limestone lochs and the
North Atlantic
you are right on the edge
it has its own social gravitational pull
and then you see Balnakiel
like it was dropped by a B-52 from
50,000 feet with these towers poking
up almost like paralysed flags...

there were just big empty spaces,
big corridors, I thought it was great,
a tonne of clay, a wheel, no money and
a space to work in, that was it freedom,
freedom to create and do what you
want without having to conform...

I did fear it... I did feel fear that the
world could be destroyed
at any time...

Balnakiel Voice Transcripts, 2006 – 2011.
Selected from an extensive archive of
recordings made by the artist of people
who live or have previously lived in
Balnakiel or the nearby village of Durness.

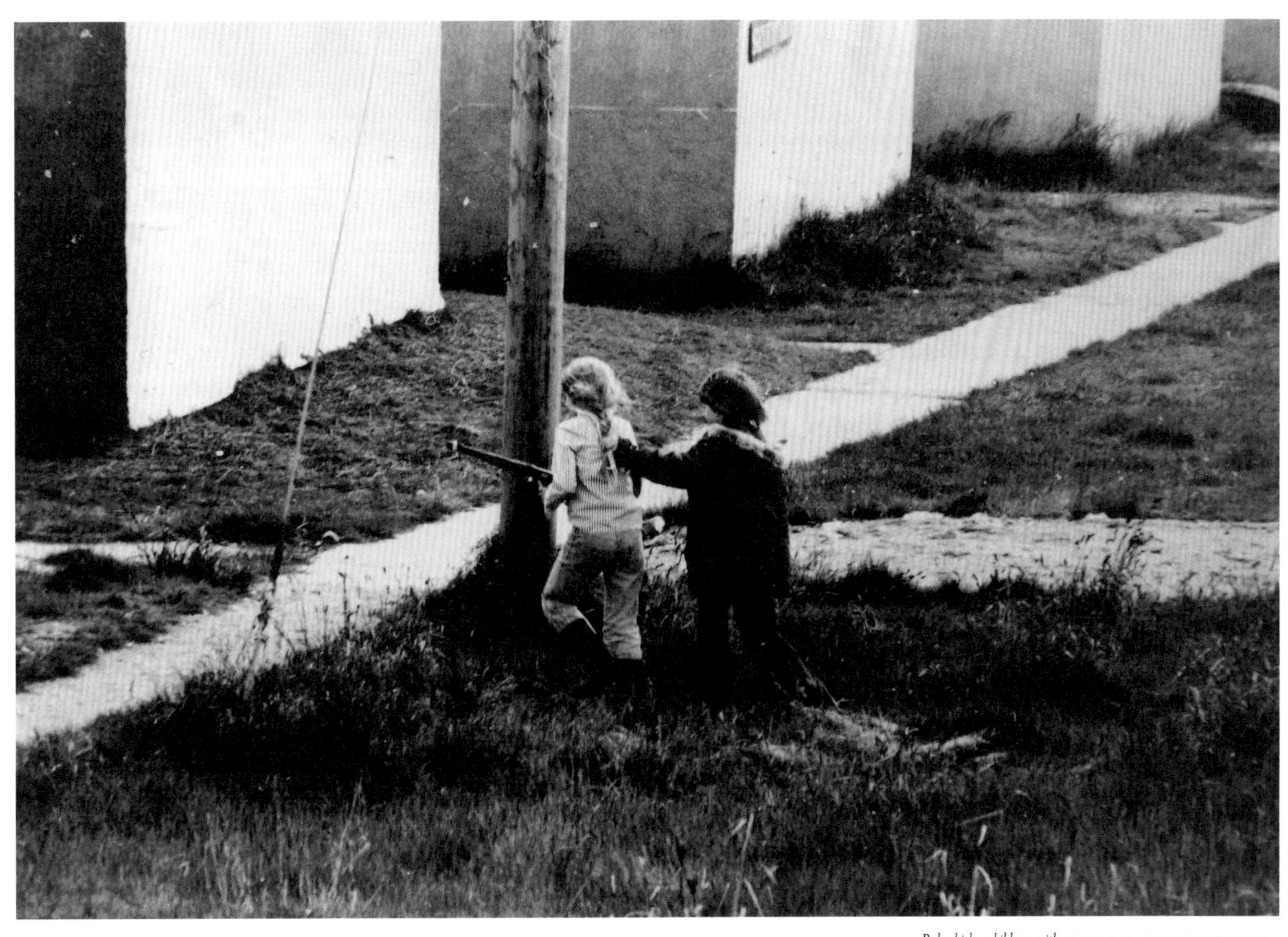

Balnakiel – children with guns, 1970s. 220 mm × 150 mm.
Photograph from the personal collection of the artist.

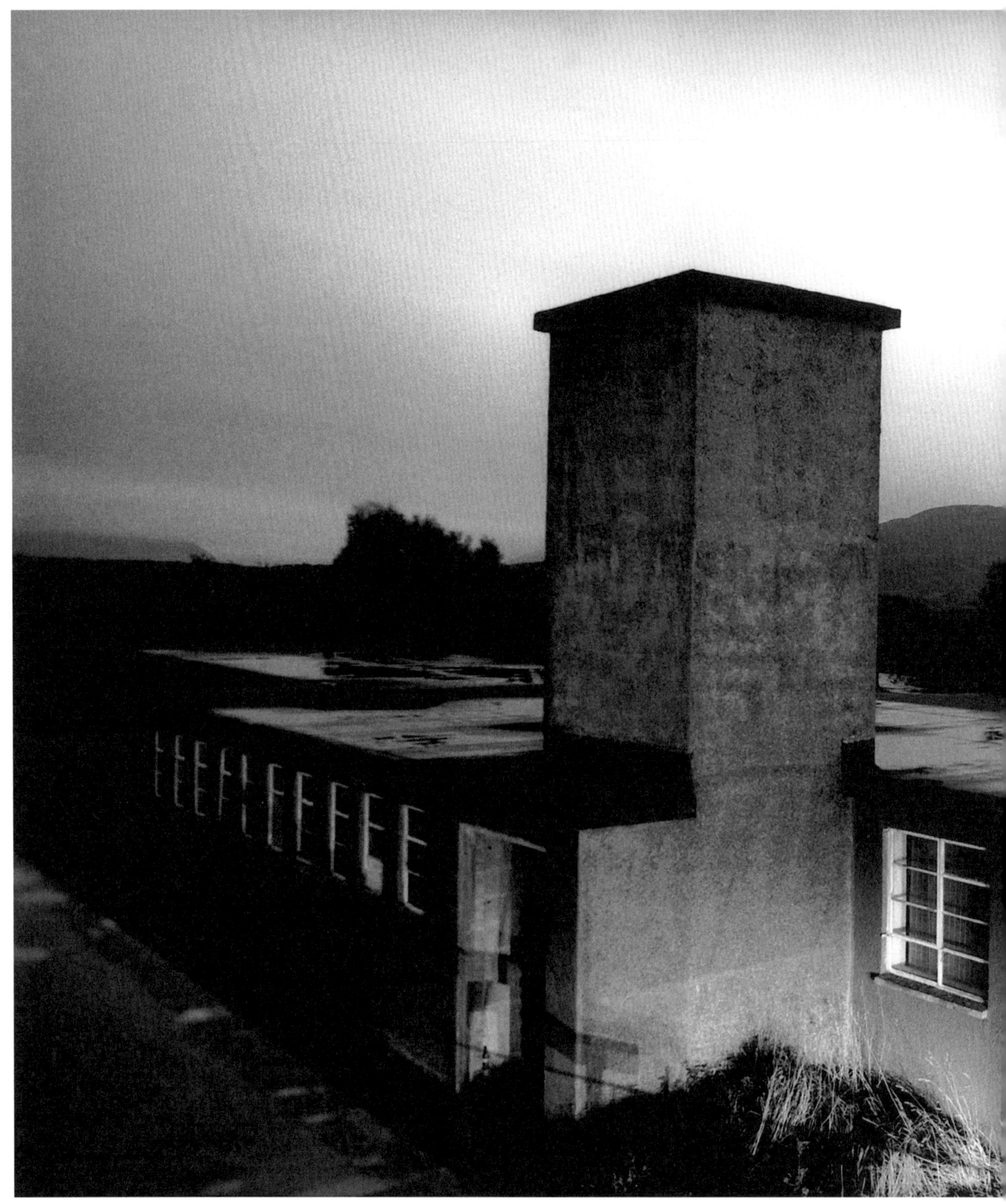

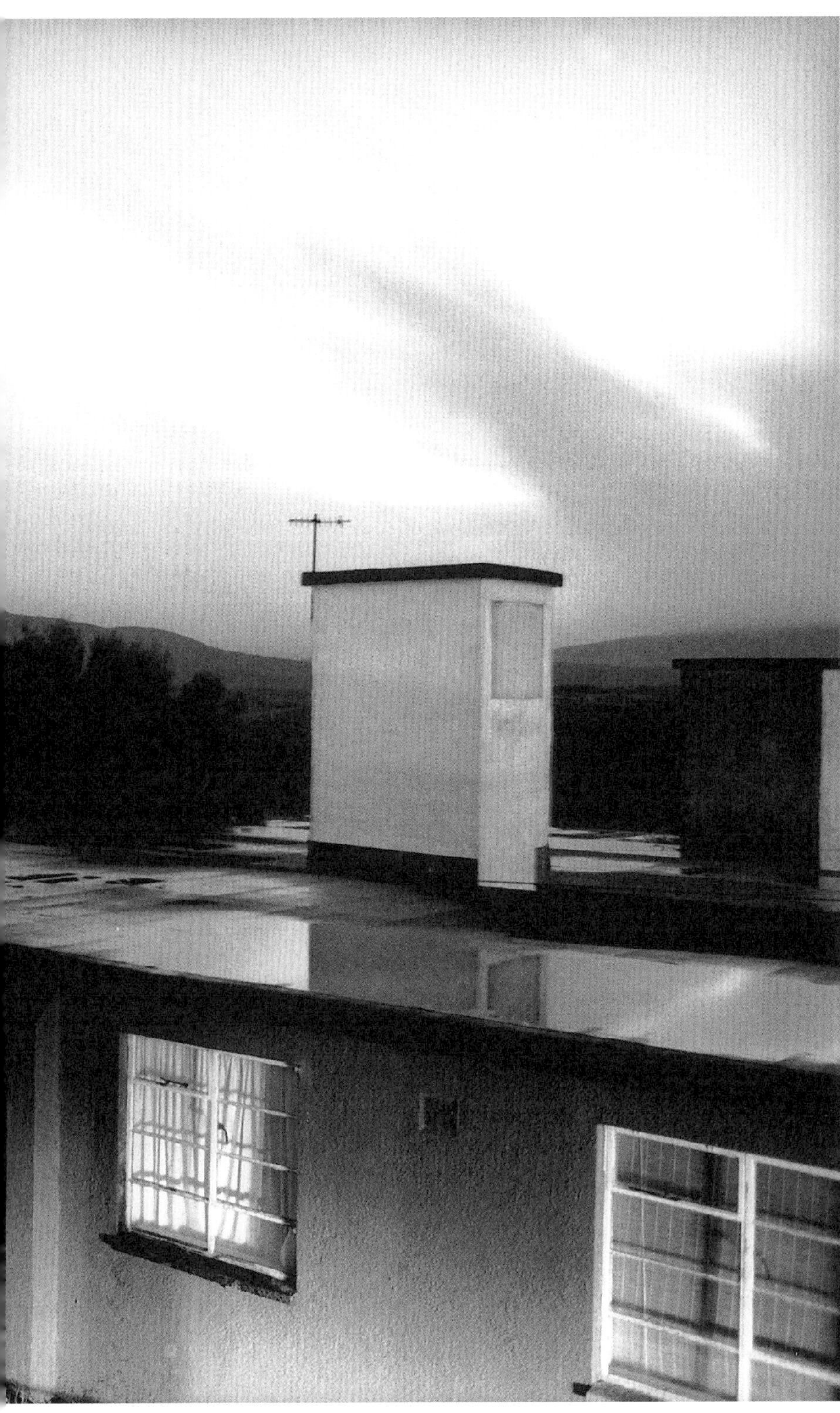

Early Warning Station – 300 sec exposure, 2010.
C-type print. 304 mm × 406 mm.
From a series of long exposure
photographs taken at night.

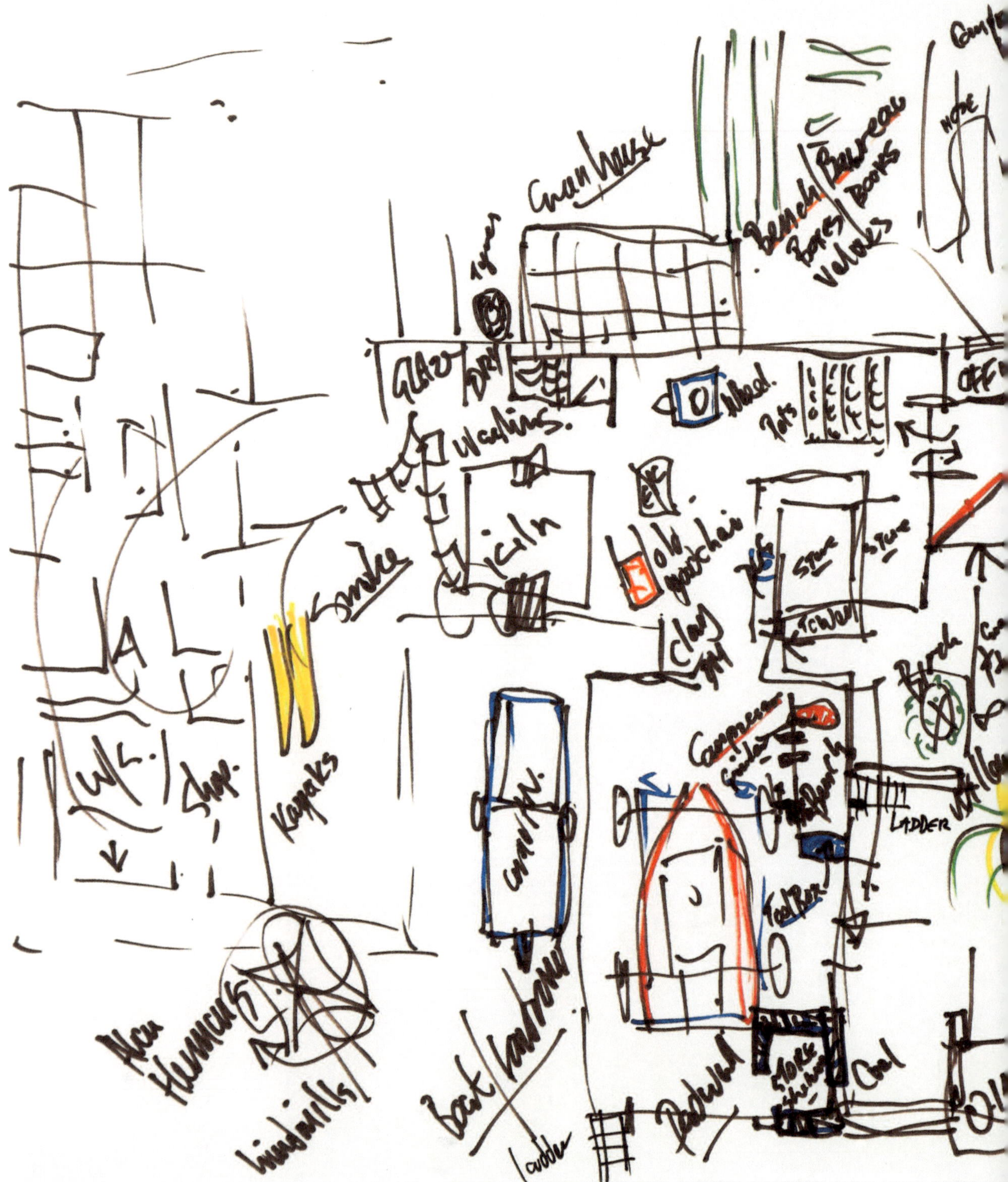

Early Warning Station – Building 15, 2008. Pen on paper. 420 mm × 297 mm. A drawing from memory of the civilian home and ceramic artist's studio and pottery created in Building 15, Balnakiel, the former Early Warning Station military hospital, in the 1970s. Made by a former inhabitant who lived there as a child. From the artist's collection of memory drawings by former civilian occupants of Balnakiel.

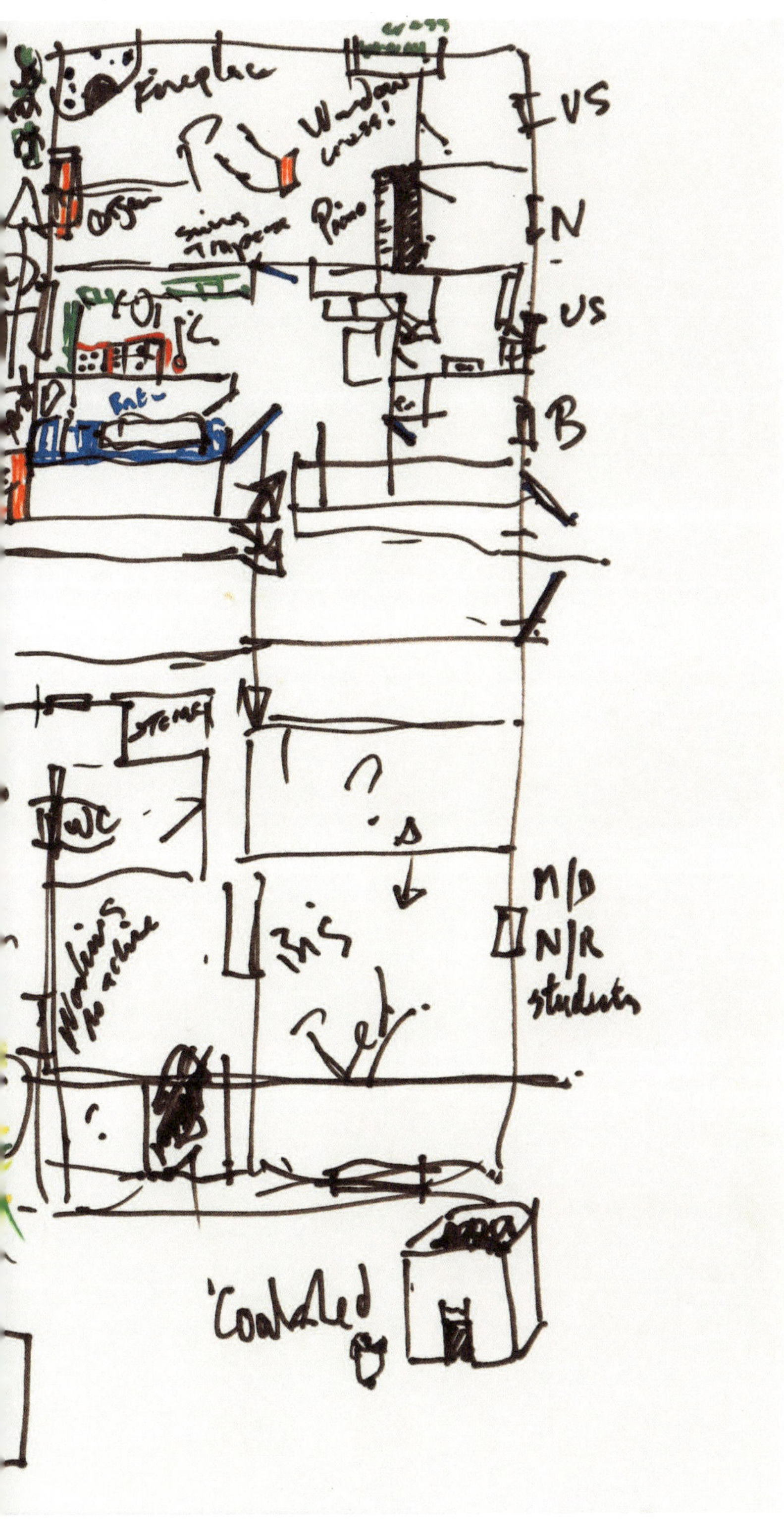

shop
kayaks
windmills
smoke
caravan
boat/landrover
ladder
kiln
glaze
dry
washing
tyres
greenhouse
wheel
pots
old good chair
clay
compressor
bench
tool box
store shelves
bench/bureau
boxes/books
valves
office
comfrey
hose
compost
fireplace
swing
trapeze
piano
oil cloth
organ
window cress
bath
big bed
coal shed
willow
oil
washing machine
birch

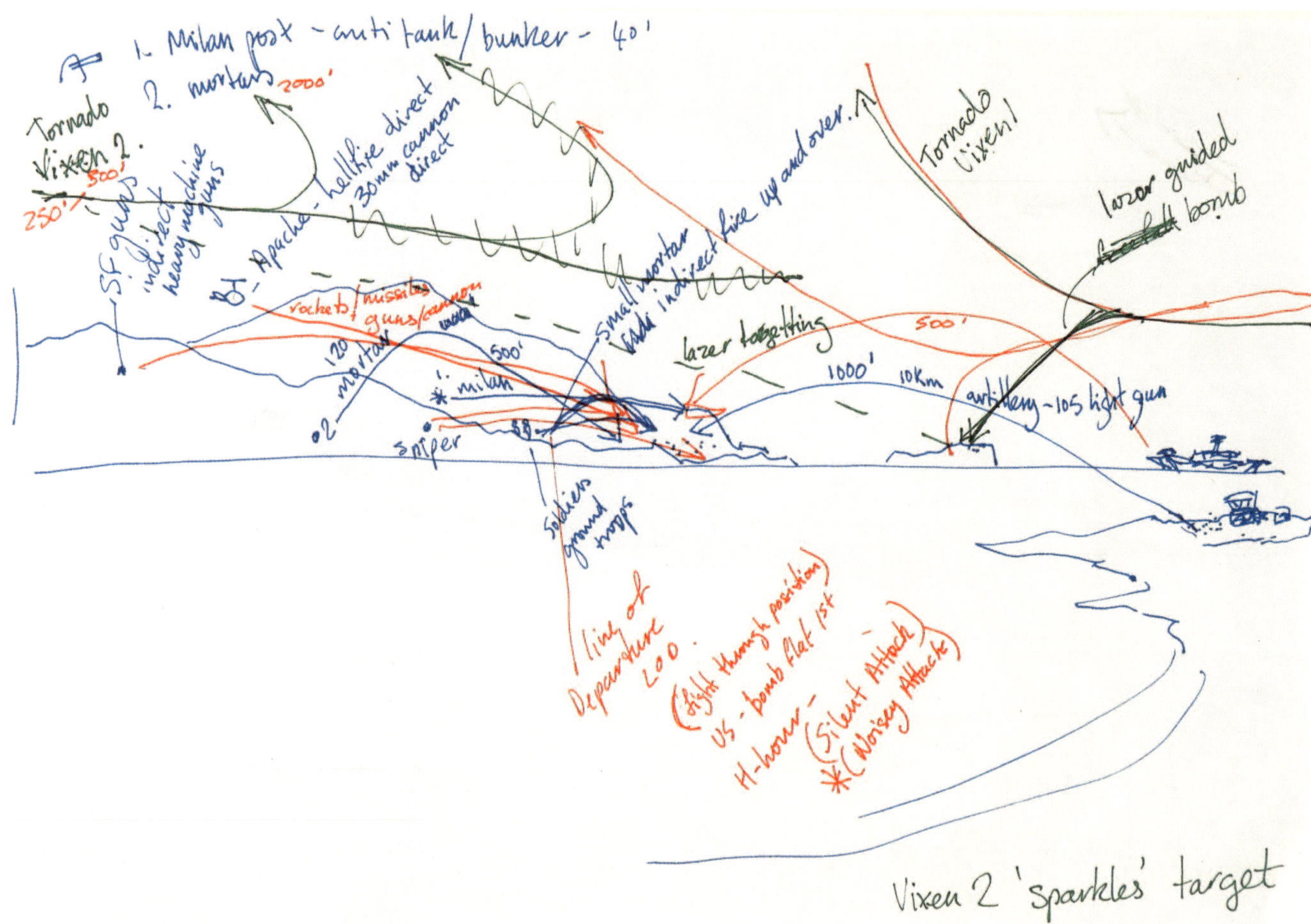

Joint Attack Mission Schematic, 2011. Pen on paper. 297 mm × 210 mm. A sketch mapping the use of 'weapons active airspace' during a co-ordinated sea-based, airborne and terrestrial exercise on Cape Wrath Bombardment Range. Made in conversation with Jason Franks, former Royal Marines Commando Officer, Helicopter Pilot, whose PhD in International Relations focuses on the nexus between terrorism, conflict and peace.

Tornado GR4	**Freefall 1000lb, laser guided and airburst High explosive bombs 30mm strafing cannon**
Apache Helicopter	**Hellfire Missiles, range 500m-8km 30mm chain gun, range 4.5km**
Heavy Artillery	**150mm High explosive/smoke/white phosphorous bombs, range 30km**
Light Artillery	**105mm High explosive/smoke/white phosphorous bombs, range 17km**
Heavy Mortar	**120mm High explosive/smoke/white phosphorous bombs, range 10km**
Naval Gunfire Support	**20mm, range 4km**
Sustained fire Heavy Machine gun	**7.62mm, range 2km**
Milan Anti-Tank Missile	**Range 2km**
Sniper rifle	**50mm, range 1km**
Light Mortar	**51mm High explosive/smoke/white phosphorous bombs, range 750m**
Light machine gun	**7.62mm, range 800m**
Assault rifle	**5.56mm, range 600m**
Pistol	**9mm, range 30m**
Hand grenade	**High explosive/smoke/white phosphorous bomb, range 10m**
Bayonet	**Steel, range 10cm**

Joint Attack Mission – Assets, 2011. Text. List of weapons available, their range and maximum arc of fire, during a co-ordinated sea-based, airborne and terrestrial exercise on Cape Wrath Bombardment Range.

Next page: *Occluded Front – Loch Eribol*, 2009. Giclée print. 406 mm × 304 mm

The controllers in the tower have directed
the jet to the appropriate point and then
what takes place after that, once the
instruction is given, is automatic, non-
conscious, beyond the executive control,
perhaps like many acts of violence when
they reach a certain point.

Another way to conceptualise these
sorts of images is as being akin to the
moment when an item of knowledge is
finally activated deep in long-term memory.
Activation then rapidly and automatically
spreads out through other networks,
activiating other knowledge and memory
details and in the case of a traumatic
memory it overwhelms current processing
sequences, and turns cognition chaotic.

Moine Thrust, 2010. Gouache and graphite on paper.
420 mm × 297 mm. Geological mapping of Cape Wrath
Bombardment Range, which sits on the northernmost
terrestrial edge of the Moine Thrust Belt, and Tornado GR4
strike aircraft. The Moine Thrust Belt was formed 430–500
million years ago in a collision zone as the Earth's tectonic
plates were shifting and two continents collided. Cape Wrath
Range Control Tower sits on an exposed edge of the Moine
Thrust Belt. The strain and deformation mechanisms in
thrust sheets and the violent disruption of the thrust belt by
post-Caledonian faulting are visible in this area.

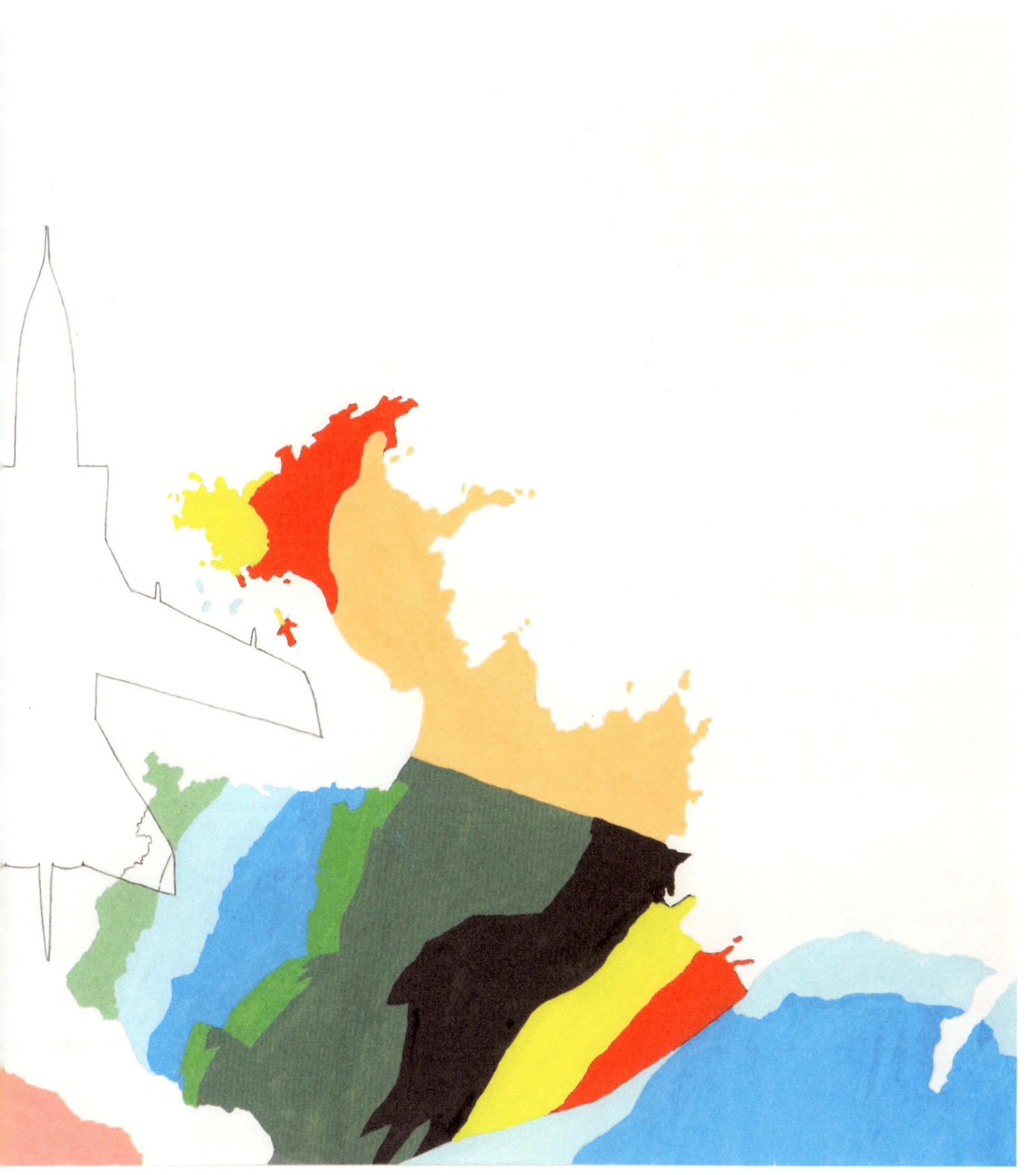

One analogy for memory is that it is like a room full of tuning forks, all tuned at different frequencies. One fork is struck, sending out sound waves throughout the room that will, depending upon their frequency when they arrive, activate another fork, or not. The pattern of acoustic frequencies in the entire room is like the pattern and activation of a complex set of neural networks that represent a memory or set of memories.

What is important is the fidelity of the signals.

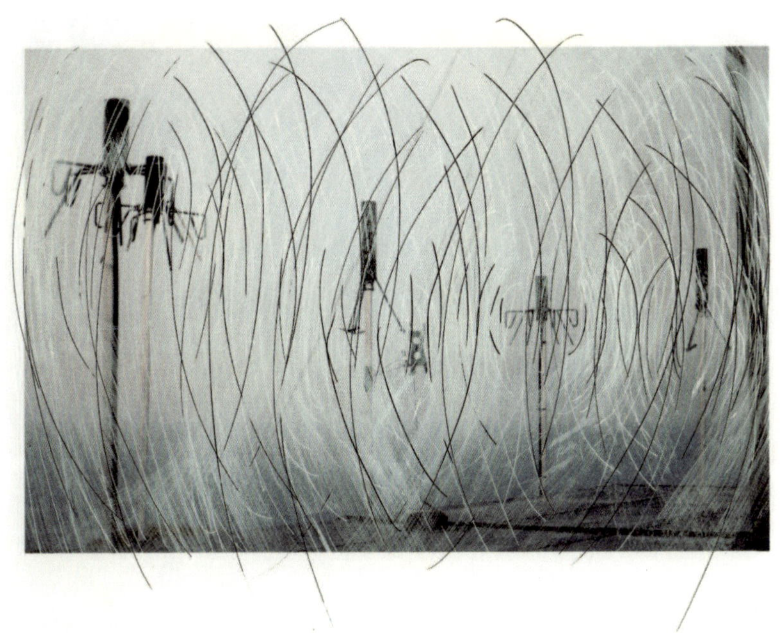

Sound Drawing – Military Antenna, 2010. 210 mm × 183 mm. Gouache and pen on photographic print. Antennae on Range Control during a bombing run when the airspace becomes live with encrypted military radio signals.

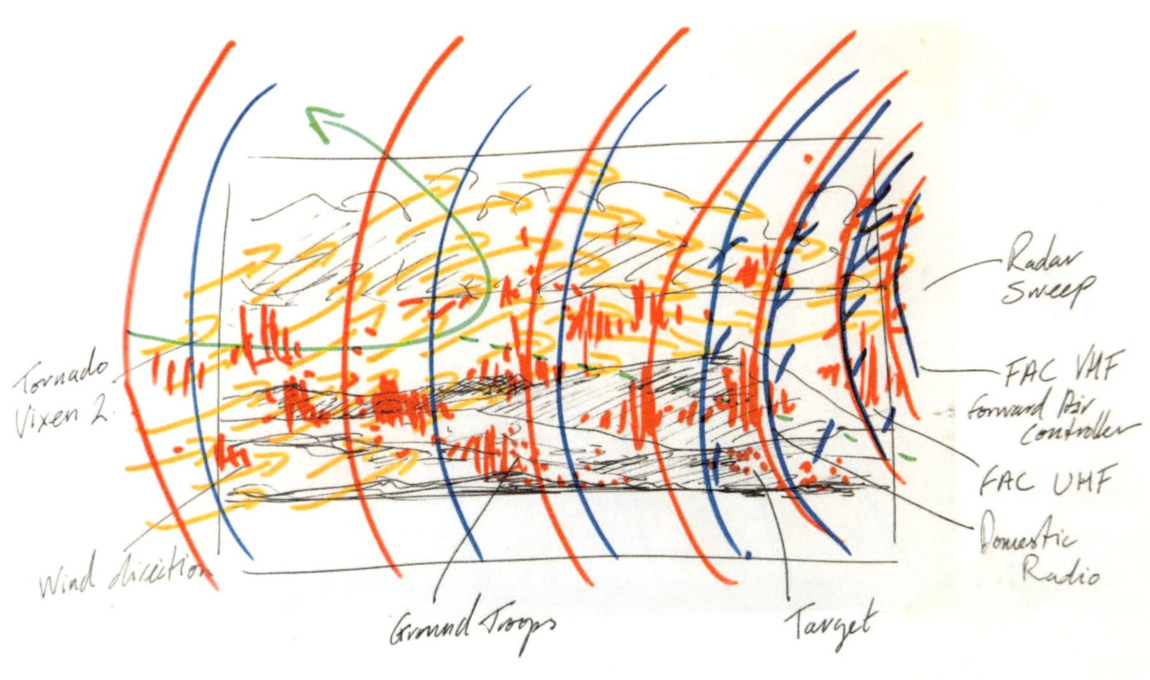

Sound Drawing – Range Active, 2011. Pen on paper and acetate. 297 mm × 210 mm. Sound drawing mapping FAC (Forward Air Controller) UHF and VHF radio frequencies, and domestic radio frequencies onto a radar sweep and the flight path of a Tornado GR4 in weapons free airspace as it laser 'sparkles' a target during a live bombing exercise on Cape Wrath Bombardment Range. Wind direction, the location of ground troops and another active target are also detailed.

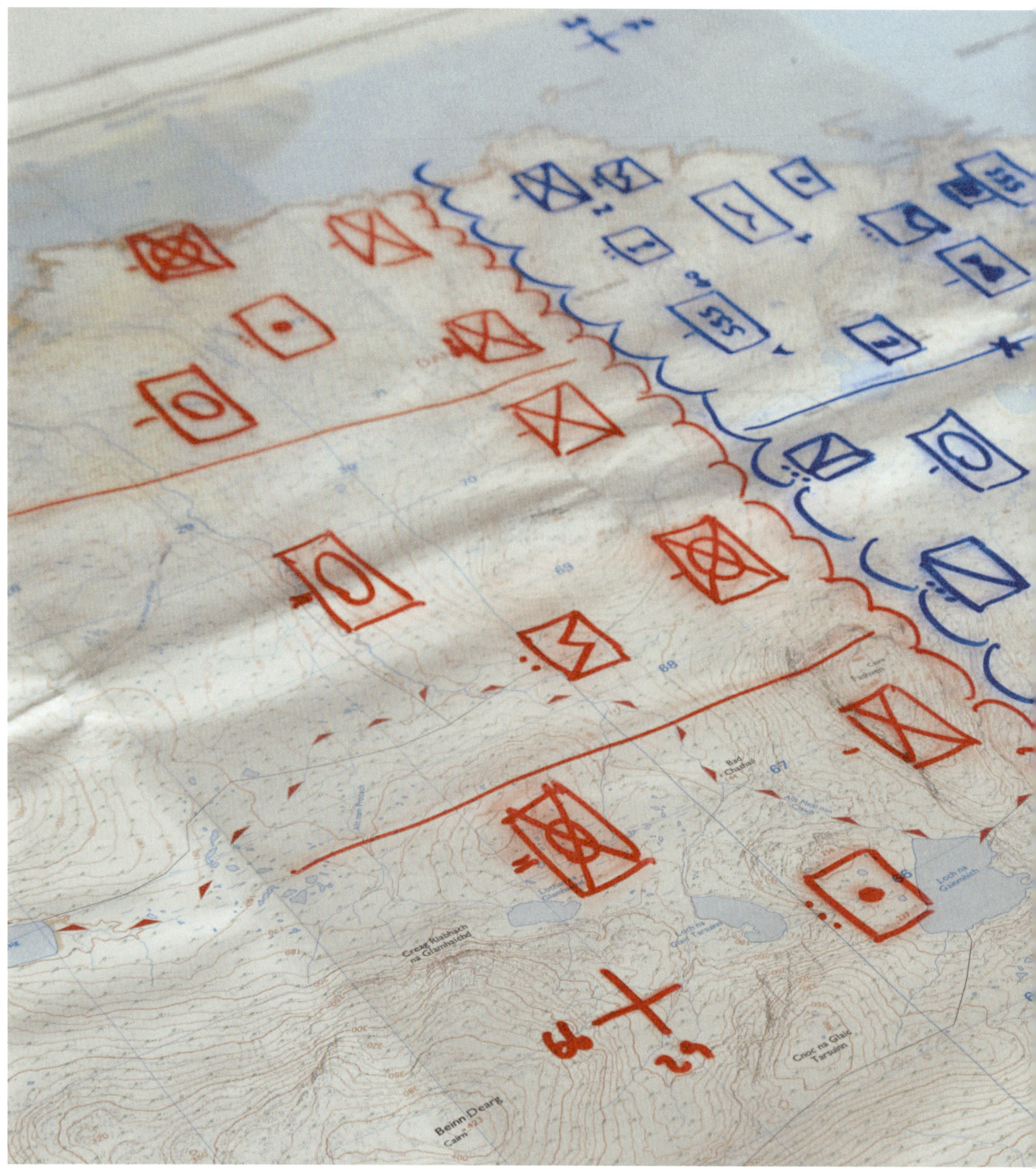

Tactical Trace Map, 2010. Pen, acetate and OS map. Tactical Trace Map created for a proposed or imagined training exercise on Cape Wrath Bombardment Range. Allied forces are represented in blue and the enemy in red. This contemporary mapping system still supports strategic military formations centred on a clearly defined territorial edge or the FEBA (Forward Edge Battle Area) determined through horizontal mapping. A dominant formation used during the Cold War era, this represents the increasingly outmoded model of a clearly defined battle front between two opposing armies reflected in the conception and configuration of the Nation State territorial border.

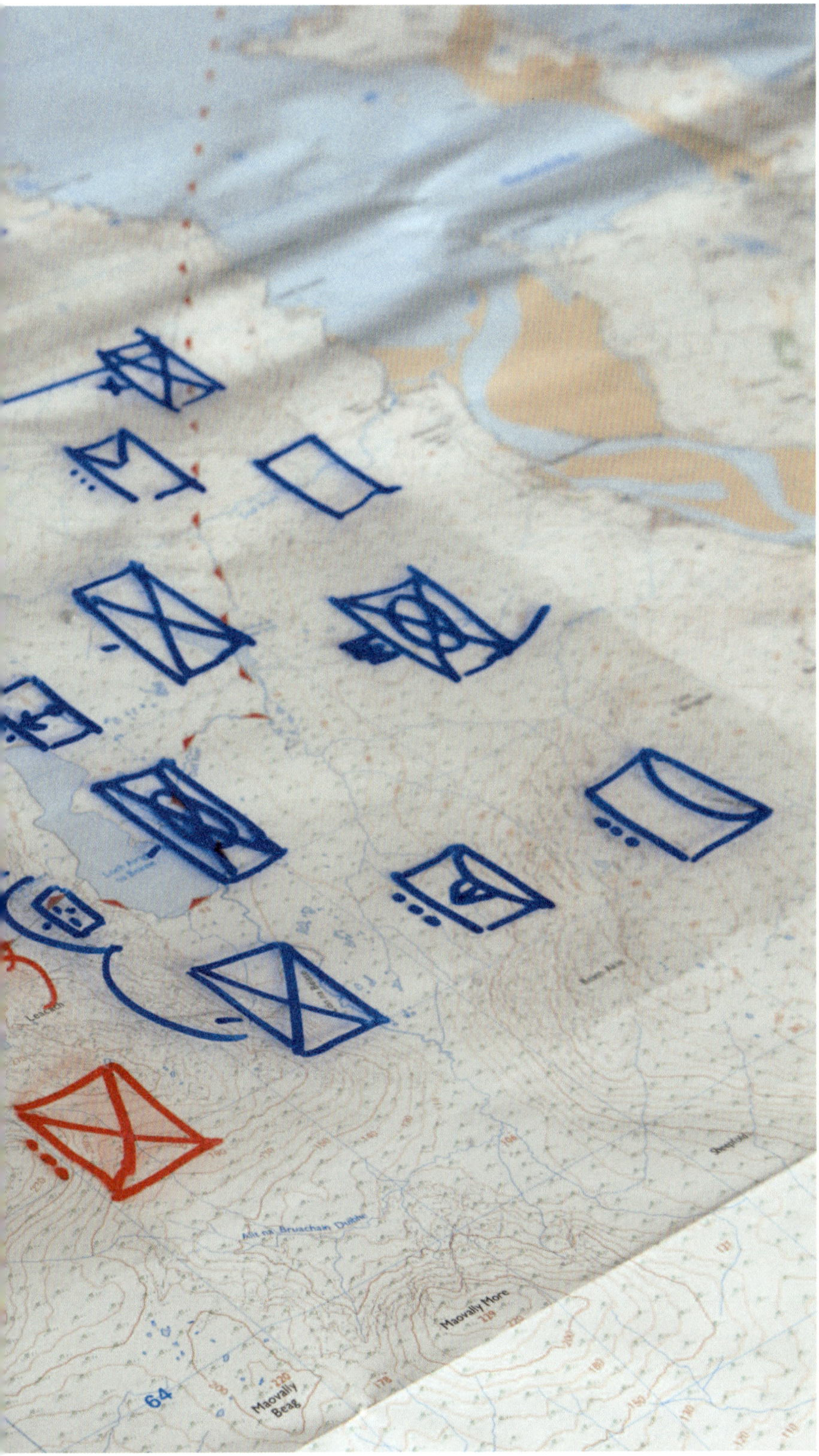

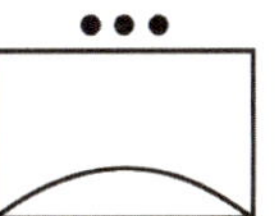

Air Defence Platoon

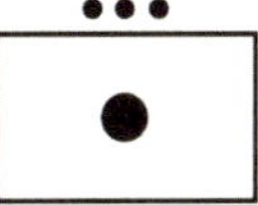

Artillery Platoon

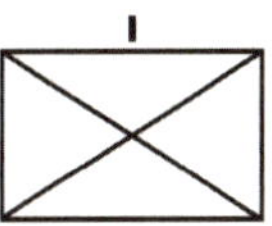

Infantry Company

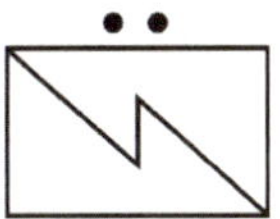

Signals Section

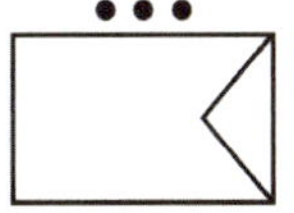

Combat Service Support Platoon

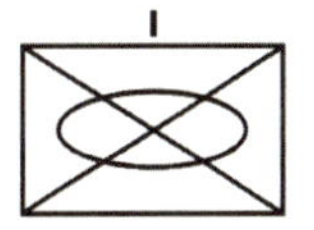

Mechanized Infantry Company

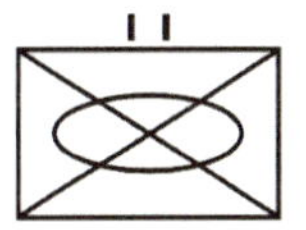

Mechanized Infantry Battalion

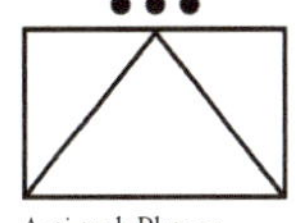

Anti-tank Platoon

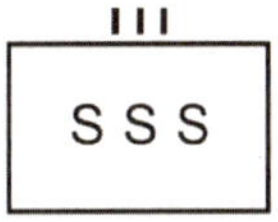

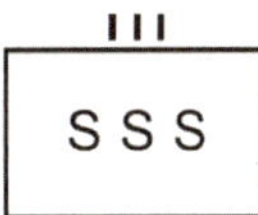

Marine Regiment

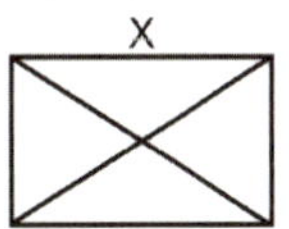

Infantry Brigade

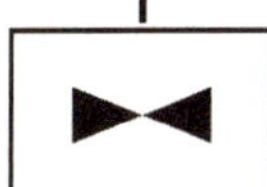

Aviation Rotary Squadron

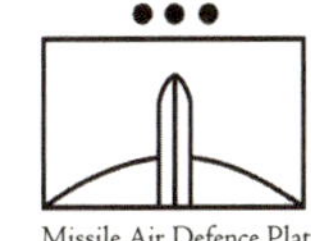

Missile Air Defence Platoon

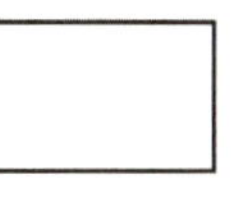

Headquarters (unspecified site)

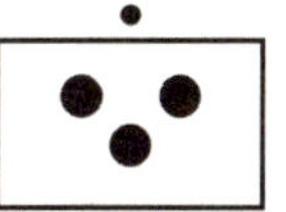

NBC (Nuclear Biological
and Chemical) Section

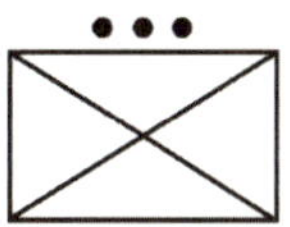

Infantry Platoon

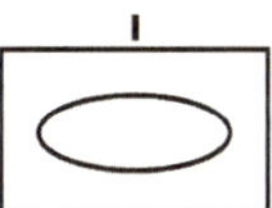

Armoured Squadron

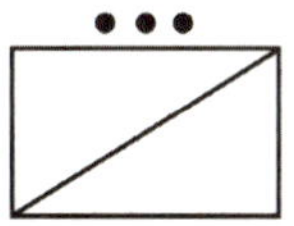

Reconnaisance Platoon

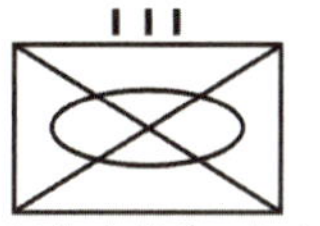

Mechanized Infantry Regiment

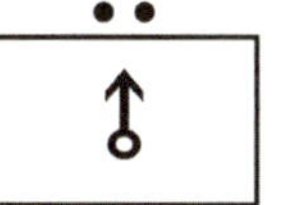

Mortar Section

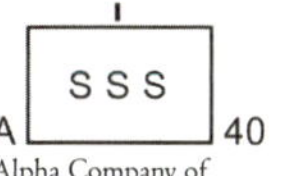

Alpha Company of
the 40 Commands,
Royal Marines

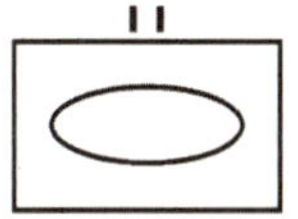

Armoured Battalion

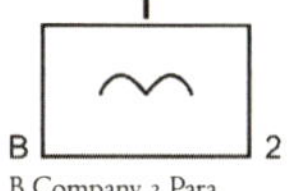

B Company 2 Para

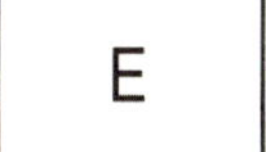

Engineer

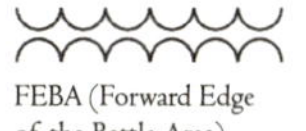

FEBA (Forward Edge
of the Battle Area)

Memories have two aspects, they have their content and then an affective component. Either one can be split off with different psychological consequences.

A landscape may be full of cues that activate memories that never get into consciousness but the associated emotion does, so you suddenly have a feeling as you are moving through a landscape but don't know why. It is very difficult to have conscious insight into these incidences of implicit cognition. When this involves negative emotion the fact that you can't accurately place these feelings can cause an even deeper anxiety.

This drawing refers to the experience of a man, recounted in the film *Balnakiel,* for whom a particular place in the landscape precipitates a profound sense of anxiety and threat. This then manifests in an intense physical reaction. He associates this with childhood experiences though he cannot bring to mind an actual event that could explain the intensity of these feelings.

The drawing depicts the proposal that in the mind, memories consist of a *conceptual frame* attached to a set of *episodic features*. Episodic features are very often in the form of static visual imageries although they can be represented in other modalities as well and sometimes may be multi-modal and occasionally may have moving images. The episodic features are represented in what we have termed an *episodic fragment*. So a *simple episodic memory* consists of a conceptual frame and an episodic fragment. This is depicted in the left-hand side of the diagram. The conceptual frame contains information about feeling intensely anxious as a child. The episodic fragment contains images generated by the fear of being bullied or attacked and perhaps other visual images as well.

The diagram depicts what might happen if one lost access to a conceptual frame but retained access to an episodic fragment. When the episodic fragment was retrieved, an individual might try to think of what part of their life this image came from and in the right-hand side of the diagram, one can see the depiction of how a new conceptual frame comes to be formed and attached to the episodic fragment. The episodic fragment now has two conceptual frames, one which is consciously accessible and one which isn't and when the memory is retrieved, the images are associated with a conceptual frame that states this is something that happened to me when I was a child. Clearly this is a new conceptual frame and maybe quite incorrect. The next diagram tries to depict how a conceptual frame might be changed to produce what is known as a *source monitoring error.*

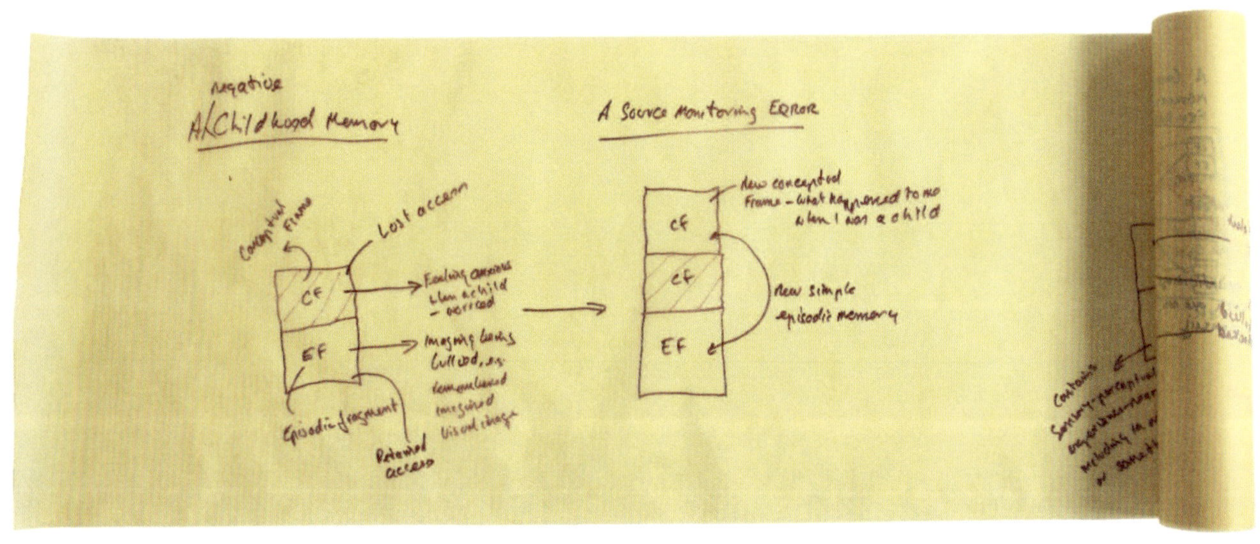

negative
A Childhood Memory
A Source Monitoring Error
Conceptual Frame
Lost access
CF
EF
Episodic fragment
Retained access
Feeling anxious when a child – overused
Imagery being bullied, eg remembered imagined visual image
New conceptual Frame – what happened to me when I was a child
CF
CF
EF
New simple episodic memory
Contains Sensory-perceptual

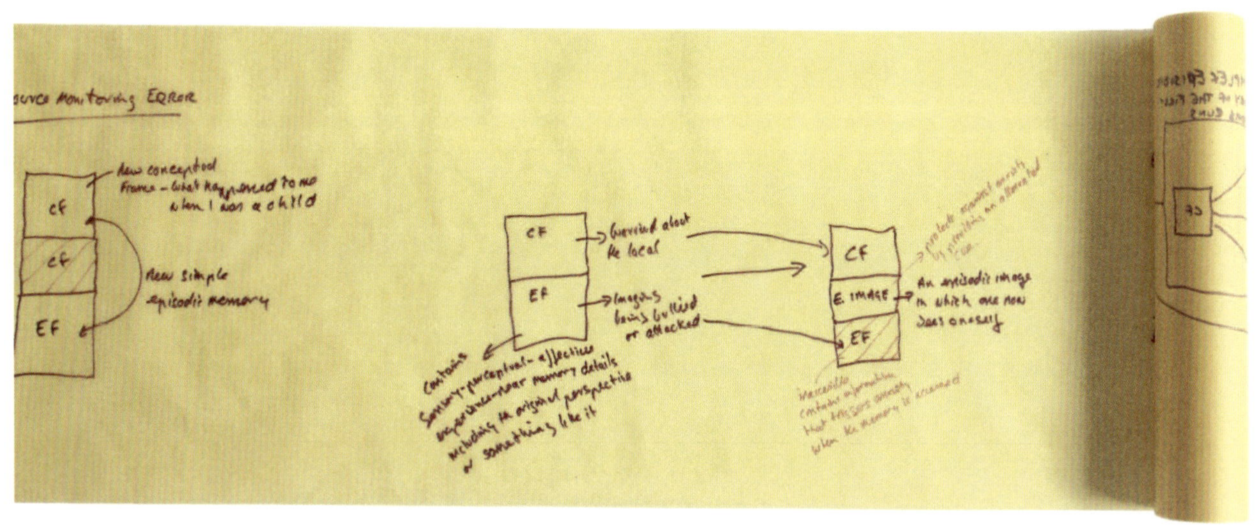

Source Monitoring Error
New conceptual Frame – what happened to me when I was a child
CF
CF
EF
New simple episodic memory
CF
EF
Worried about the local
Imagery being bullied or attacked
Contains Sensory-perceptual-affective organised-near memory details including the original perspective or something like it
CF
E. IMAGE
A. EF
An episodic image in which one now sees oneself
CF

The third diagram shows how military training in this landscape is used to create a mental schema devoid of individual memories that can then be transferred to sites of war and conflict elsewhere in the world. On the left-hand side of the diagram, several bombing runs are depicted and each gives rise to a conceptual frame with an episodic fragment. As these rather similar memories proliferate in memory, they become attached to a more complex conceptual frame that organises them and it is that conceptual frame of bomb runs in general that form the schema. It is the creation of the schema that is important. Here the landscape serves the purpose of allowing the military through repeated similar experience in training to build up a schema for what is a complicated and coordinated set of actions by several different groups of combatants. This also allows these military units to generate a collective sense of becoming masterly and being accomplished so that they can feel ready for action when they go into a war zone and systematically carry out those sets of actions.

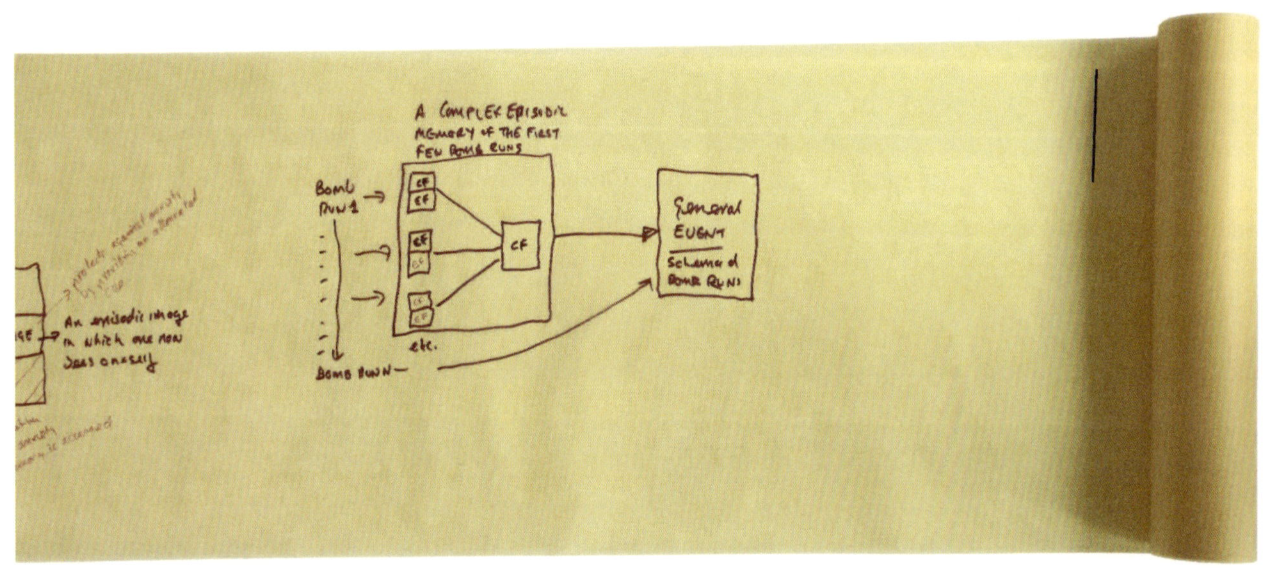

Memory Drawings – Mental Schema and Source Monitoring Errors, 2010. Pen and Canary paper. Roll 304 mm wide. Made by Martin A. Conway in conversation with Shona Illingworth.

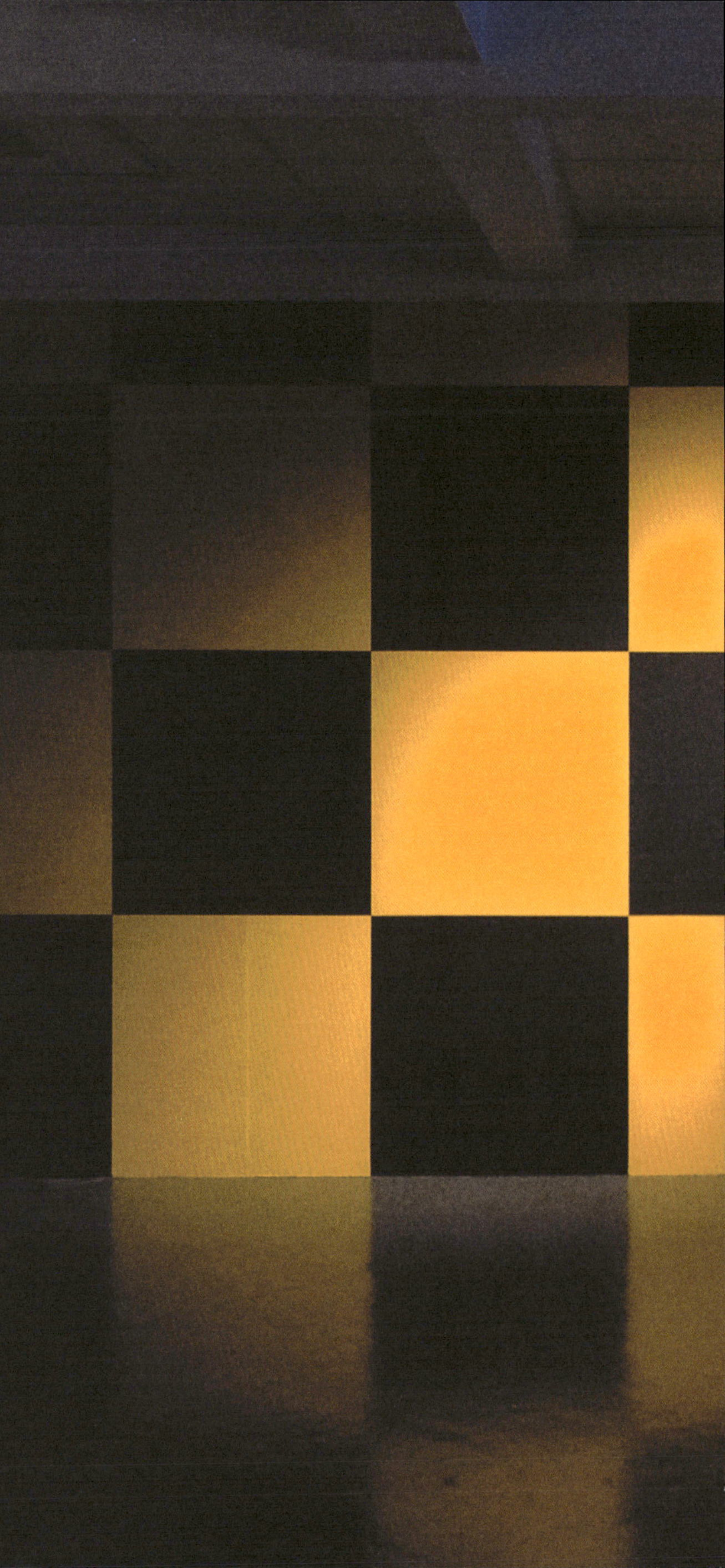

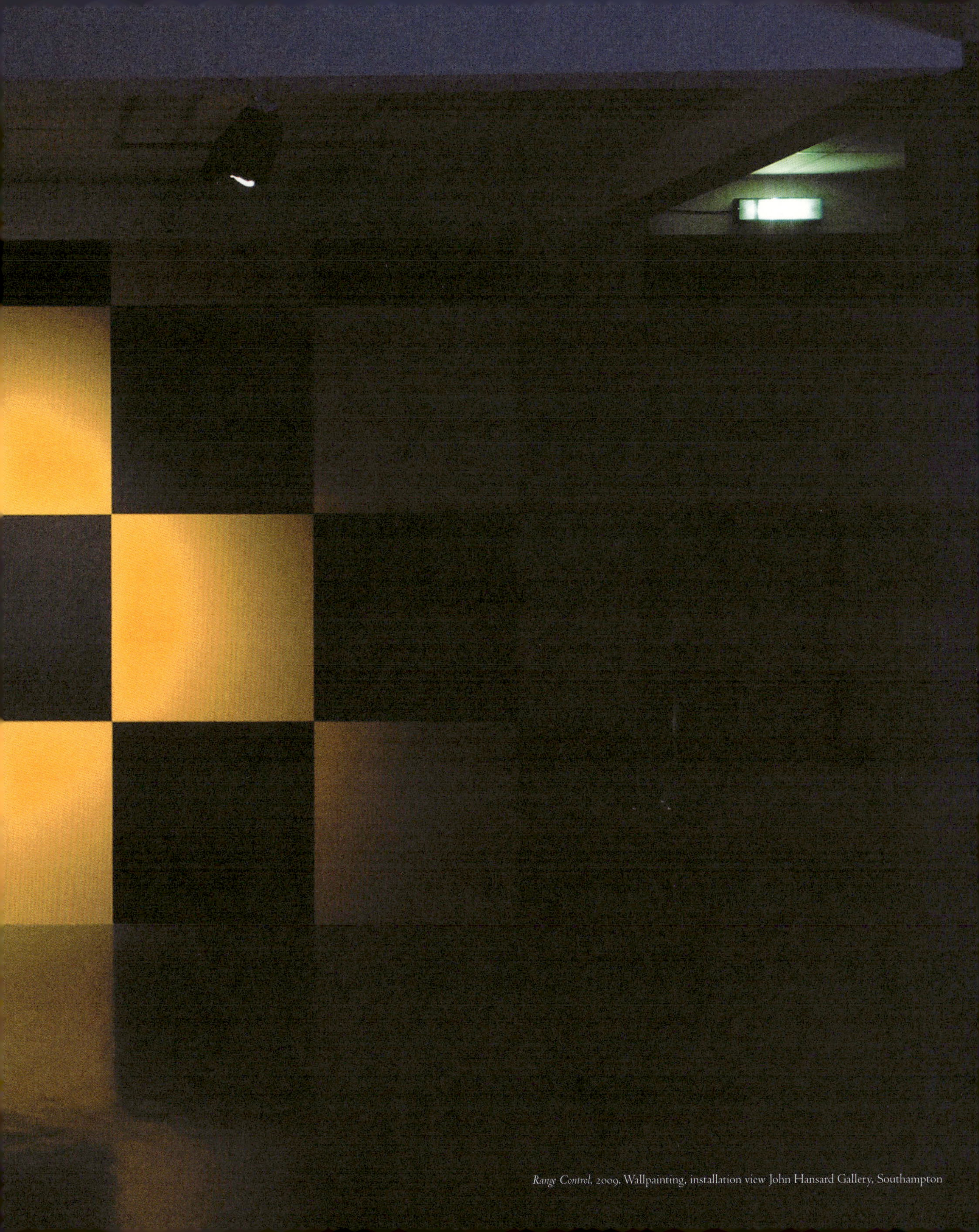

Range Control, 2009. Wallpainting, installation view John Hansard Gallery, Southampton

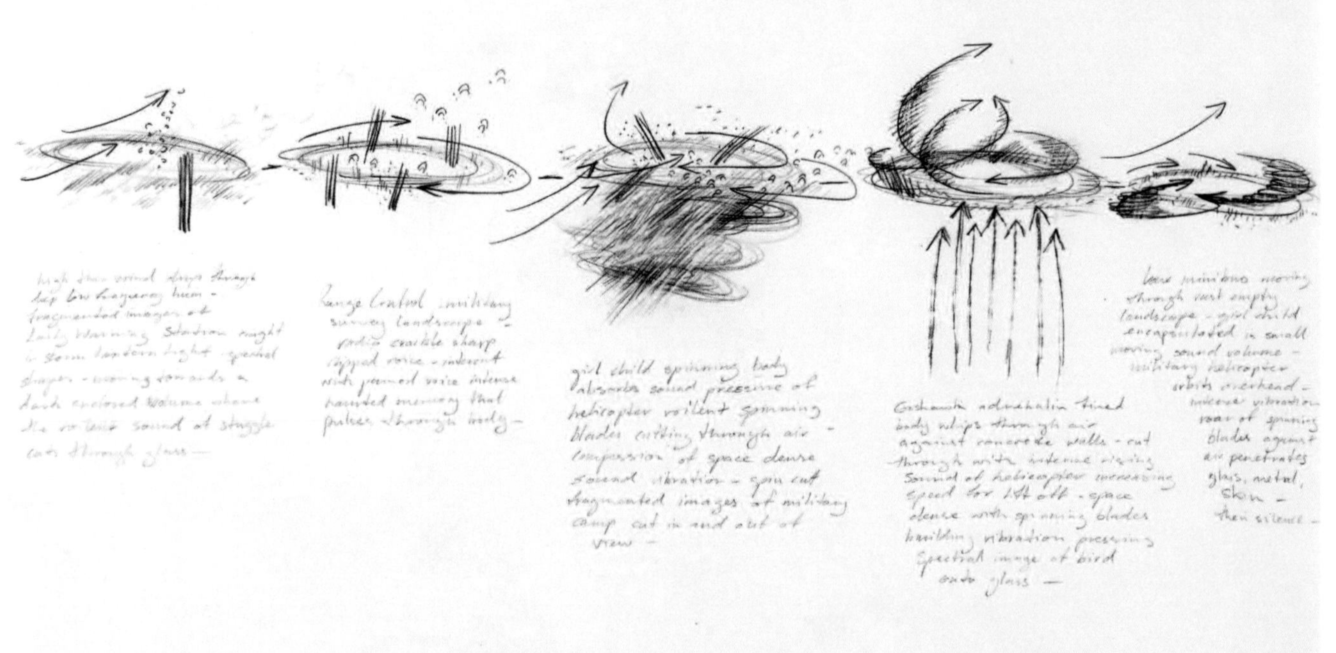

Balnakiel – Sound Drawing With Notes, 2009. Graphite on paper, 415 mm × 290 mm, depicting the forward temporal order of the video and sound installation *Balnakiel*, interrupted by volumetric compositions of sound.

The images viewed from the Range Control Tower are like control processes embodied by the tower looking out expectantly into the future, they are based on what has gone on before. They are based on the communications which permeate the atmosphere and the landscapes surrounding the tower. The military jets might be thought of as plans about to be executed, plans which have to be organised and sequenced to come in at the right time and at the right pace. The Watch Tower has a plan for how this is to be achieved and that plan is based upon memories, expectations and an anticipation of the future. Thus the action in Balnakiel takes place in what we might call 'the remembering-imagining system' in which the past can be constructed and those mental constructions used to guide the future action. Without a past there will be no future actions.

Caterina Albano

BALNAKIEL: IN THE SPACES OF MEMORY

Every image of the past that is not recognised by the present
as one of its own concerns threatens to disappear irretrievably.
Walter Benjamin[1]

Like a cinematic sequence, the image of the past flashes up and dissolves, precariously steering towards irretrievability. This eminently modern image is both disturbed and disturbing. It is an image that, as Benjamin hints, is implicated with the processes of memory. But what is the nature of such an image? Can this image of the past be also one of memory? And if so, how does it concern the present? How can the danger of irretrievable loss that so potently mars Benjamin's idea of an image of the past be accounted for? Perhaps drawing on an unusual interpretative standpoint, I would like to rethink Benjamin's 'image of the past' in the light of current neuro-psychological models of memory whereby memory is conceived spatially rather than merely temporally and is subject to various forms of disturbance during retrieval, making the threat of irretrievability and its consequences a condition of memory, and arguably of the imageries of the past that it forms. The focus of my discussion is Shona Illingworth's sound and video installation *Balnakiel*, which presupposes the spatial plane of memory as a tangible and figurative location of disturbance. The work is set in Balnakiel, a Cold War outpost on the coast of the North Atlantic originally intended for the protection against a potential nuclear threat, and is concerned with the historical legacy of the location at the interface of broader geopolitical strategies of control, both past and present.

Developed in dialogue with cognitive neuro-psychologist and memory researcher Martin A. Conway, *Balnakiel* is part of Illingworth's ongoing exploration of the modalities of memory and space through sound and the moving image.[2] Conway's scientific research underlines the spatiality of memory as a dynamically changing space whose temporal co-ordinates are neither the past nor the present, but rather at the intersection of past moments and events with the present, since memory helps us to make sense of the present and to imagine the future.[3] Hence, the image of the past with which we are concerned – whether in terms of memory or history – pertains to the present and is situated at temporal and perceptive boundaries, at the threshold of recognition and loss, of recollection and dissipation, of disturbance and irretrievability. We shall envisage this image as one of space as the shifting realm of perception at the edges of conscious and non-conscious processes of memory formation, recollection and dissipation. As with physical space, scale, perspective, and plane intersections are similarly topographical parameters for charting the mental territory of memory and the figurative dimensions in which an 'image of the past' unfolds.

Scale, Intensity and the Quality of the Image

Balnakiel opens with a high-ground view of the area of Balnakiel. The image then moves to the close-up of the metal frame of a semi-open window. The first sequence shows an encompassing bird-like perspective of the landscape, the second one focuses on a single detail. Both sequences present us with a space: the territorial borderline of Balnakiel and then the threshold of one of the concrete barracks of the military camp built during the Cold War. Throughout, the expansiveness of space and its liminality are the sensorial focus of Illingworth's work, and the perceptive co-ordinations through which the artist unravels her exploration of a place situated at geographical and geopolitical boundaries.

In *Balnakiel*, distant aerial perspectives of the landscape, often black and white, alternate with middle ground views of the land and of the barracks, and lingering close-ups of details: a hanging cloth moved and wrapped by the wind, a piece of paper or a string floating gently, a small plant swirled by the breeze. The slow aerial scanning of the landscape is reminiscent of a surveillance view from which the regimented layout of Balnakiel stands out with its low modular constructions erected one next to the other within a fenced perimeter. Abstracted and distant, we can associate this panoramic perspective of the horizontal plane below with the military control of the area, signalled in the past by an Early Warning Station and listening post for early detection of nuclear attack and in the present by a Range Control Tower that surveys a vast area of the nearby bay and land used for the training of British, NATO and allied forces in combined air, land and sea exercises. Such a view contrasts with the intimate intensity conveyed by the focus on single isolated objects. It is as if the remote observer of the aerial view were drawn into the landscape and made almost a participant of the scene. Distance dissolves and the feeling of what we see and hear intensifies. Disturbance is already subtly apparent, suggesting the disquieting quality of the image and hence of the space of memory that unravels.

Throughout the work, the juxtaposition of distance and proximity, large and small scale, separation and intimacy, visually modulates and nuances the emotional intensity not only of what we see, but also of what we hear. The sound of the rain and wind can be relentless and the roaring engines of Tornado fighter-bombers and helicopters, at times distant and hardly audible, and at times deafeningly close. The shifting scale and intensity of both the visual and acoustic landscapes can be compared to the sensory perceptual data of event-specific details that compose the raw material of memory formation: memories arise in the present from different configurations of memory details or episodic features. Hence, the modulation of scale figuratively intimates the continuous transition from the sensory flow of perception to the mental representation of experience in sequential, discrete pictures that the mind recomposes to recall an event, including the emotional charge that accompanies both the event and its recollection. Indeed, the images and sounds that the mind stores and recomposes through memory processes are the details that forge the emotional landscape of the mind and its inherent experience of the external environment that it references.

The mutability of scale also denotes a range of points of views and ways of experiencing the place that indicates the overlaying of different types of mapping that are pertinent to the social-history of Balnakiel and the 'cultural differences' within it, as they are evinced in the fragmented and disjointed voiceovers that punctuate the work. The voices are those of the 'people' of Balnakiel and the nearby Clearance village of Durness – whose inhabitants divide respectively into the incomers and local people – mixed with the intermittent crackle of military radio transmission. Each group relates to the location differently using memory to invest the place with a range of meanings that are embedded in their personal and collective histories. These meanings diverge from 'sense of belonging' in the voice of one person, to 'displacement' in that of another. Closeness and distance, familiarity and extraneousness, act as the parameters through which the external environment acquires its internal configurations and can be claimed as one's place. They are like the compass that defines the territory that one inhabits in memory and the image of the past that the external environment ensues within oneself. Intersecting this view of the landscape is the aerial mapping of the territory – the distant airborne view of the place – and the close scrutiny of the concrete buildings that testify to the militarisation of the area.

Covert reminders of conflict are apparent throughout *Balnakiel*. The work overlays the voiceovers onto close-ups of the barracks and empty landscape suggesting that their presence is intimately woven with the life of the inhabitants, with their stories and experiences. The barracks infer the psychological charting of a past marked by antagonistic relations between the locals and the incomers, and the military; a past that entraps, determining the present. A past, also, that like the present, is conditioned by external distant threats that push against the boundaries of this secluded location rendering it both peripheral and central to international hegemonic concerns. It is as if history were disturbingly (sub)liminal to Balnakiel. The actuality and media attention of the Cold War in the 1950s and of today's War on Terror is removed from this harsh landscape. Balnakiel's military importance has been and is generally unknown and the relevance of this location is part of expert knowledge. The place is remote, peripheral, and geographically marginal to international geopolitics, though strategically positioned at the frontline of one of the zones of surveillance during the Second World War and the Cold War, and an important site for military preparation for combat action at present. The horizontal line of the barracks that persists across the vertical margins traced by the descending and ascending Tornado fighter-bombers reminds us of the intersecting of deeper-lying structures of power, and produces an image of the past that is visually potent for the present: it intimates a potential threat that lies elsewhere; it is conducive of a feeling of 'being under attack'.

VERTICALITY AND RESONANCE

Formally, *Balnakiel* develops around a series of circular sequences in which visual and acoustic features are layered to create vertical volumes that disrupt the internal narrative, creating figurative boundaries within the structure of the work through the interplay of horizontal and vertical configurations. Here, the juxtaposition of planes, and hence of scale and perspectives, becomes even more apparent.

One such potent moment of verticality occurs halfway through the film when an adolescent girl, who acts as a silent observer, is shown spinning with a rope on the roof of one of the barracks and the camera turns with her as the deafening downward engine noise of a helicopter mixes with rising acute thin notes and the intermittent horizontal whipping sound of the rope slicing through the air. The effect is ominously threatening. Close-ups and broad-angled views seamlessly intercut producing a visual vortex in which the viewer is apparently caught up. The focus rapidly shifts from first to third person point of view and vice versa, from an internal and intimate way of seeing to an external, surveying perspective. This visual dissociation is disconcerting and deeply affects the feeling of the image, which becomes highly perceptual and hence emotionally disturbing. The use of low frequency sounds in relation to the images imparts a sense of dissonance. One is under the impression that installation space compresses while seeing on screen a low aerial view from the helicopter over the village. The overall effect of the sequence is one of vertigo and disorientation, of being cognitively thrown out of balance. It is a moment of impasse, frightfully disconcerting and potently vivid.

This is consistent with the internal dissociation of points of view (from first to third person) that occurs in memory processes during retrieval when memories not normally accessible interfere with normal recollection, thus altering the experience of memory itself. The space of memory and the images that relate to it become fractured and disorienting, emotionally disturbing and acutely problematic, since something that seemed lost (or forgotten) impinges on the present and latently disturbs the image of the past that the mind forms. In *Balnakiel*, disturbance results from a tension between the topography of the place and the intimate, almost claustrophobic dwelling on details that figuratively shreds the internal geography of the work to a point in which disturbance almost 'bursts through' the image. The crossing of ways of experiencing, and hence remembering and knowing the place, is momentarily reconfigured rendering palpable the boundary separating what is visible and what remains peripheral, what is clearly perceivable and what is hazy, uncertain, concealed. What appeared as objective (the place of Balnakiel) becomes a subjective experience of the landscape (and with it of the installation environment). Two forms of experiencing and hence of knowledge seem to be at stake. The psychoanalyst and critic Suely Rolnik defines this in terms of a 'subcortical' or non-conscious form of knowledge as distinct from a cortical one that is congruent with the categories of language and meaning. [4] As she writes:

> I refer to the capacities of perception and sensation that allow us to
> apprehend the otherness of the world, respectively as a map of forms
> on which we project representations, or as a diagram of forces that
> affect all the senses in their capacity for resonance. [5]

Rolnik's concept of the 'resonant body' as the figurative trope of 'subcortical knowledge' is suggestive of the immersive space of *Balnakiel* when the physical and figurative room we are in compresses and pushes toward verticality, creating what we may describe as the 'resonant space of memory'.

For Rolnik, the 'resonance' is imbued in the mapping of identity and power, and is central to a notion of territorialisation that invests the subject and the individual's appropriation of the structures of power that codify the charting of reality and the contested sites of political hegemony. [6] Spatially the surfaces and boundaries on which forms of separation and enforcement operate are the result of vertical rather than solely horizontal spheres of control. In his discussion of the territorialisation of the West Bank, Eyal Weizman argues that within the current panorama of geopolitics, airspace is no less prominent in the definition and monitoring of boundaries, rendering borders volumetric constructs that operate across and within the territories through a variety of forms of separation and seg-regation that are both physical and metaphorical.[7] A vertical 'architecture' incorporates both airspace and land delineating the physical and psychological 'territorialisation' of space by both the civilians living there and the military.

Extending Weizman's theorisation to our discussion of memory and space, we can suppose a similar intersecting of lines within the volumetric configuration that underpins cultural processes of recollection. Indeed, if memory operates by structuring temporary sensations of the past in relation to the present, in order to enable a coherent narrative of the subject through their re-presentation into an internal image of the past, similarly the historical past interacts with the present to give visibility to its cultural manifestations. In *Balnakiel,* this visibility reveals a concealed, suppressed, traumatically painful substratum that disturbs the coherence of a historical narrative of hegemony and of its horizontal organisation of space, since it introduces ambivalence and contradiction, threading on the resonance of what remains liminal, peripheral, and at the edges of knowledge. The landscape is thus layered with visible and non-visible lines that organise its topography according to over-imposed frameworks of appropriation and knowledge.

Such lines run through and across the landscape in Balnakiel. They include horizontal solid demarcations of the land that constitute the historical topography of the area according to a mapping of the land established during the successive colonisation by various waves of migrations, and the intangible boundaries of surveillance of the Range Control Tower that criss-cross and intersect with the dry stone edges (or dykes) on the ground. The horizontal demarcations are reminders of the physical and emotional appropriation of the landscape over time and act as traces of the controversial history of the local community. Deeply embedded in the environment, these edges are almost invisible to the eye of an outsider. They intimate the haptic knowledge argued by Rolnik that affects the subject's non-conscious experience of place, as a memory imbued both in the body of the individual and in the physical texture of that landscape. Both physically and metaphorically, these edges already indicate structures of power and an image of the past whose historical relevance has however been superseded by current hegemonies of control, which equally traverse the landscape as the invisible trajectories of jets and other forms of combat training.

The aerial vertical boundaries of control iterate and at the same time contrast with the haunting presence of the concrete buildings that stand like ghostly 'empty shells', creating latency that envelops the landscape in less perceptible though equally disquieting ways. This is epitomised in another of the vertical volumes in the work that occurs when the sound of the flapping of wings and screeching of a goshawk trapped in one of the buildings is overlaid with the roar of the engine of a helicopter at take-off. While the sound rises in intensity towards the pitch of flight, the film shows the bird pressing against the windows in an attempt to escape. This rising tension in the sound of the helicopter generates the feeling of a vertical push. It is as if, like the bird, the viewer was also pressed against the opaque barrier of the window, and entrapped with it in the deafening sound of the engine. No less than the walls and windows of the barracks, the sound similarly erects a figurative wall. Here, the surfaces of the interior of the building and the vertical volume of the installation merge becoming like edges of confinement, pushing the limits of perception. The resonant space that the work achieves claustrophobically compresses the visual space of the projection vertically. Fear is made palpable in a feeling of physical discomfort heightened by the agonising screeching of the bird. Verticality and the supposed lines of control that it intimates overlay with existing structures of power (the barracks) and the histories of control that they represent. It is this latency and interference that resonates when we think of the space of *Balnakiel* as one of memory, making the image of the past that the work evokes disturbed and disturbing.

Interference

One of the most moving sequences in *Balnakiel* is a voiceover recollection of a childhood memory that still brings feelings of fear and physical pain.

> In my stomach. In my chest. Breathless. It's like being breathless with
> your heart pounding at the same time. Feeling sick [...] Almost a silent
> hissing in your head. It's like adrenaline. So wired. So completely wired.
> And... and the crazy thing is – not once – was there an incident – for
> me to fear walking through the village.[8]

The man's account unfolds against the camera's roaming view of the landscape from inside the Range Control Tower. The memory that per se is irretrievable is cued by the landscape, as a non-conscious experience that disturbs with its unsettling feeling. As the physical pain and fear of the man's recollection unfolds, we hear the air traffic controller's exchanges of spatial co-ordination on the radio. The 'cortical' forms of knowledge of the military – to use Rolnik's analogy – interferes with the 'subcortical' experience of a place, a kind of knowledge within the body that is deeply troubling. The visual and auditory interference of this sequence reminds us of what remains latent and yet overwhelmingly present. As Conway explains,

> The voice of the air traffic controller in the Range Control Tower cuts into an auditory dialogue of an interview with a man who experiences feelings of anxiety when in the vicinity of a wall in a village nearby. This was a wall that he used to walk past when he was a child, a wall where something may have happened that he cannot place. We might think of this as an example of 'retrieval failure' in which the control processes cannot generate the appropriate cue and therefore the knowledge which is in some sense apprehended cannot be brought into consciousness. The blocked retrieval seems to give rise to and then exacerbates these profound feelings of anxiety, which are also manifest in an intense physical/sensorial response, as the memory which is sought for is somehow locked and cannot be opened.[9]

The individual's feeling of entrapment brought about by blocked memories is alluded to throughout *Balnakiel,* as the underlying 'blocked' experience of the place and the anxiety that it ensues.

The interfering sound of engines, the background hauling of the wind, and the radio transmissions of the military are consistent insinuating noises throughout *Balnakiel* that act as a pervading and significant component of the work. Like the horizontal and vertical lines of demarcations that can be read as interfering boundaries on which the work articulates a preoccupation with the latency of current geopolitics, similarly these interfering sounds are an instance of a disturbance that remains liminal though ever present and disturbingly affecting. Hence, the recurring disjunction of images and sound throughout *Balnakiel* whether in terms of scale (the intimate and delicate lingering on a small plant falling and the potent crashing sound that accompanies it) or of perception of the place rendered through the fragmented, overlapping and juxtaposed voiceovers that are overtly disconnected with the images on screen. Illingworth's landscape is dense with visual and acoustic dissonance, with the distressing interpolation of historical, social and hegemonic lines that cut through and across the landscape and interfere with its sub-cortical if not cortical knowledge.

From a cognitive point of view, the visual and acoustic haziness of sensory perception is problematic since it affects the 'fidelity of the signals' and the retrieval of experiences and events. Interference concerns the ability to remember and hence the capacity of forgetting in relation to long-term memory.[10] We could compare the sensory-perceptive stimuli on which memories are formed to signals that vary in strength and can even deteriorate and disappear not in relation to their original vividness but rather to the internal mental processes that make knowledge available. Emotion is one of the factors that affects the strength or fidelity of the memory signal, thus interfering not only with what is remembered but also with how something is remembered or forgotten. Emotional interference thus impinges on the image of the past to a point of irretrievability, yet leaving a trace of the distressing feeling that a memory may have caused.

The airspace of *Balnakiel* is full of interference. Some of it is overt, as in the adolescent girl's attempt to tune in with portable domestic radio; some encrypted, as in the radio communications between the Range Control Tower and the military aircraft, and the ships and ground troops that we do not see but whose presence persistently and pervasively lingers at the margins of the camera's lens; and some concealed, as in the case of the emotional perceptive networks of inhabitants and which denote the feelings of belonging and dis-placement that run through the work. As Conway argues,

> One could draw an analogy between the inaccessible in memory
> contained within networks of activation across dynamic mental space
> and the inaccessible in the communications that resonate throughout
> this airspace. Both processes are influenced by something which
> cannot be accessed but which nonetheless has an effect.[11]

The notion of 'something which cannot be accessed', that is blocked within but nonetheless can be felt, is inherent to cultural as well as psychological memory processes whereby places are imbued with the traces and reminders of the past, whose significance remains concealed, half hidden and liminal. This is the case of Balnakiel whose local history is saturated with the reminders of an utopian pursuit of freedom – as for the incomers, who moved to this remote location to escape the constraints of growing capitalism – and of the century-long strategies of control – the hegemonic lines that cut through the land and sky. They are the remainders on which feelings of belonging and dislocation are iterated and mark the distance that set the local community, the incomers and the military apart. Ultimately, these traces are the signs that separate Balnakiel from other international histories – those to which it is intrinsically connected but that happen elsewhere and from which this secluded place is remote, blocked out, unheard of, despite the fact that it is an important NATO training ground. We could argue that its history is part of an image of the past that – to borrow Benjamin's words – is not made a concern of the present and hence steers towards disappearance and the danger of irretrievability. Yet, not without consequences, since the traces of this history can subliminally interfere.

In *Balnakiel*, the image of the past that emerges intimates both a spatial and temporal latency toward that which resists remembrance and yet affects memory with its insinuating fear and emotional disturbance. In this sense, the past latency of the supposed threat of a foreign nuclear attack repeats itself in the present in the military training for combat action. As a result, the confluence and overlapping of perspectives that the film achieves figuratively renders the boundaries on which retrieval, interference and irretrievability dynamically interact to chart an evolving place and its history. In this context, different scales of territory – from geopolitical to local – overlap in both space and time. The images of the past are telling of histories but also of their location, of their physical, ideological and symbolic environments. Balnakiel, not unlike Afghanistan on the global scale, is removed from the 'target rich environment' that makes the current War on Terror distinct from the visually charged locations of the Cold War.[12] Its physical and historical latency is yet of concern to the present: the image of the past signals a liminal place whose environment is saturated with the impinging presence of contemporary fears.

1

Walter Benjamin, 'Theses on the Philosophy of History', in *Illuminations*, trans. by Harry Zohn (London, Collins Fontana, 1973), pp.255-266, p.257. Benjamin's quote refers to his discussion of historical materialism and we consider it within a broader context.

2

Elsewhere in this volume, Martin A. Conway considers the functions of memory and draws attention to the psychological configuration of the work in relation to memory formation and retrieval. He charts a complex territory in which different types and modalities of memory are equally active. This notional framework is also evident in the visual and acoustic mapping of *Balnakiel* and in the broader concern with the current debate on geopolitics of space.

3

See Martin A. Conway, 'Sensory-perceptual episodic memory and its context: autobiographical memory', in *Episodic Memory: New Directions in Research*, Alan Baddeley, Martin A. Conway, and John P. Aggleton, ed. (Oxford and New York: The Royal Society and Oxford University Press, 2002) pp.53-70; Helen L. Williams, Martin A. Conway, & Alan D. Baddeley, 'The Boundaries of Episodic. Memories', in *Understanding Events: From Perception to Action*, Thomas F. Shipley and Jeffrey M. Zacks ed. (Oxford: Oxford University Press, 2008), pp.589-616; Martin A. Conway and Catherine Loveday, 'Accessing Autobiographical Memories', in *The Act of Remembering: Toward an Understanding of How We Recall the Past*, John H. Mage ed. (Oxford, Wiley-Blackwell, 2010), pp.56-70.

4

Suely Rolnik, 'The Body's Contagious Memory: Lygia Clark's Return to the Museum' (2007), translated by Rodrigo Nunes, http://eipcp.net.transversal/0507/rolnik/en5 Ibid., http://eipcp.net.transversal/0507/rolnik/en

6

Suely Rolnik, 'The Geopolitics of Pimping' (2006), translated by Brian Holmes, http://eipcp.net/transversal/1106/rolnik/en

7

See Eyal Weizman, *The Politics of Verticality* (2002), www.opendemocracy.net; Peter Sloterdijk, *Terror from the Air* trans by Amy Patton and Steve Corcoran (Cambridge Mass. and London, MIT, 2010); W. J.T. Mitchell, *Cloning Terror: The War of Images, 9/11 to the Present* (Chicago and London, The University of Chicago Press, 2011).

8

Voiceover, *Balnakiel* (2009).

9

Martin A. Conway, unpublished notes in conversation with Shona Illingworth.

10

Alan Baddeley, *Human Memory: Theory and Practice* (Hove and London, Lawrence Erlbaum Associates Publishers, 1990), pp.43-50; 246-256; 'Memory researchers talk about fidelity rather than accuracy in relation to memory and discuss memory as a signal that varies in strength – not according to how the state of the world once was but to how the mind is working – making knowledge available – emotion and other cognitive processes contribute to the fidelity of that signal' Martin A. Conway, unpublished notes in conversation with Shona Illingworth.

11

Martin A. Conway, unpublished notes in conversation with Shona Illingworth.

12

W. J. T. Mitchell, op.cit., p.3.

One might view the aerial images of *Balnakiel* and the surrounding landscape as being impersonal, a different organic aspect of memory, a set of images at the surface of the brain. As the sequence progresses we move into an area of memory that is more personal, connected to the individual, the self through the image of the girl.

The image of the girl in the dark room with a storm lantern that is carried through a window and around the former Early Warning Station might be thought of in the context of some kind of theory of attention, particularly the so called 'spotlight' theory of attention, in the way that controlled networks search through the darkness of below-activation-threshold sets of networks in which memory information may be represented.

But then the search seems to be abandoned and the processes return to some sort of resting state; the images of the remote countryside reappear representing something that is distant and impenetrable, perhaps like a memory or set of memories that cannot be accessed.

BALNAKIEL

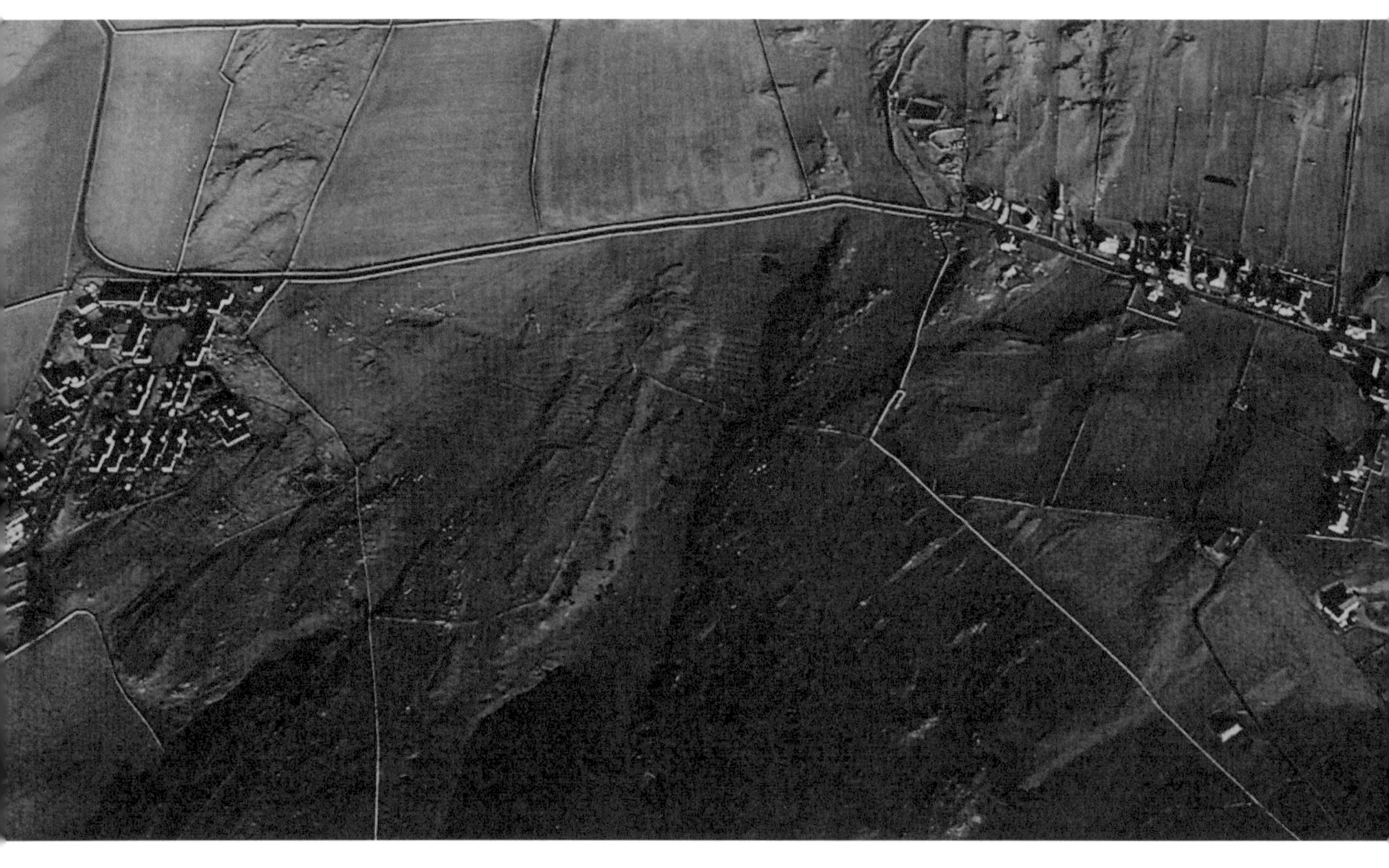

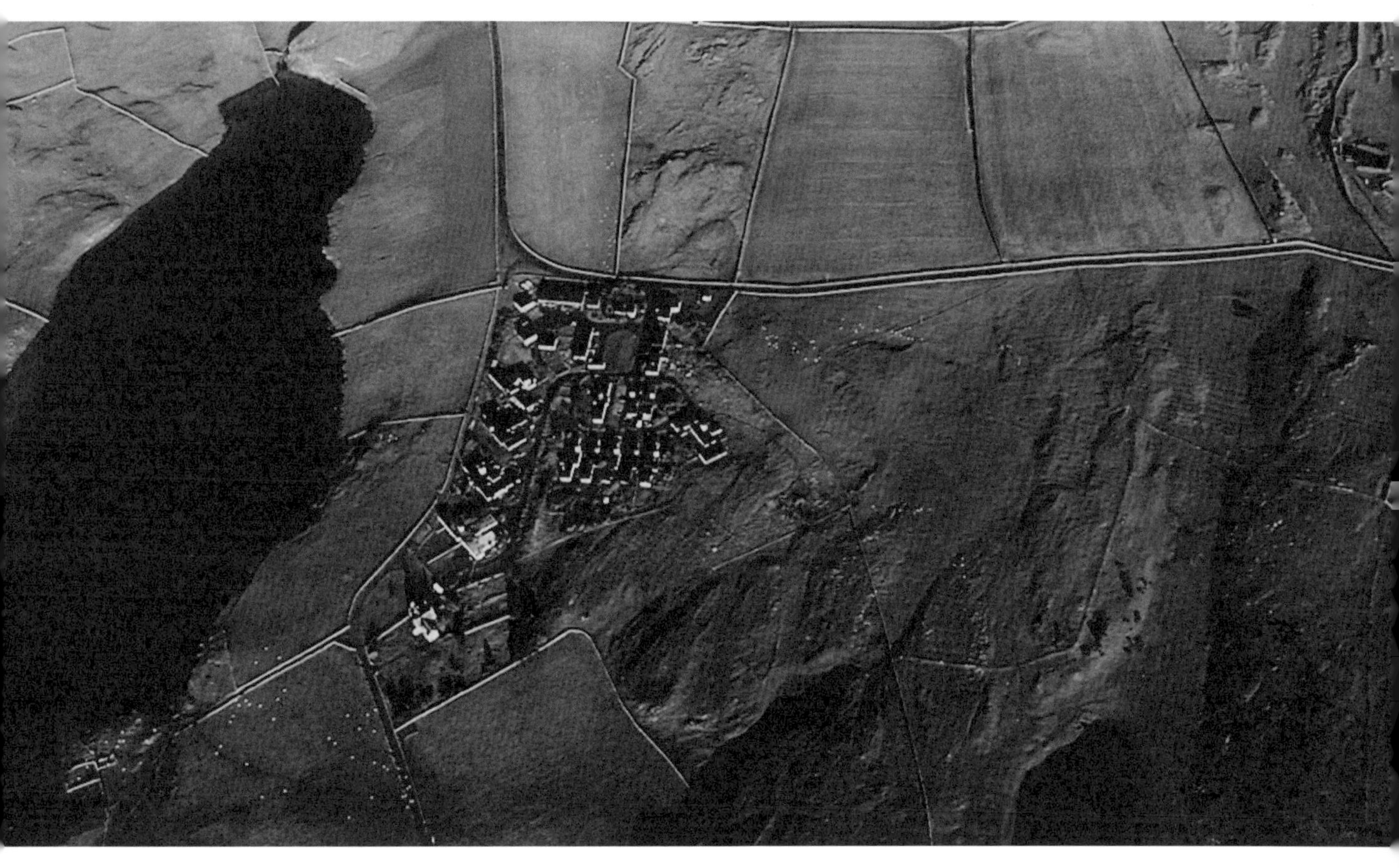

Digital video stills and selected voice transcripts from *Balnakiel*, 2009

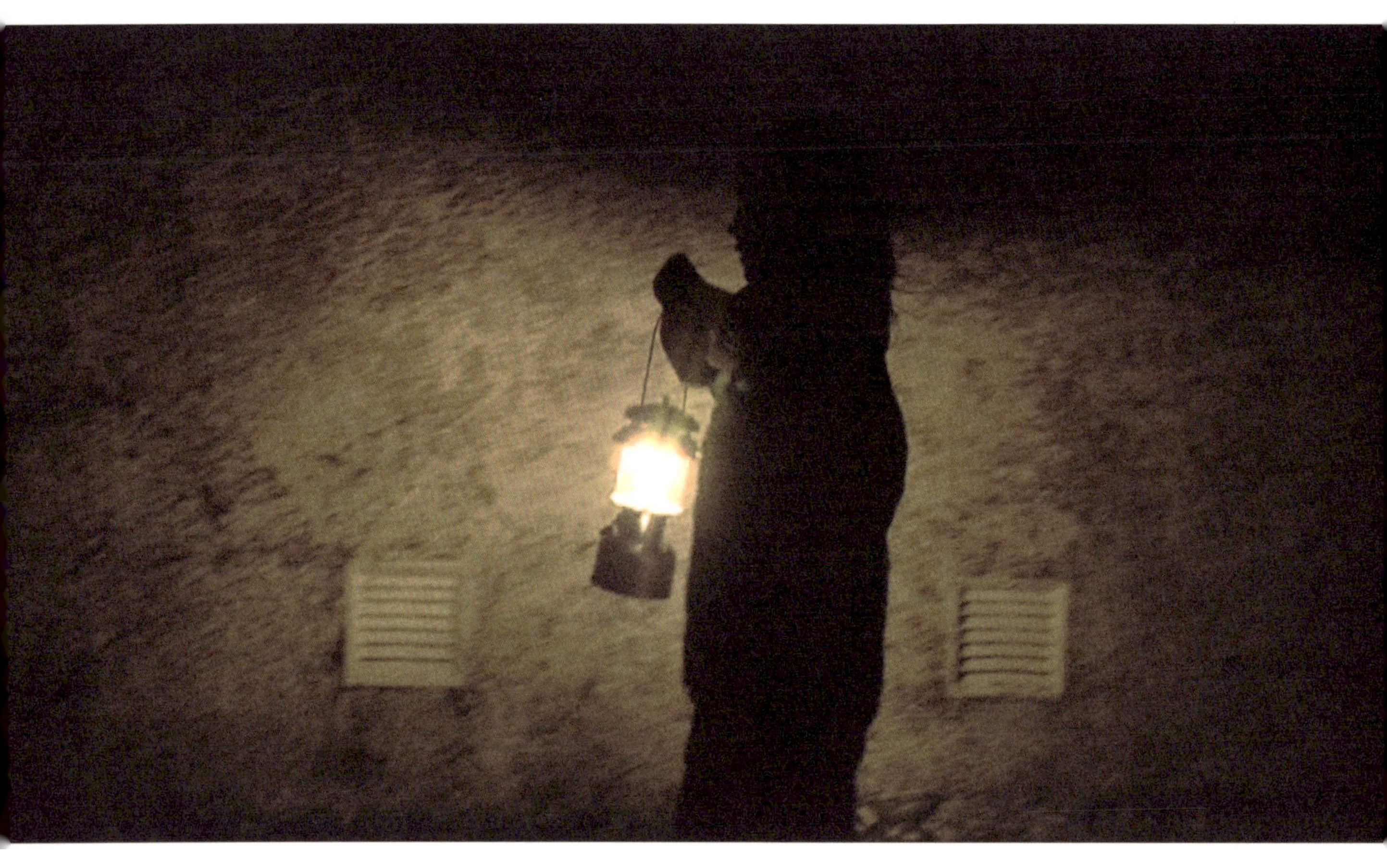

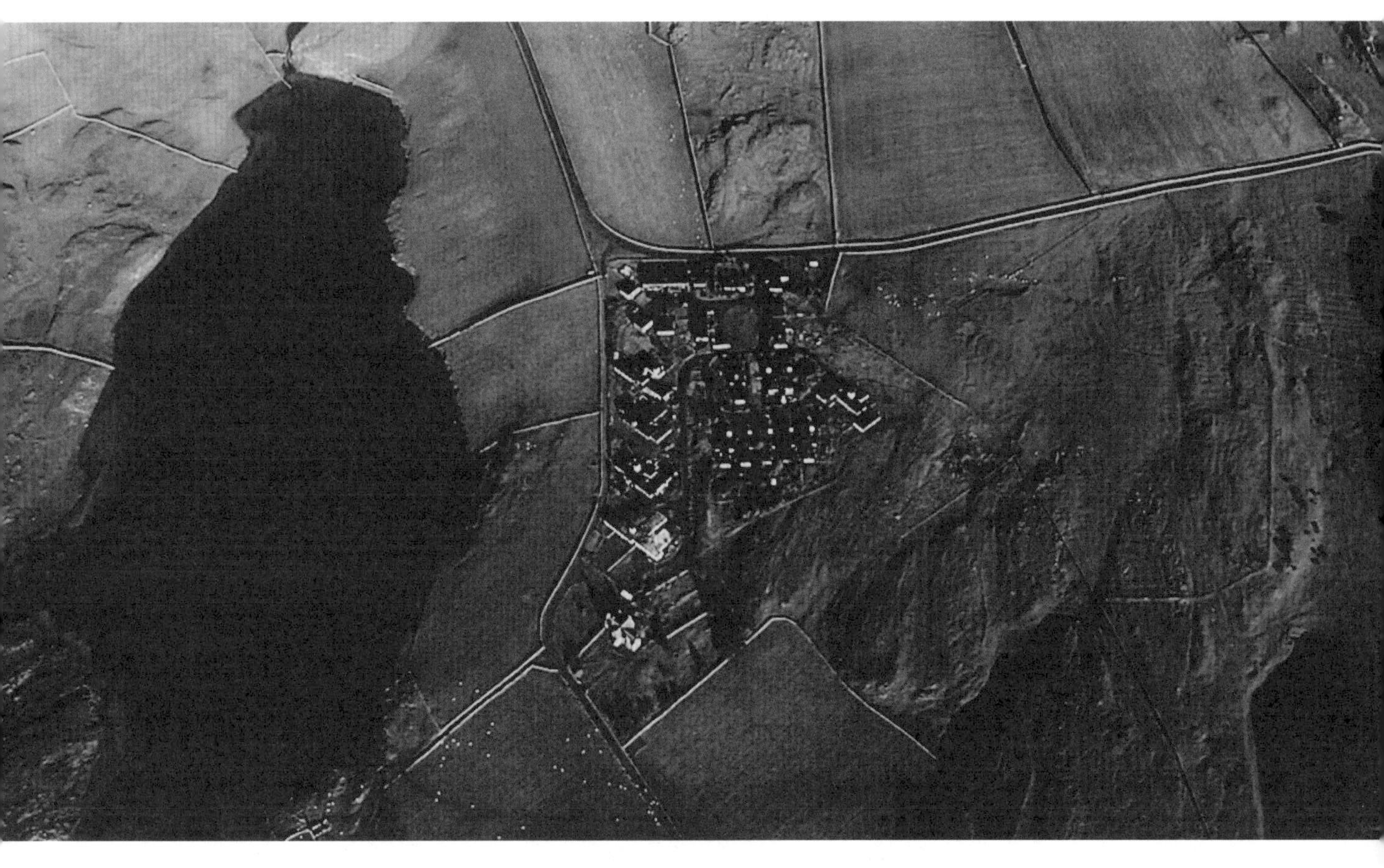

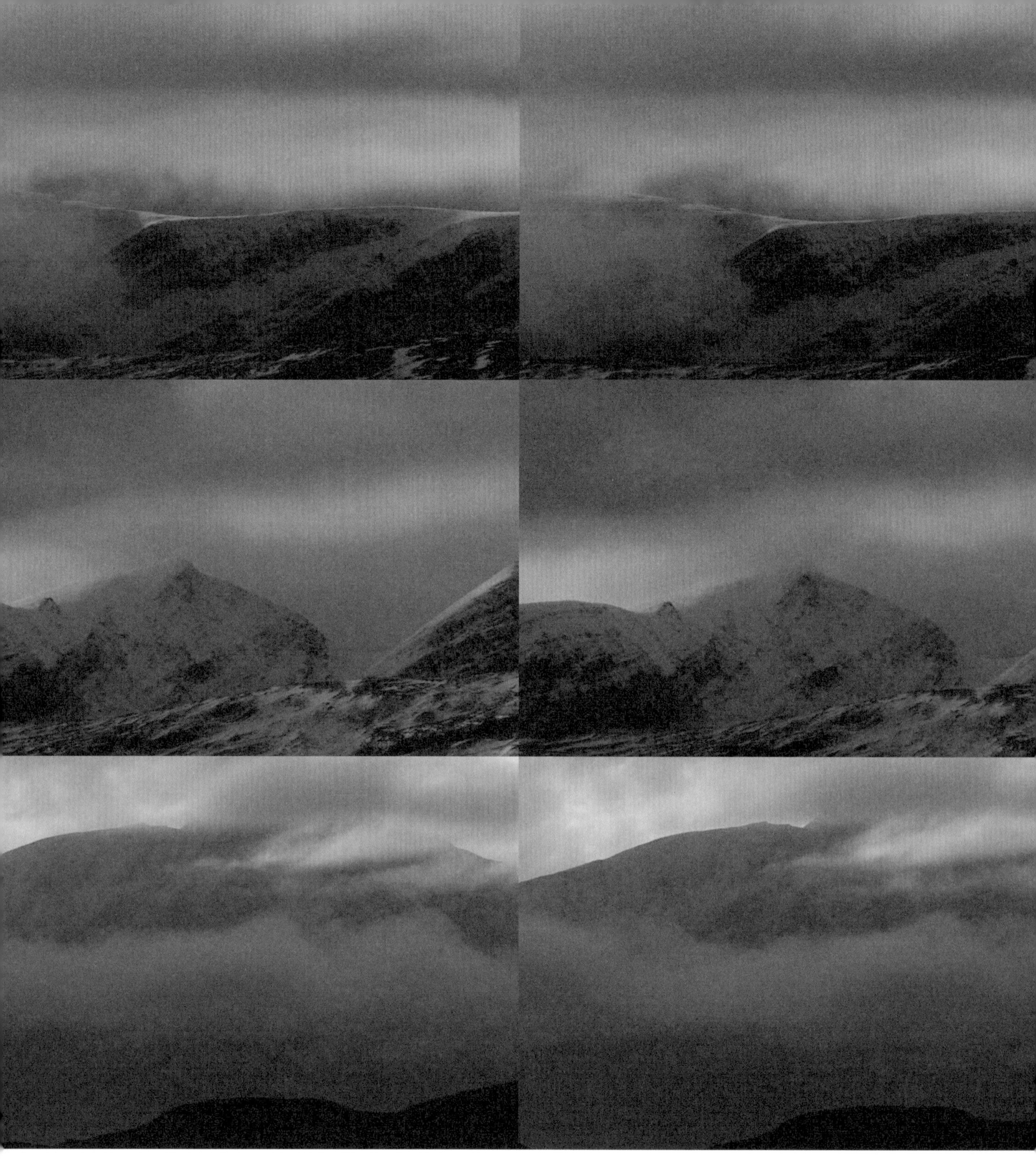

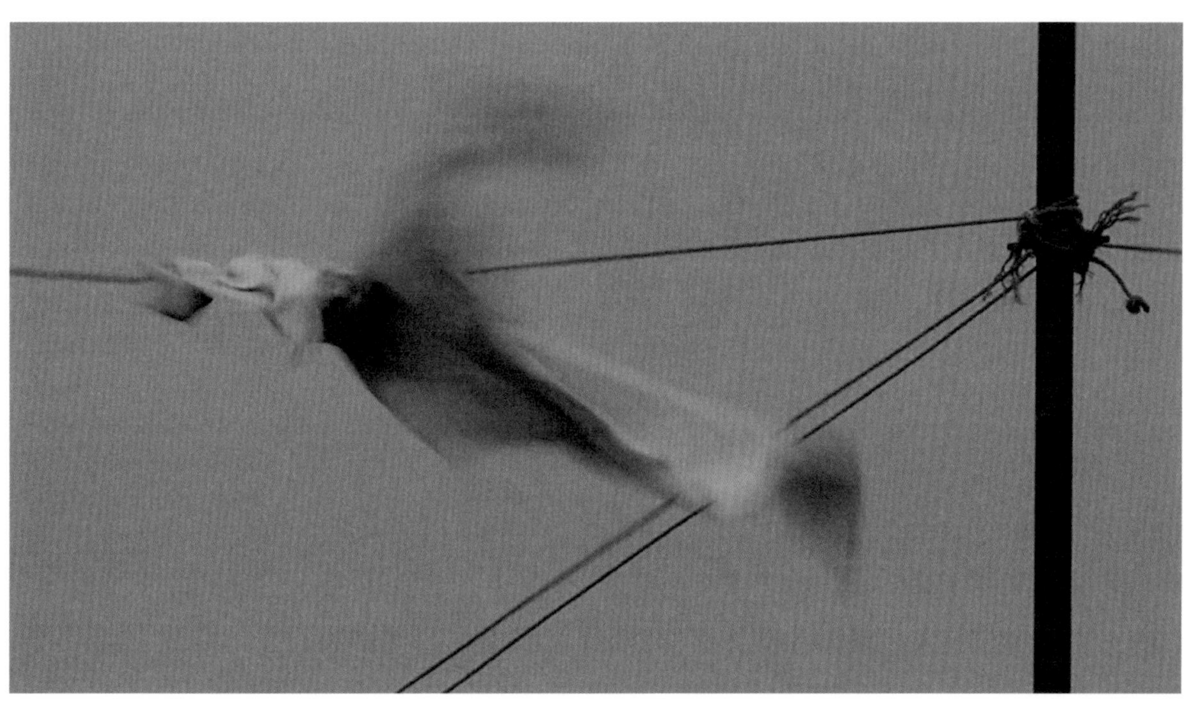

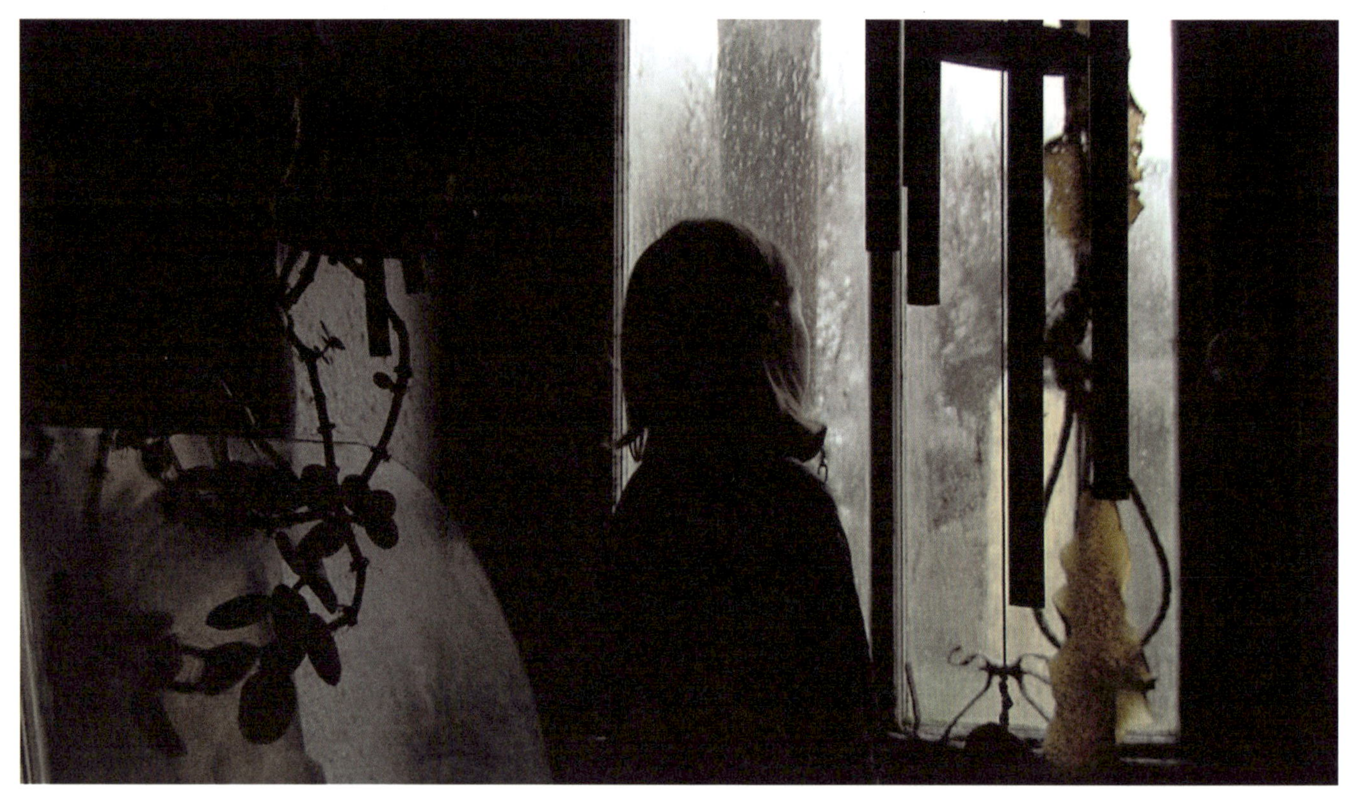

Woman
The incomers were all escaping something

Woman
They'd come to the edge of the country
to escape something

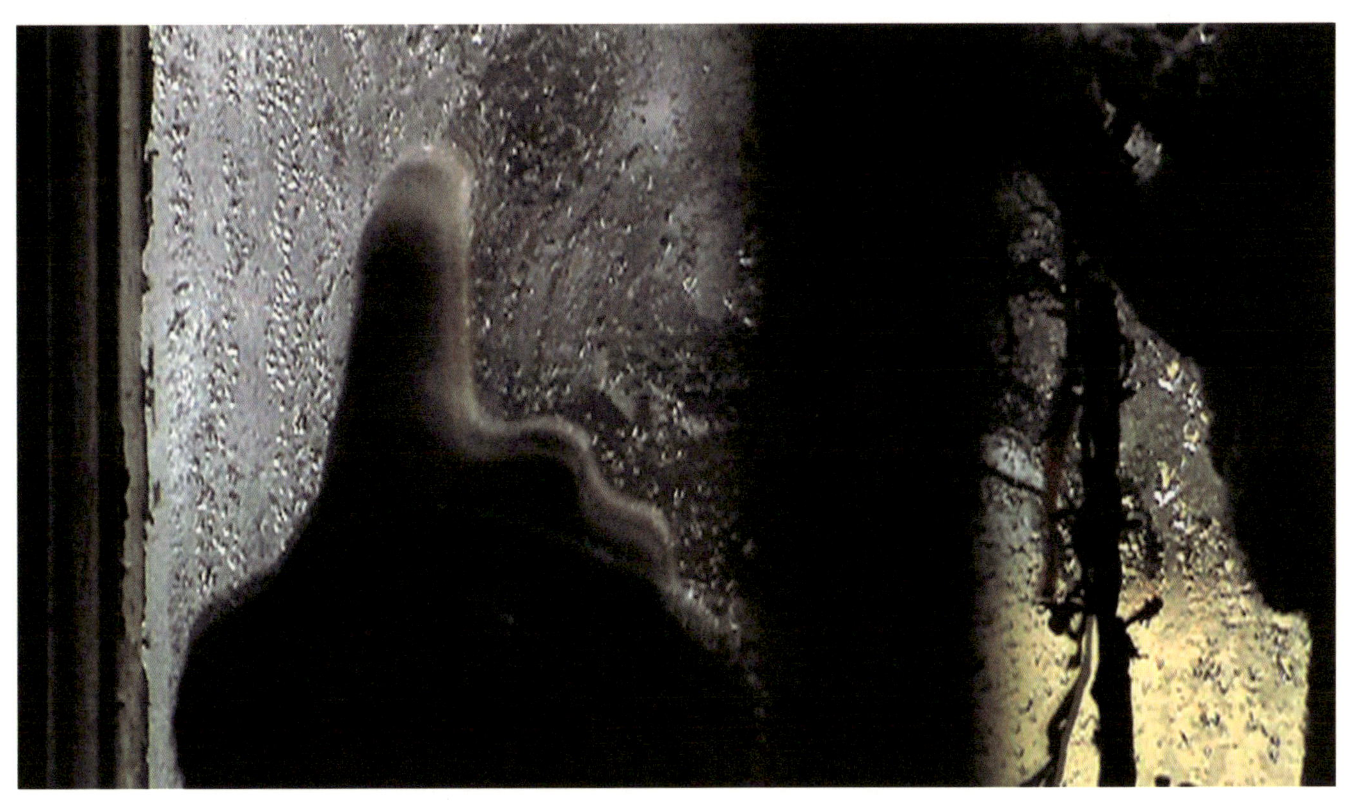

Woman
They wanted to absent themselves
from the pressures of urban living

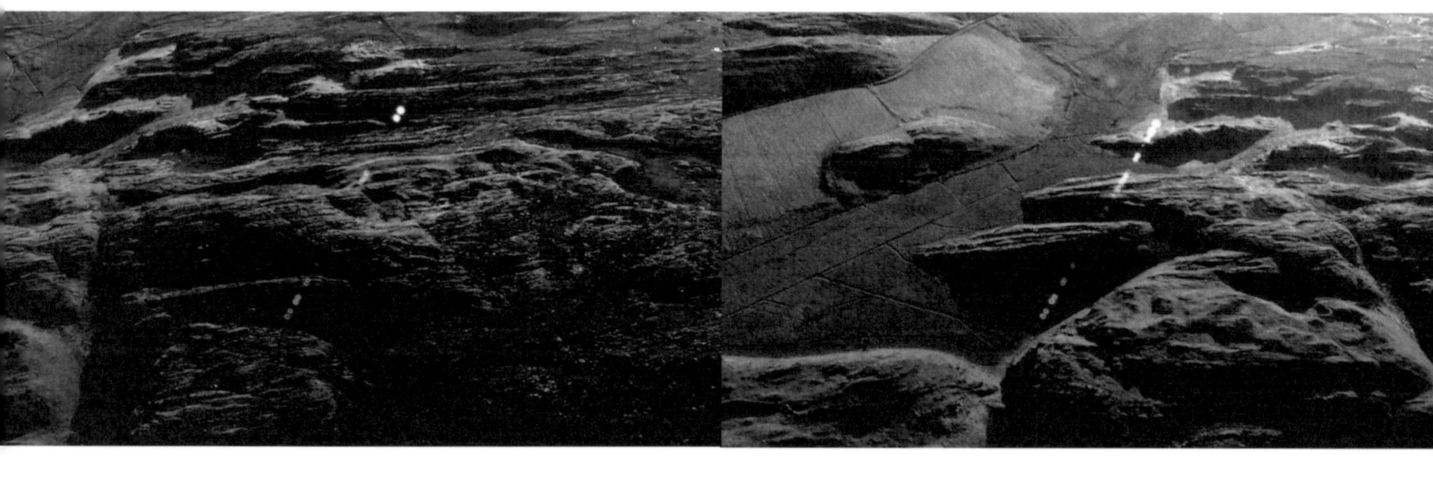

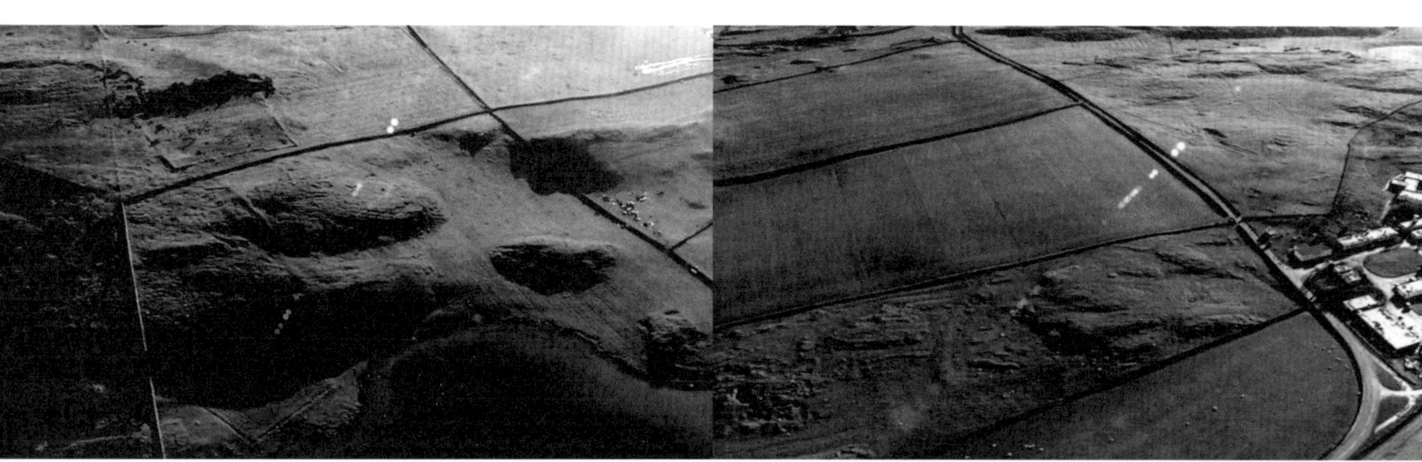

Range Control
Hello safety. This is range control did you get my last 'Over'?

Safety
Safety. Roger, request permission to proceed. Over.

Range Control
Range Control, wait out.

Aircraft
Climbing to zero – still climbing to zero – safety watch just started.

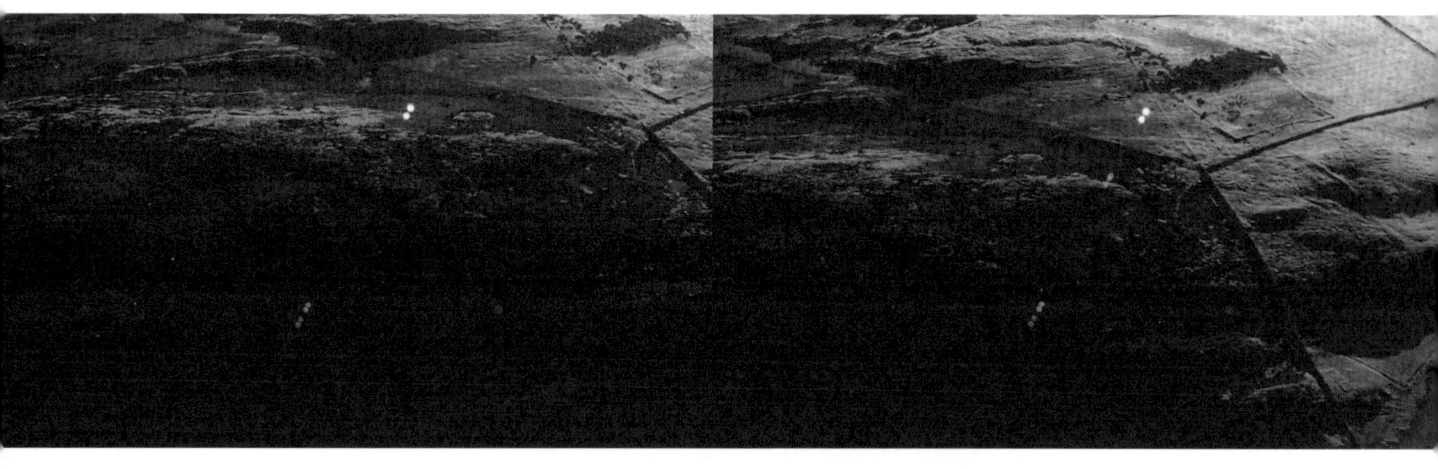

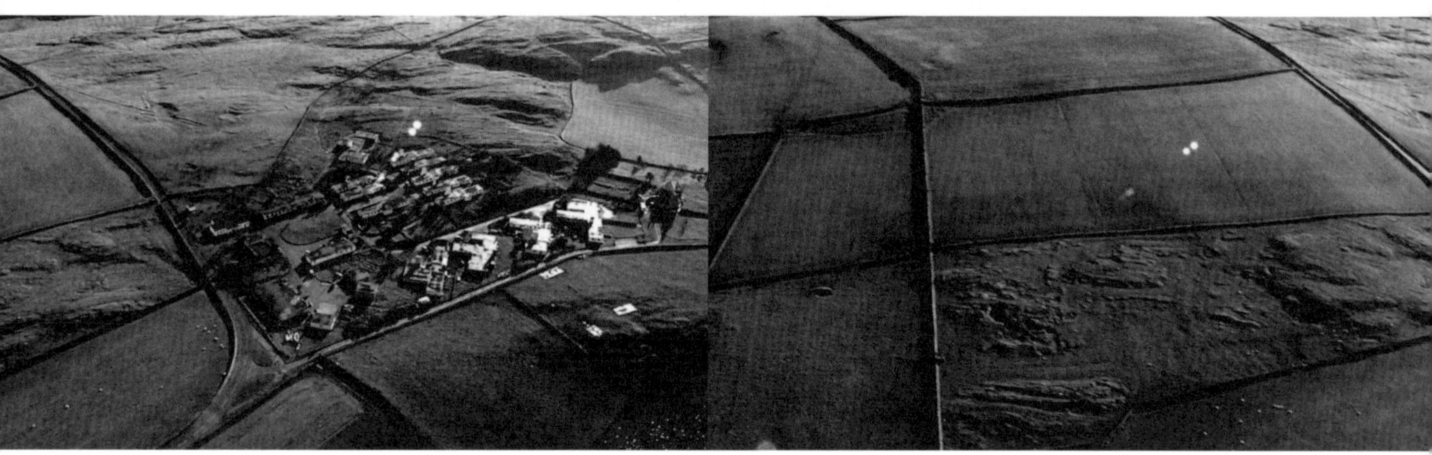

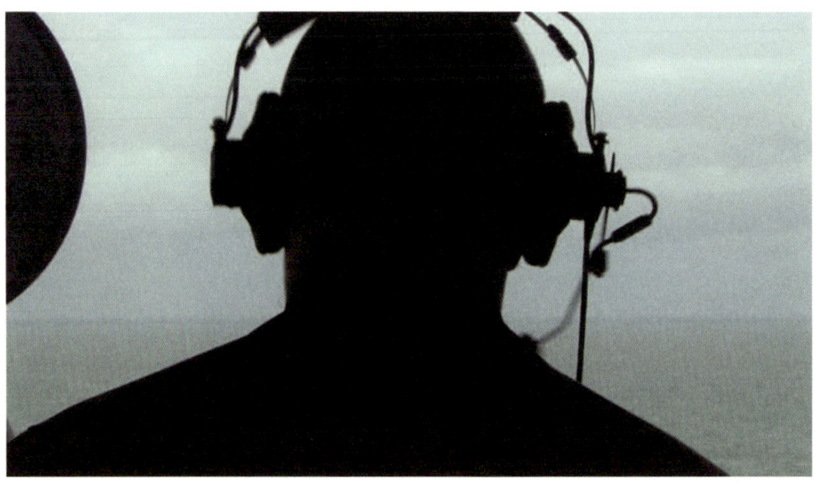

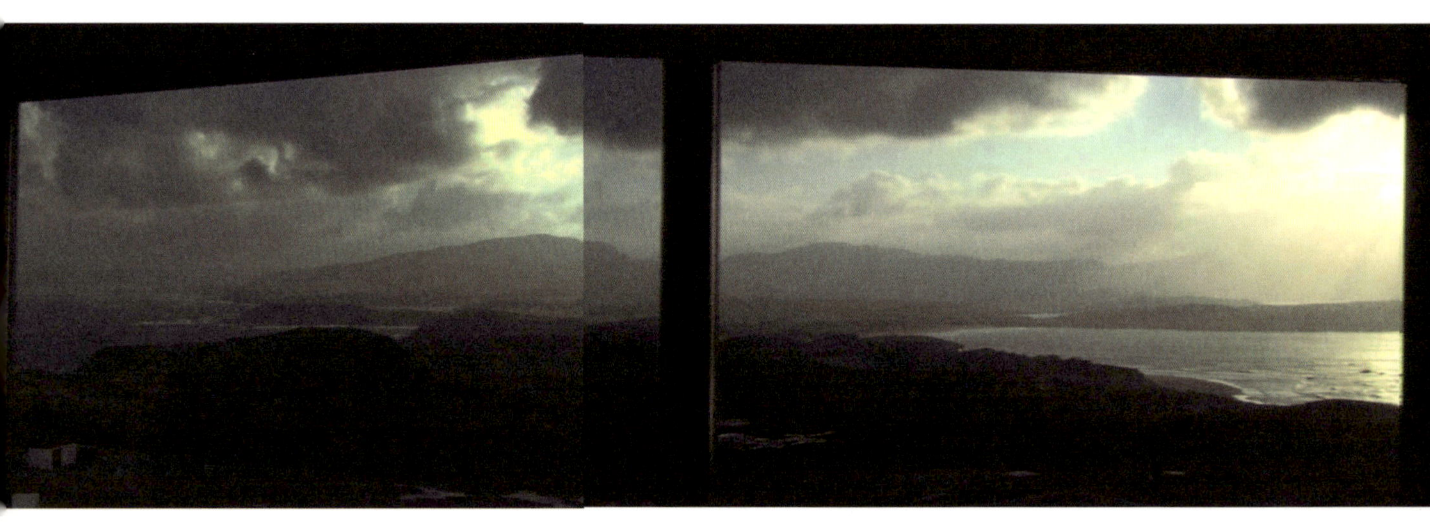

Range Control
Few at six hundred primarily to the south of the target area scattered
at one thousand five hundred going up to two thousand five hundred.

Man's voice
In my stomach and my chest – breathless – it's like being breathless
with your heart pounding at the same time – and feeling sick –
almost like hunger, and having this almost silent hiss in your head –
it's like adrenaline – it's like.

Range Control
Few at six hundred climb out to south of the attack area scattered
at fifteen hundred few at two thousand.

Man's voice
You're so wired – so completely wired, and and the crazy thing is –
not once – was there ever an incident – for me to fear walking
through the village.

Range Control
Roger visual roll right of my position is the Control Tower at the end
of the main peninsula. Just to south of my location – two small
buildings – troops in contact that location.

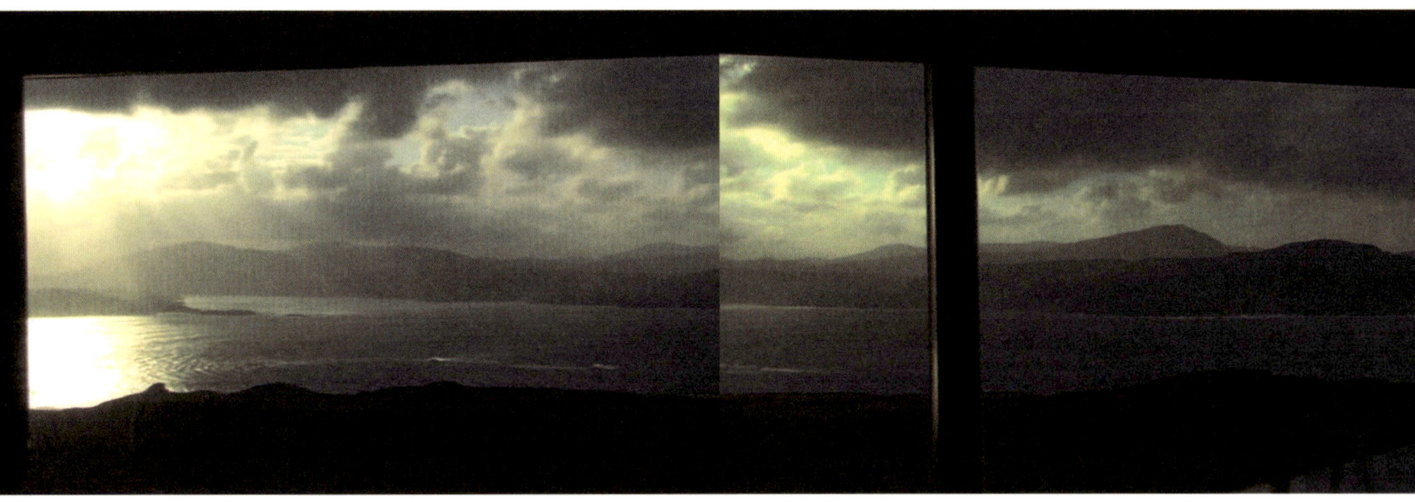

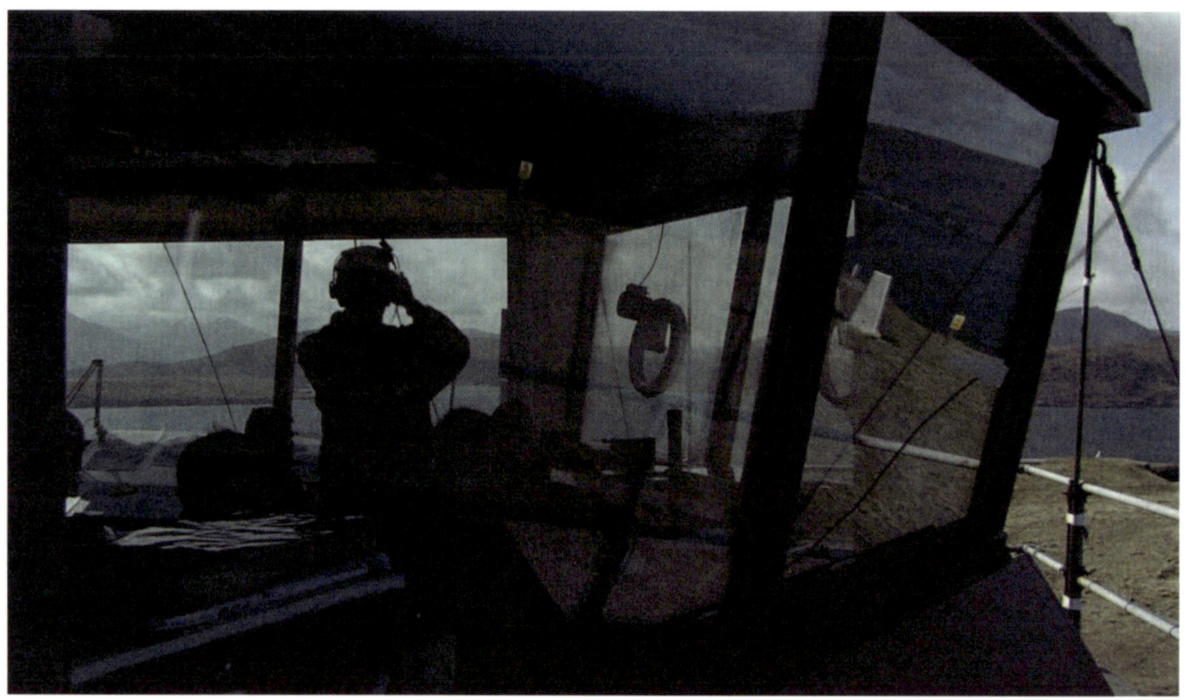

Aircraft
Cape Wrath Range good afternoon Vixen 2.

Range Control
Vixen 2 Cape Wrath Range good afternoon.

Aircraft
Good afternoon Gav a bit late now about ten miles to run to our
range clearance pass.

Range Control
Roger. Are you in communication with Vixen 1?

Aircraft
Roger. Yes I am, we start the target run and aim the bombs when
we get there.

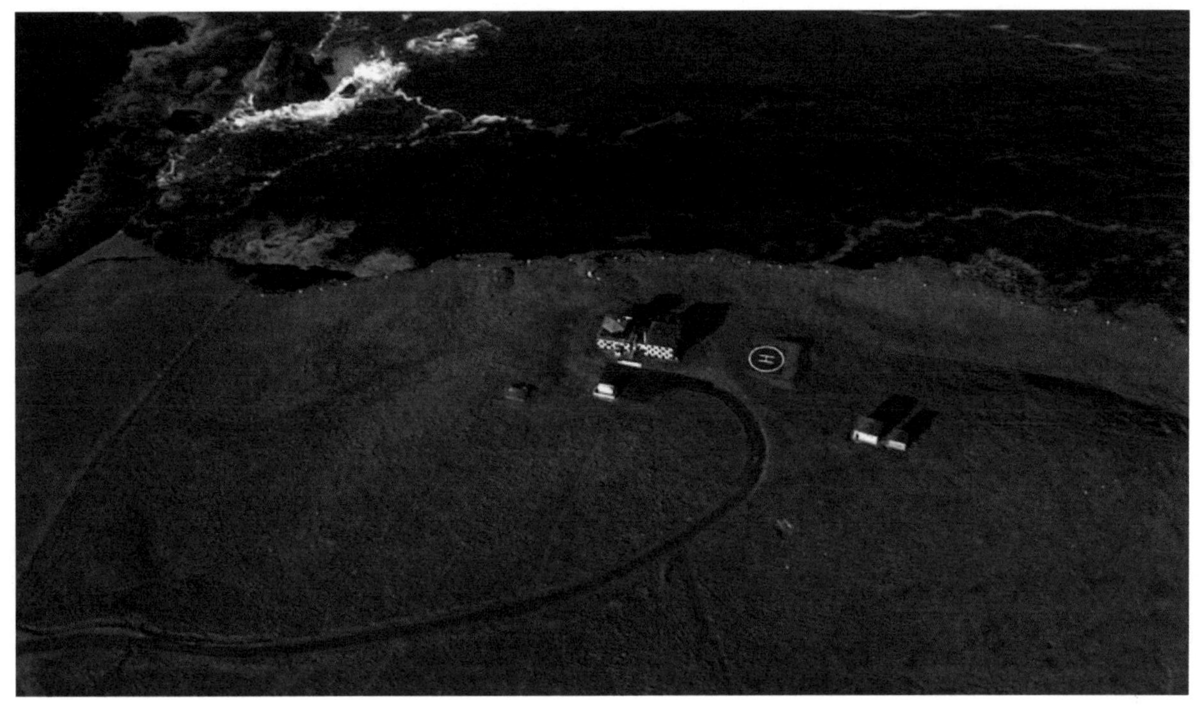

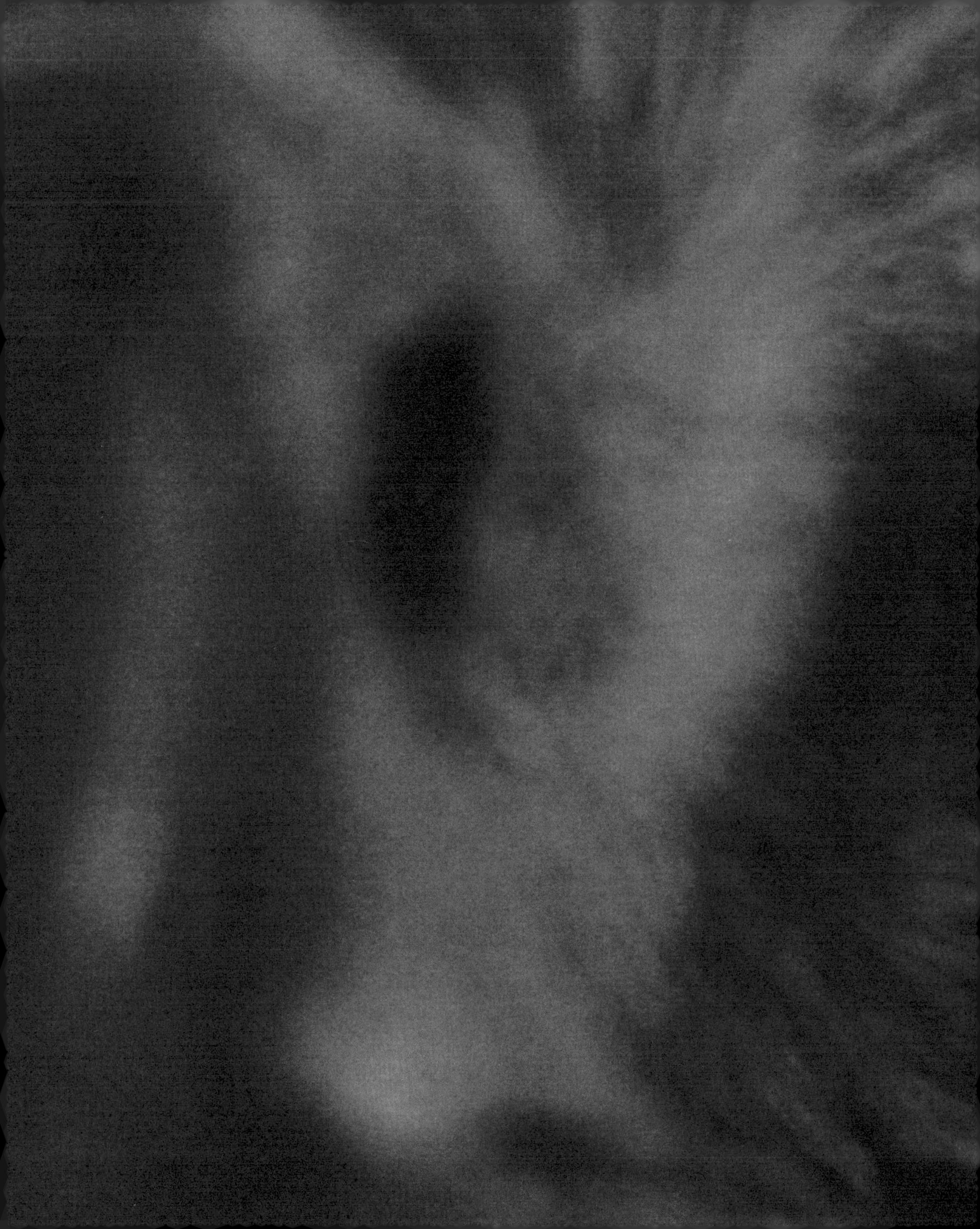

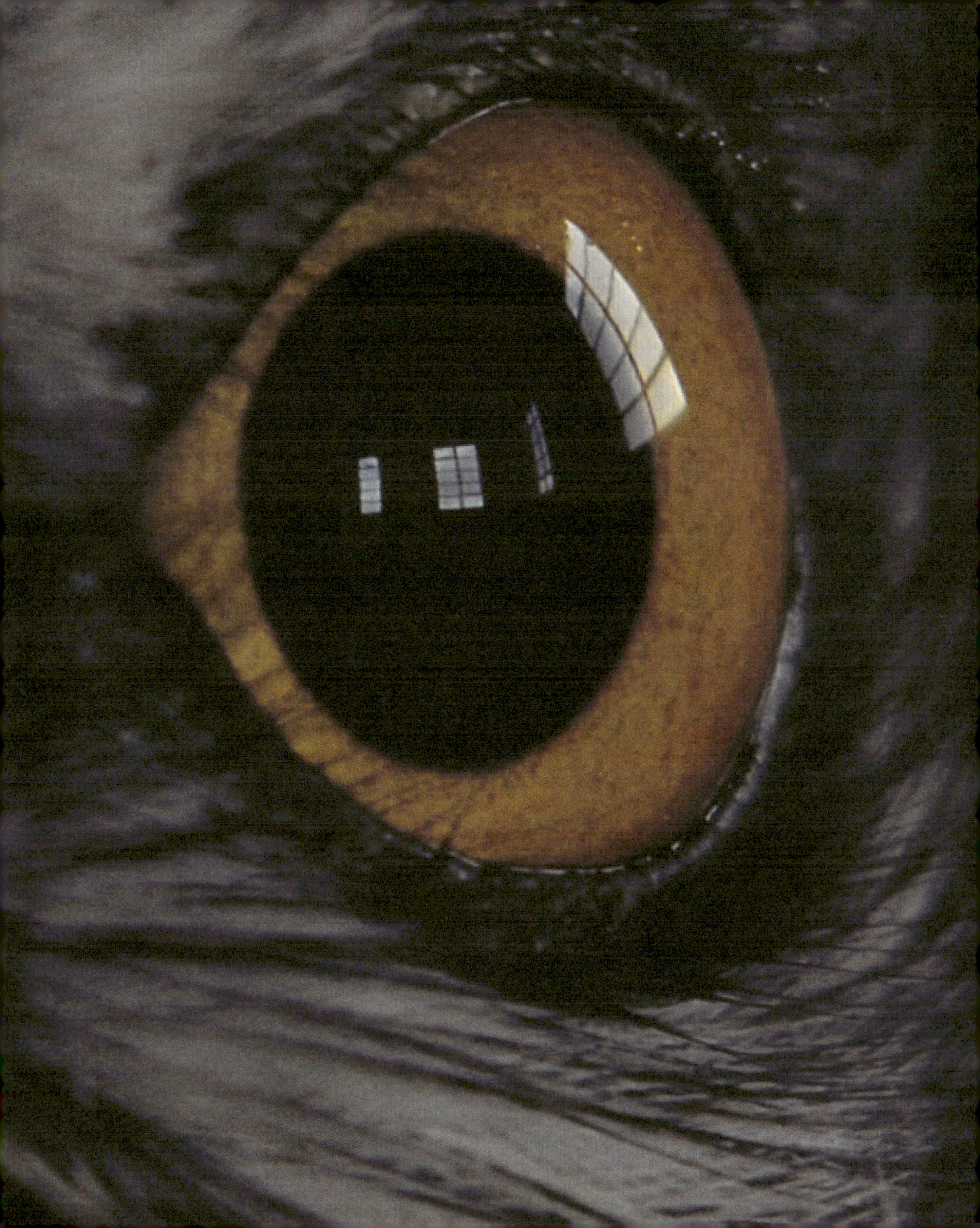

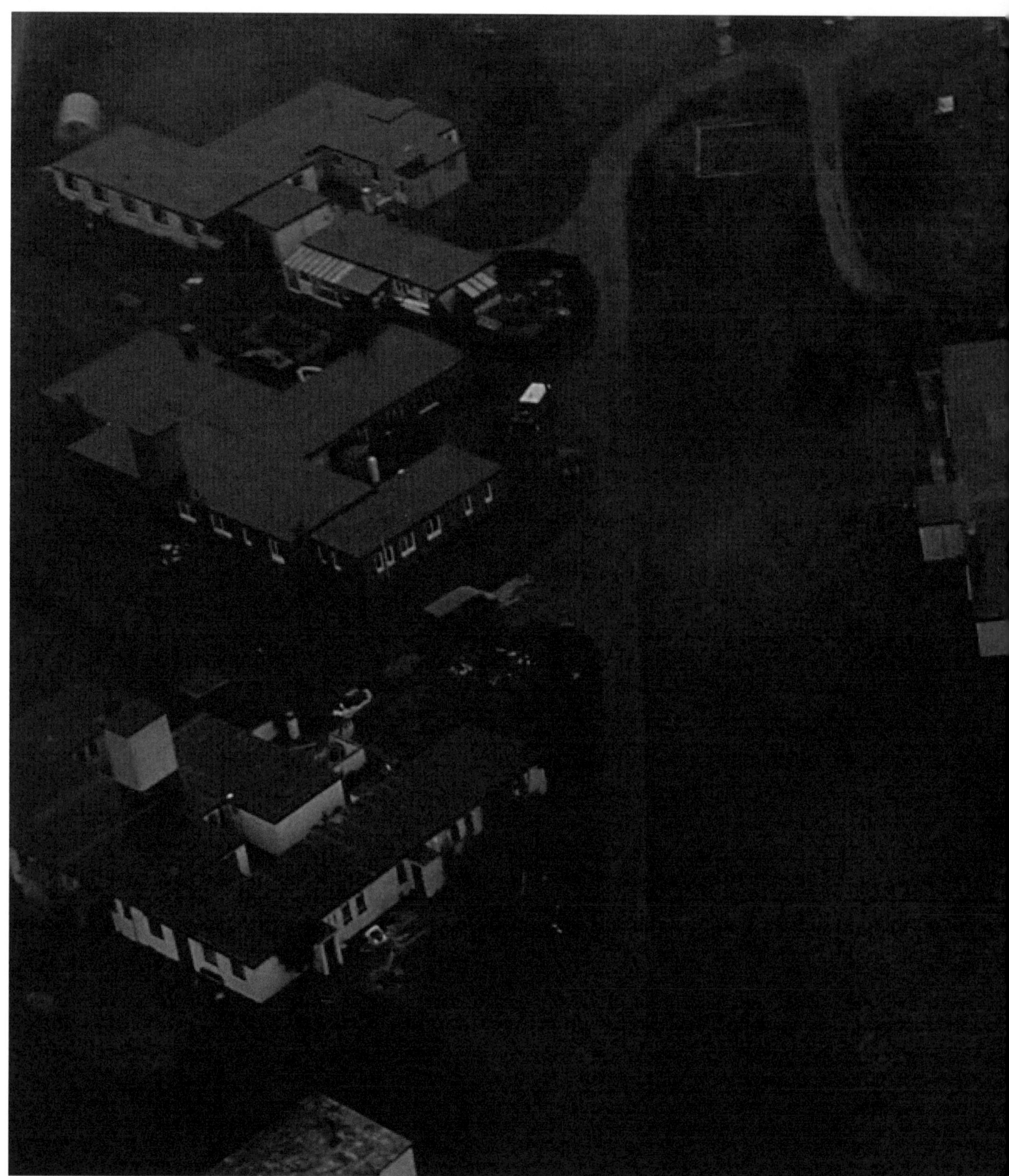

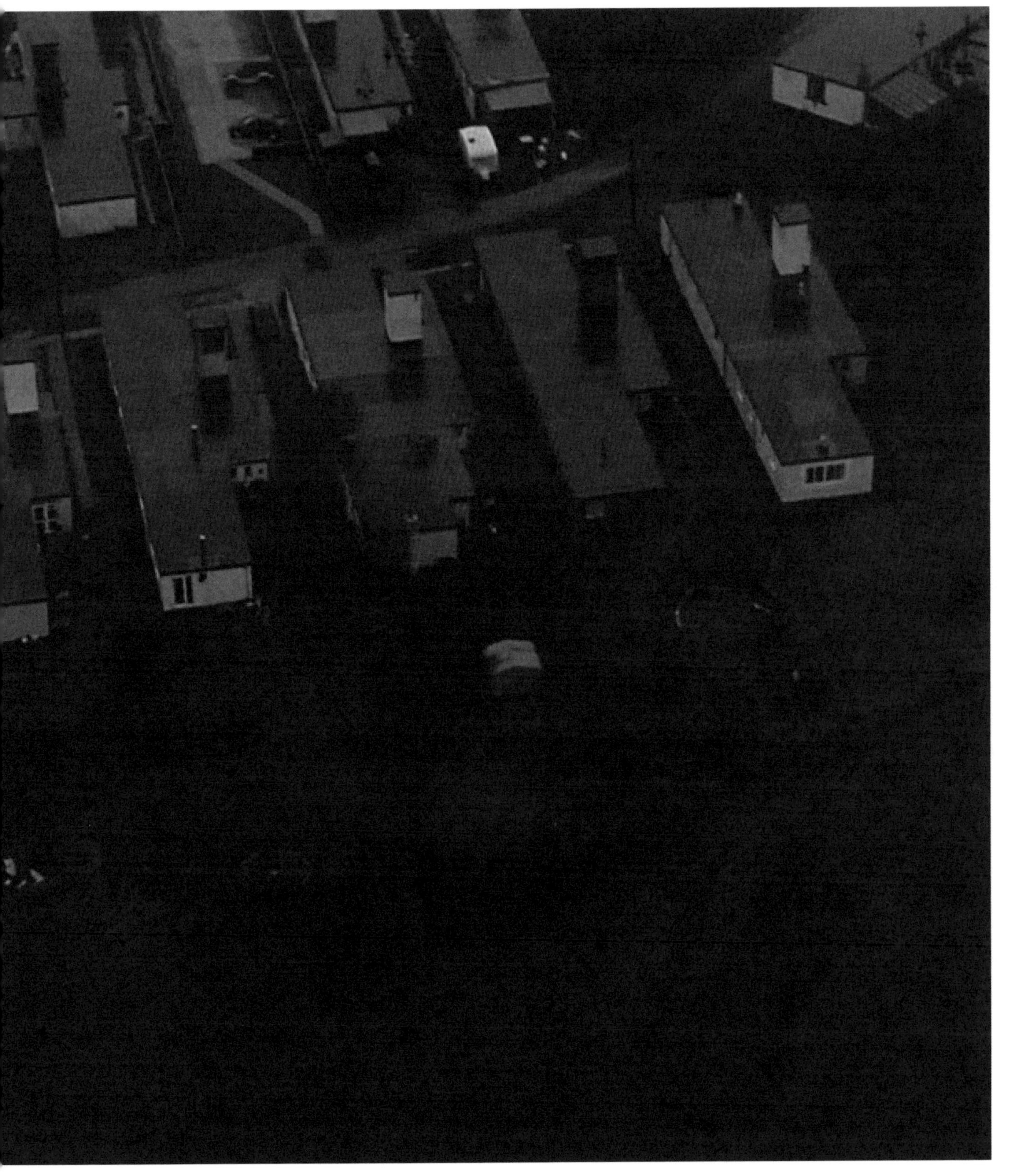

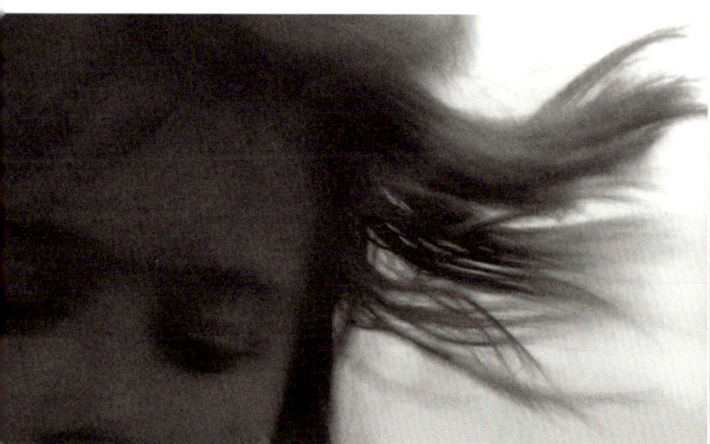
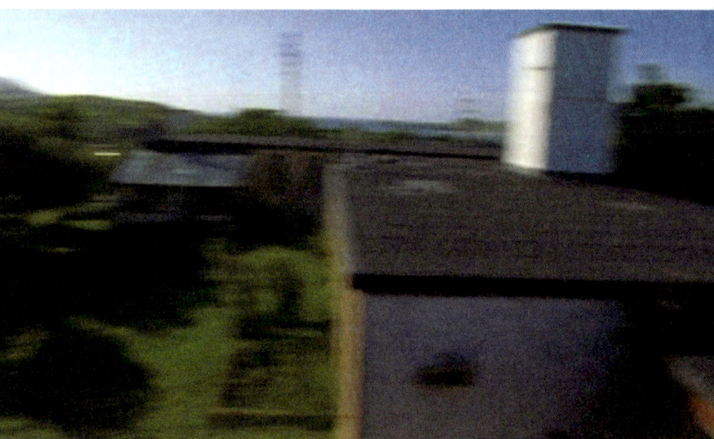
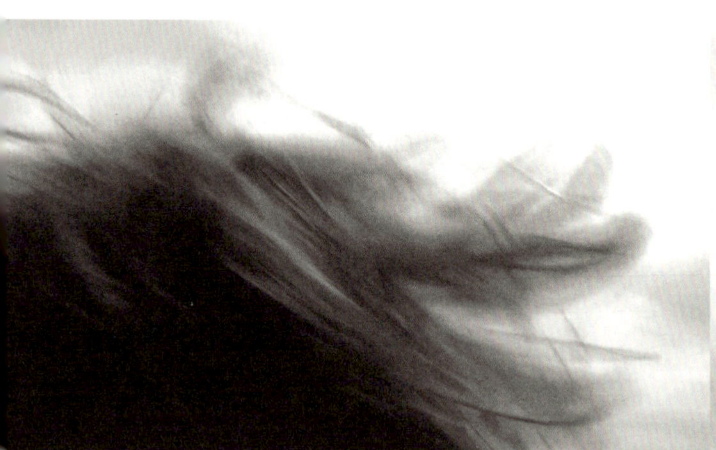
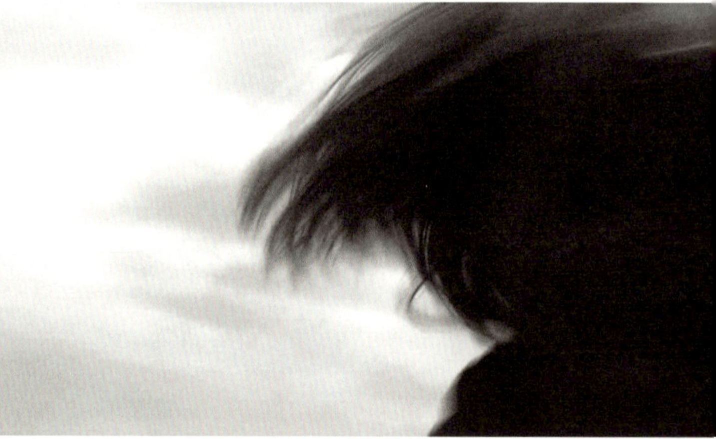

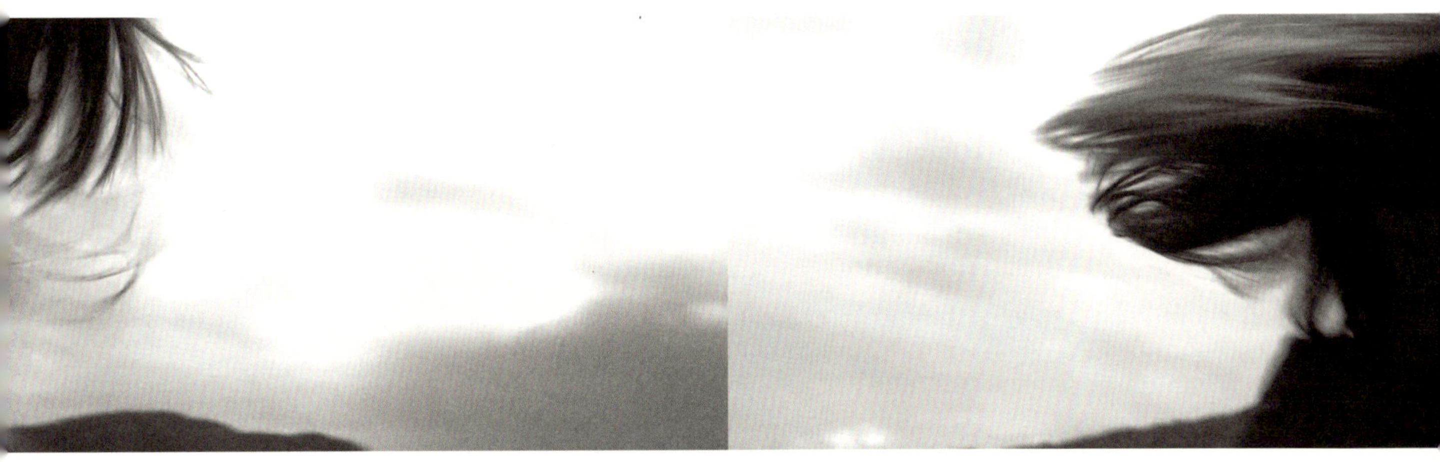

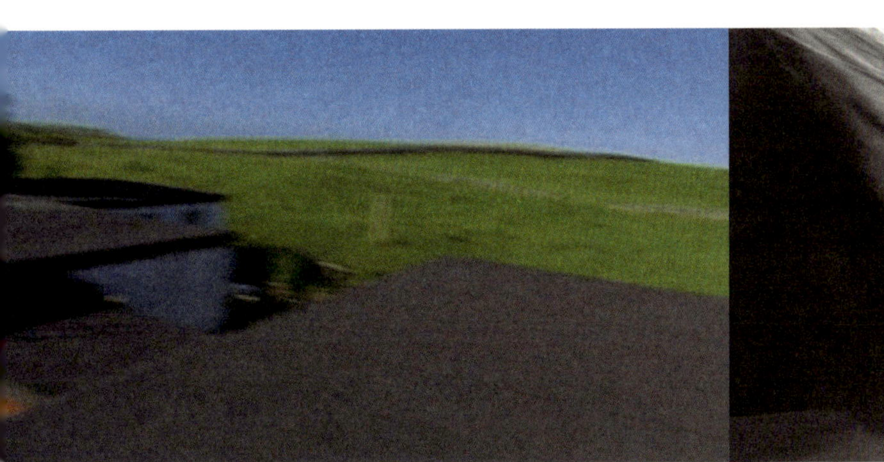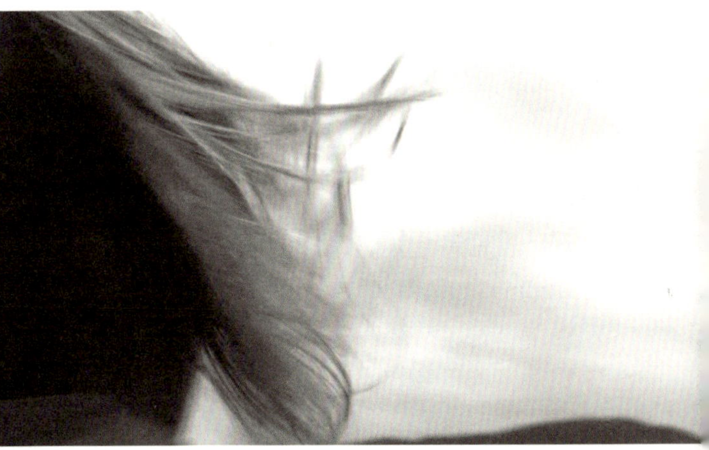

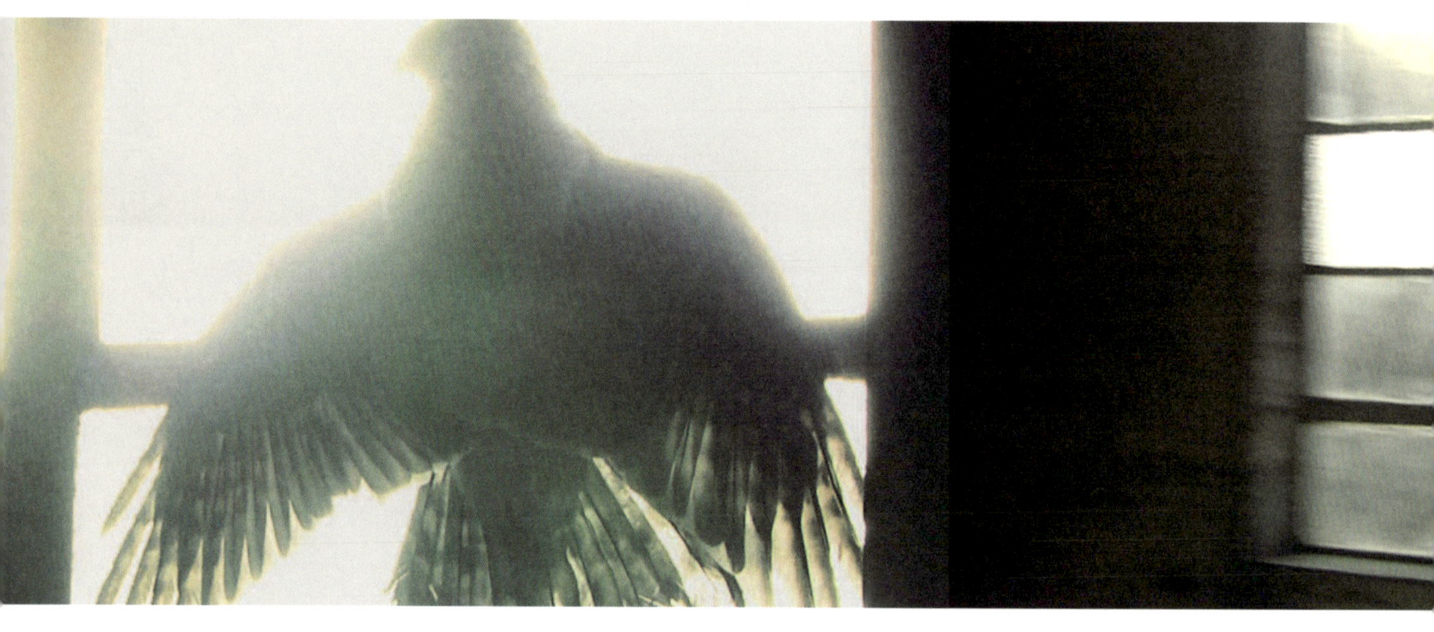

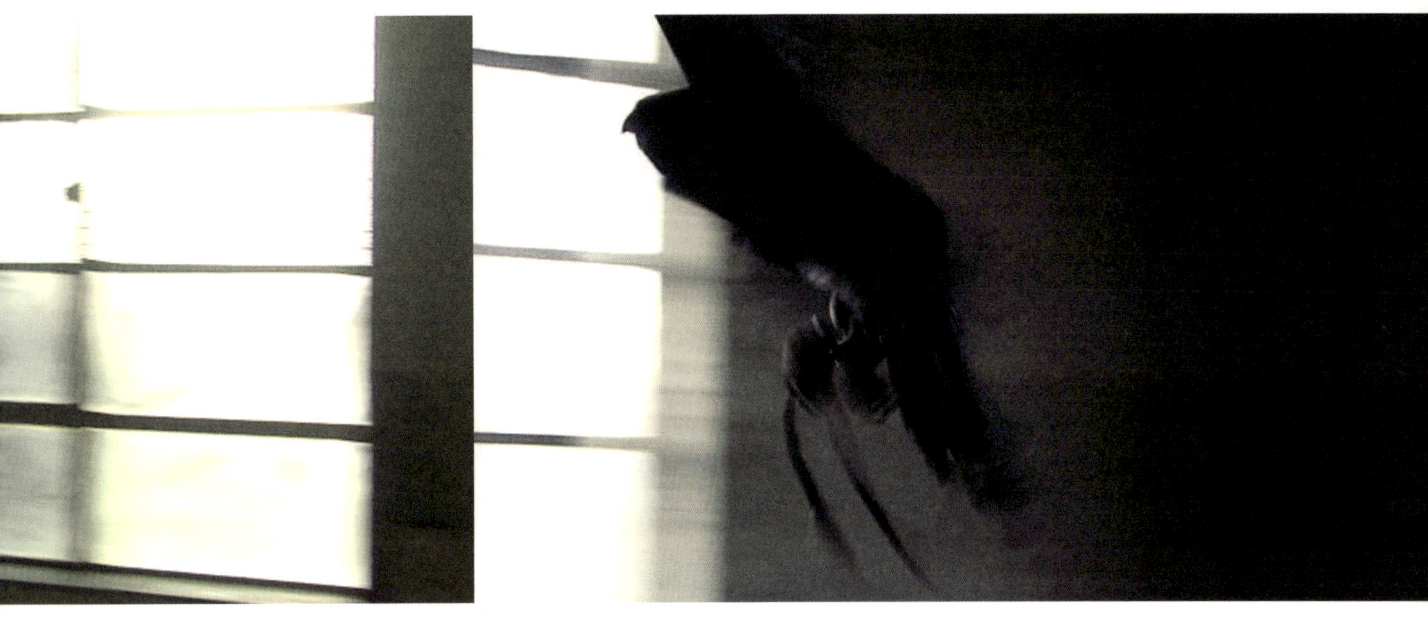

Woman
She had a corner stove – a corner fire and lots of
books – I remember that was a lovely room – and it had
lots of kids things in there and drawings on the wall

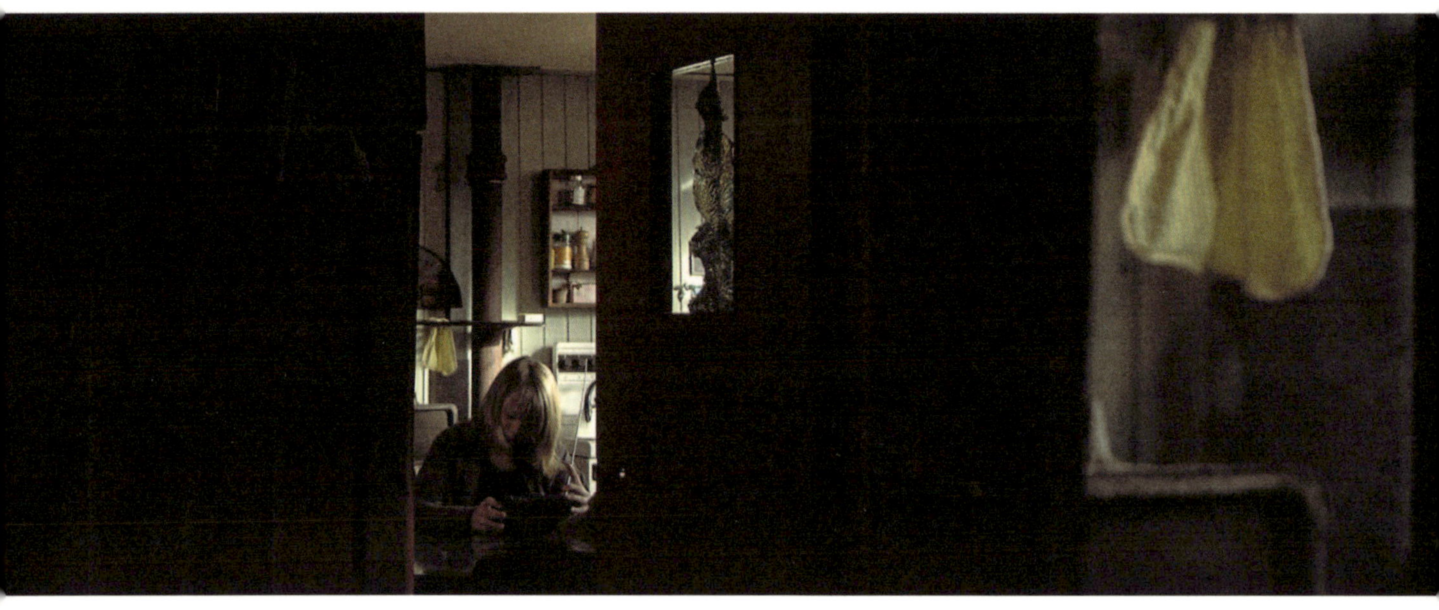

Woman
...and most of the time it's actually a kind of a kind of dusk for most of the day

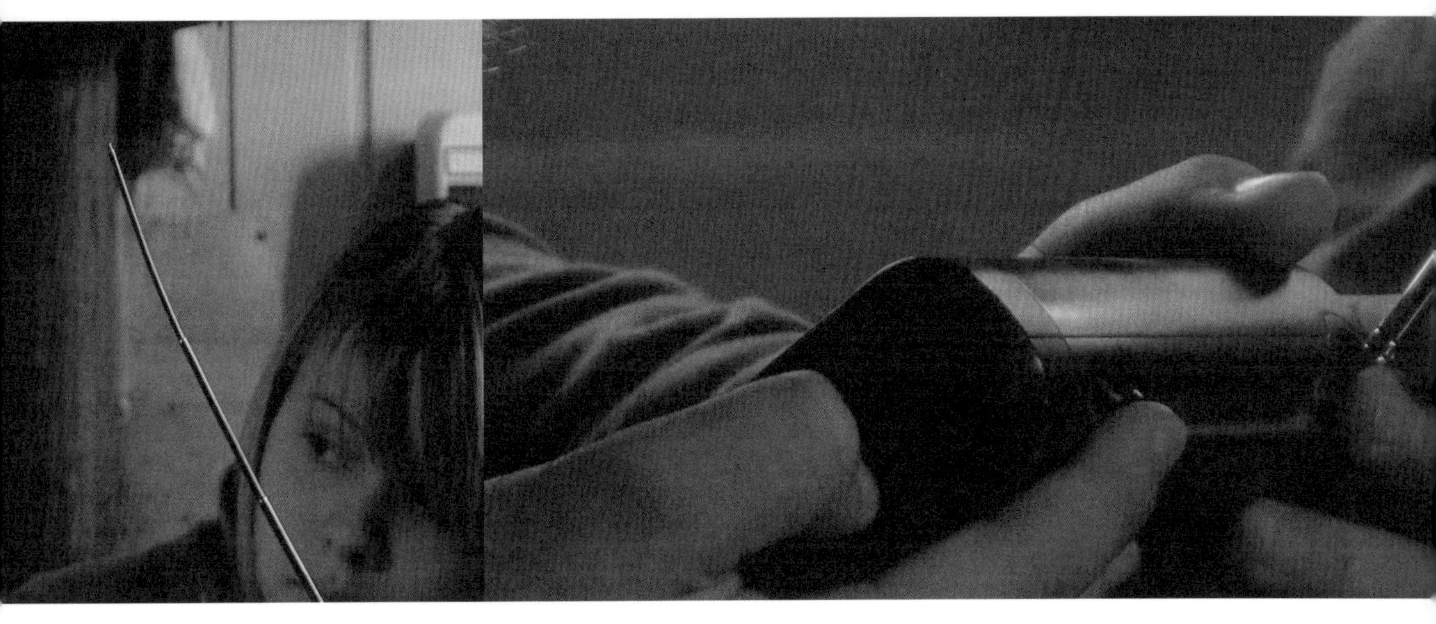

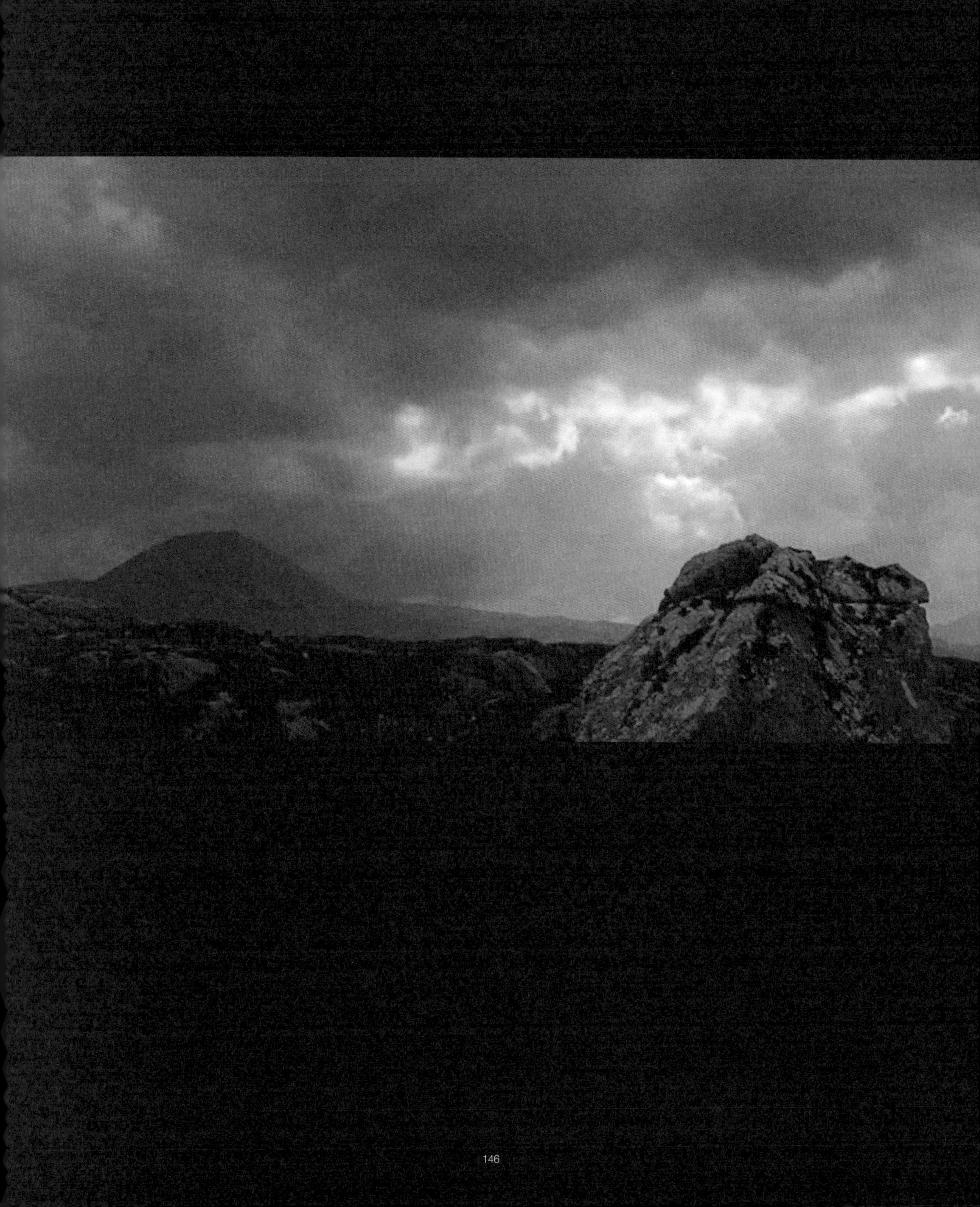

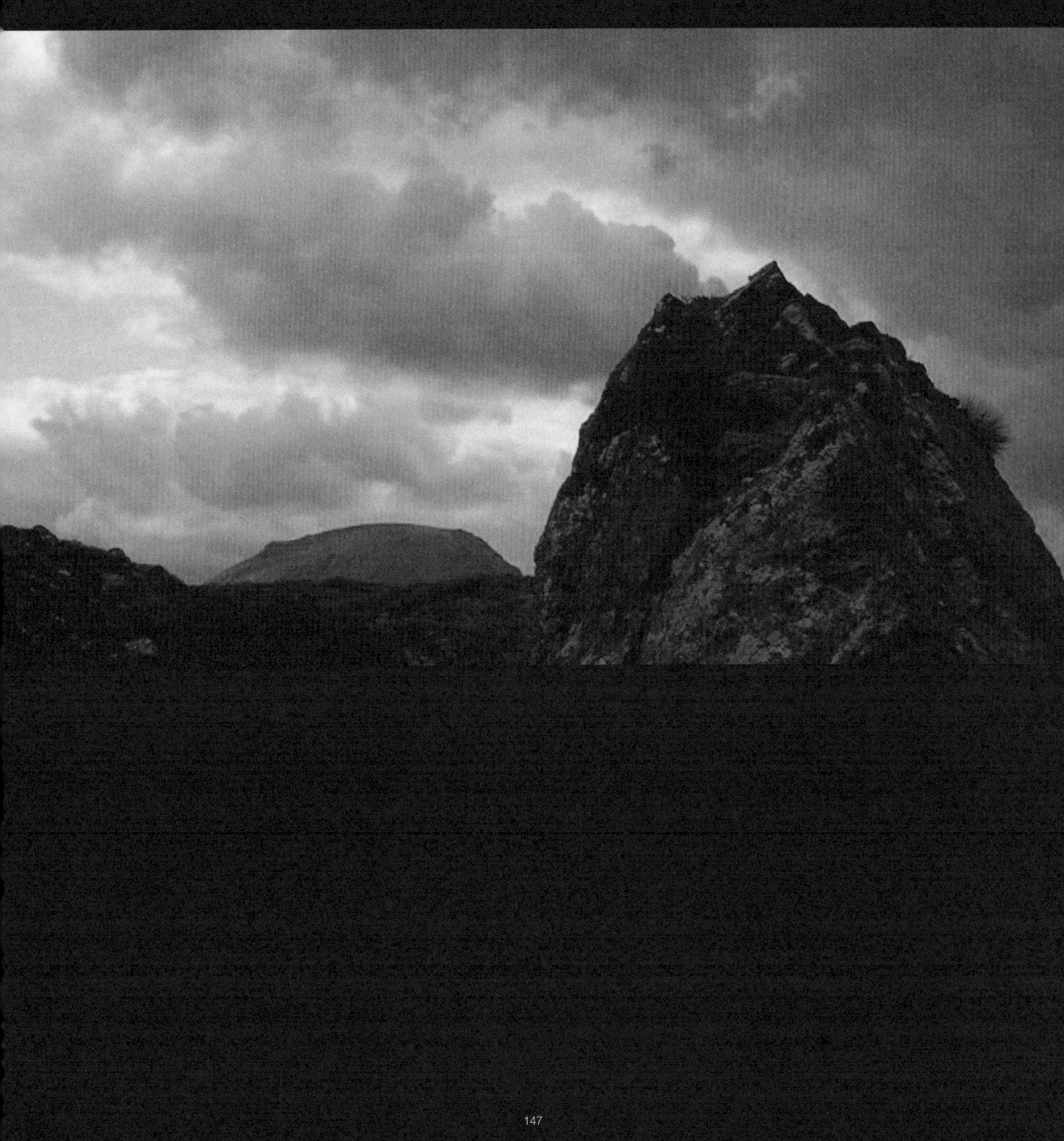

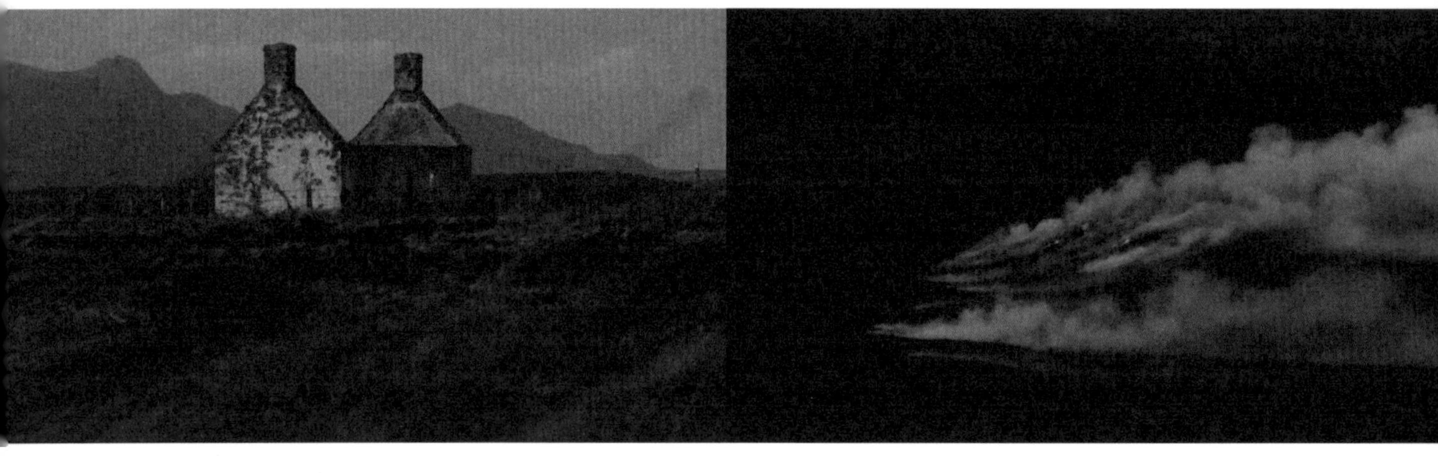

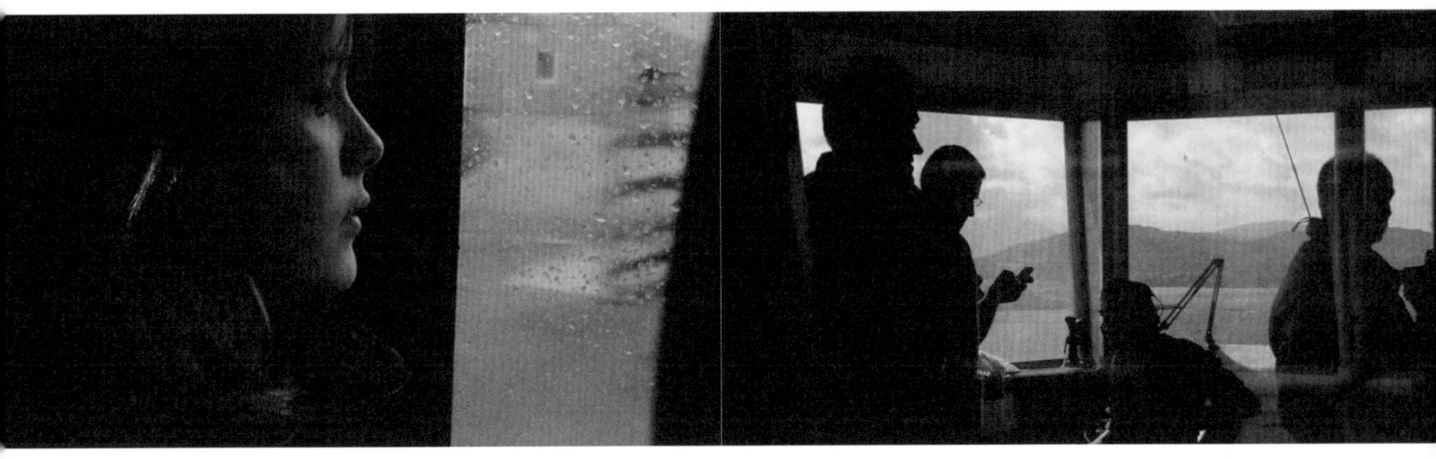

Woman
The people that pioneered to Balnakiel were people that
wanted freedom

Man
I never thought of it as being isolated at all

Range Control
'Nastar 11', 'Nastar 11' this is Range Control. Out

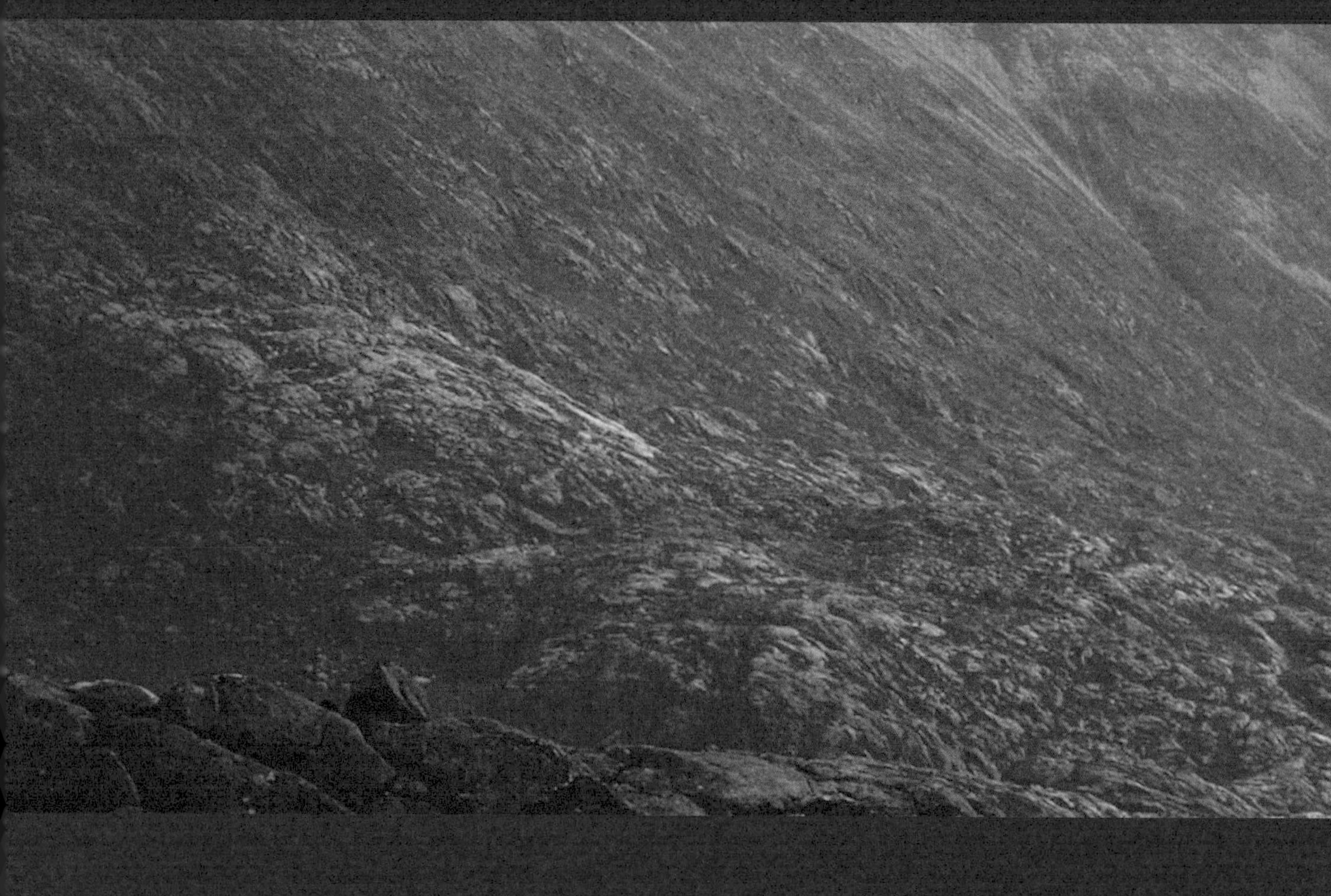

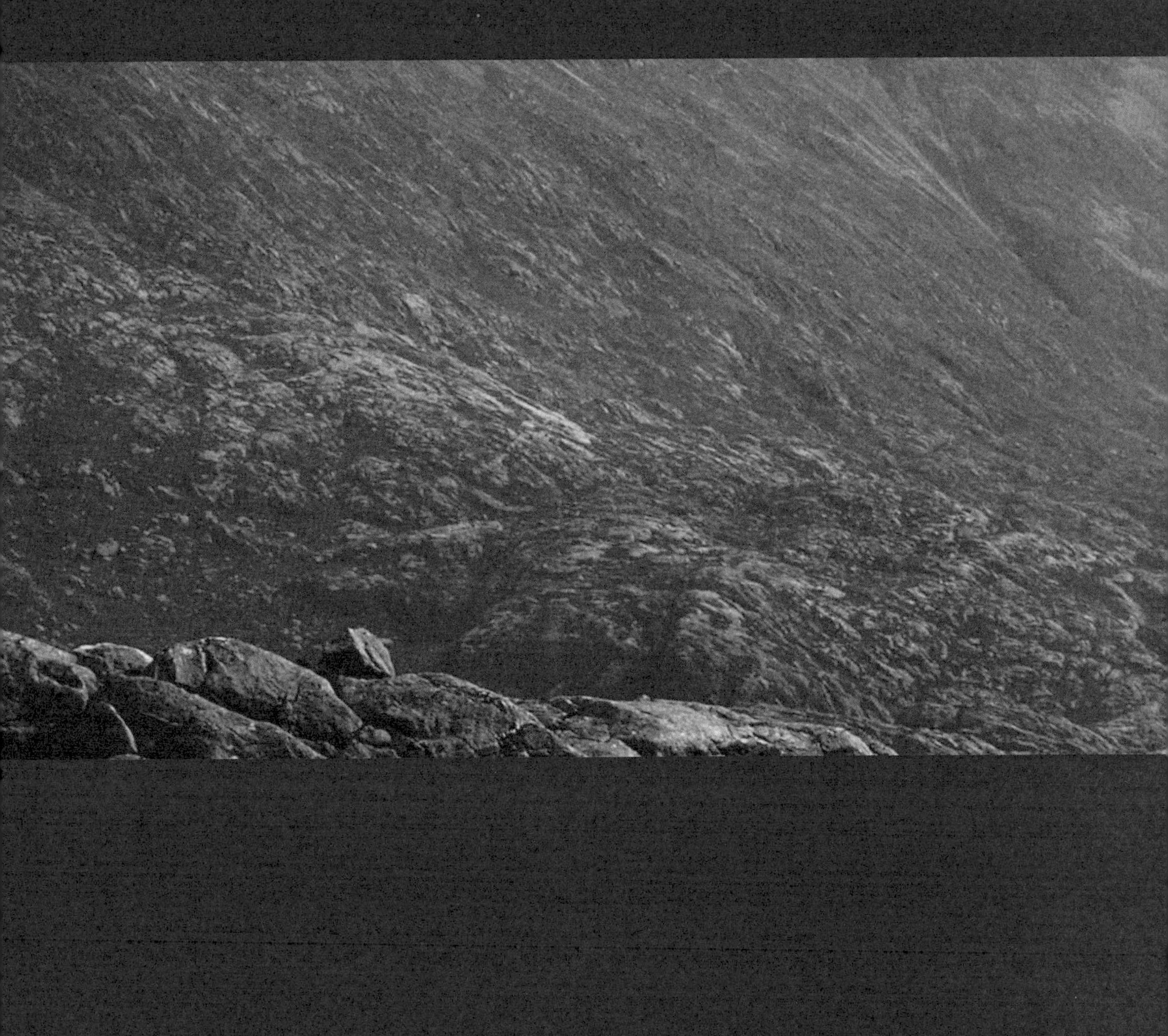

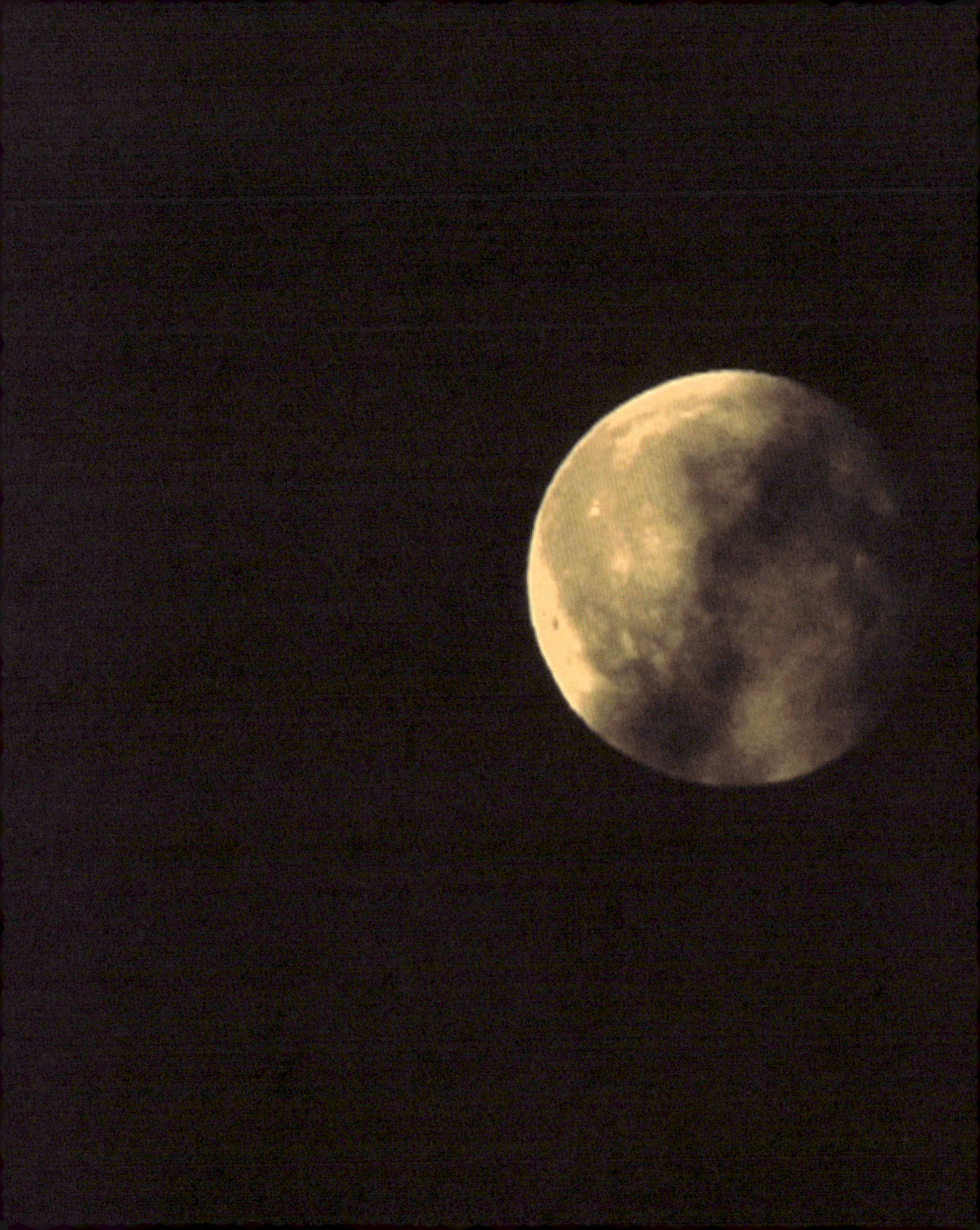

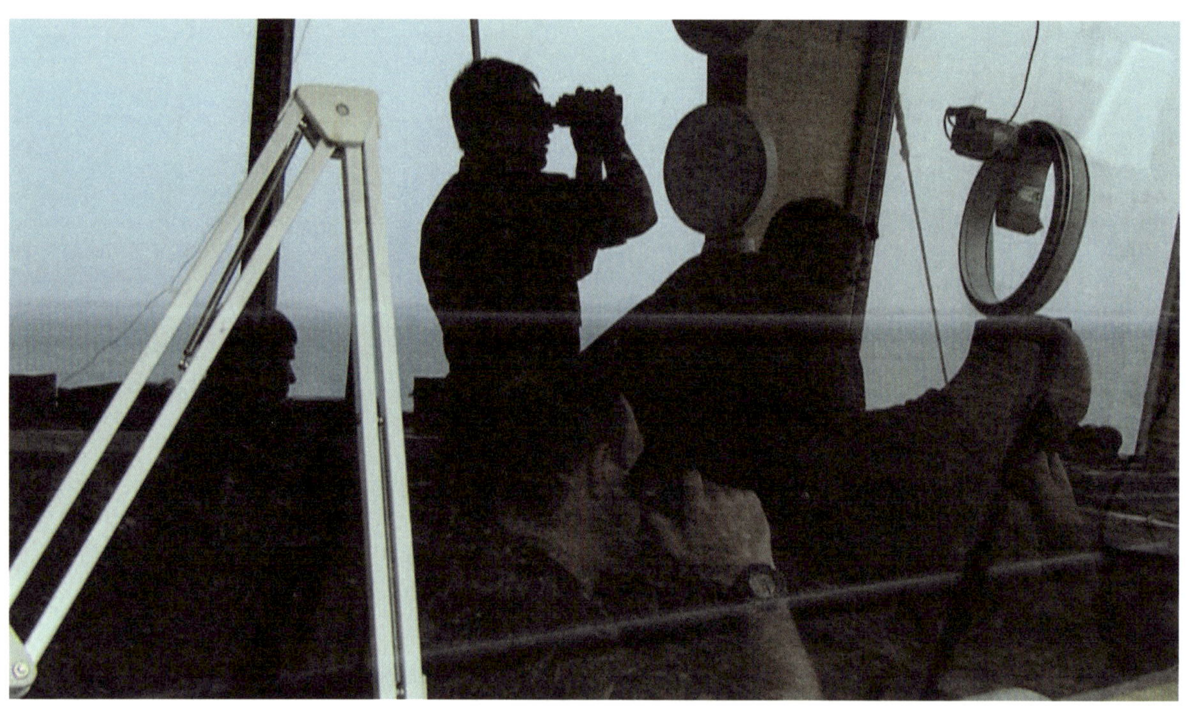

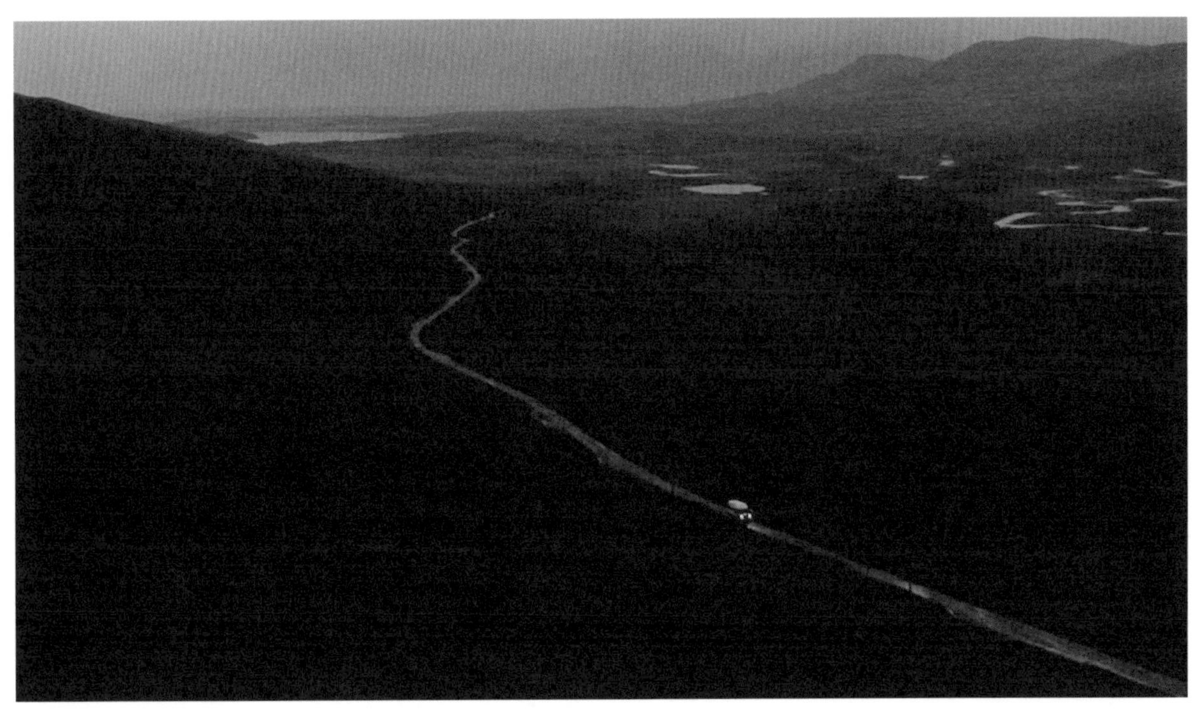

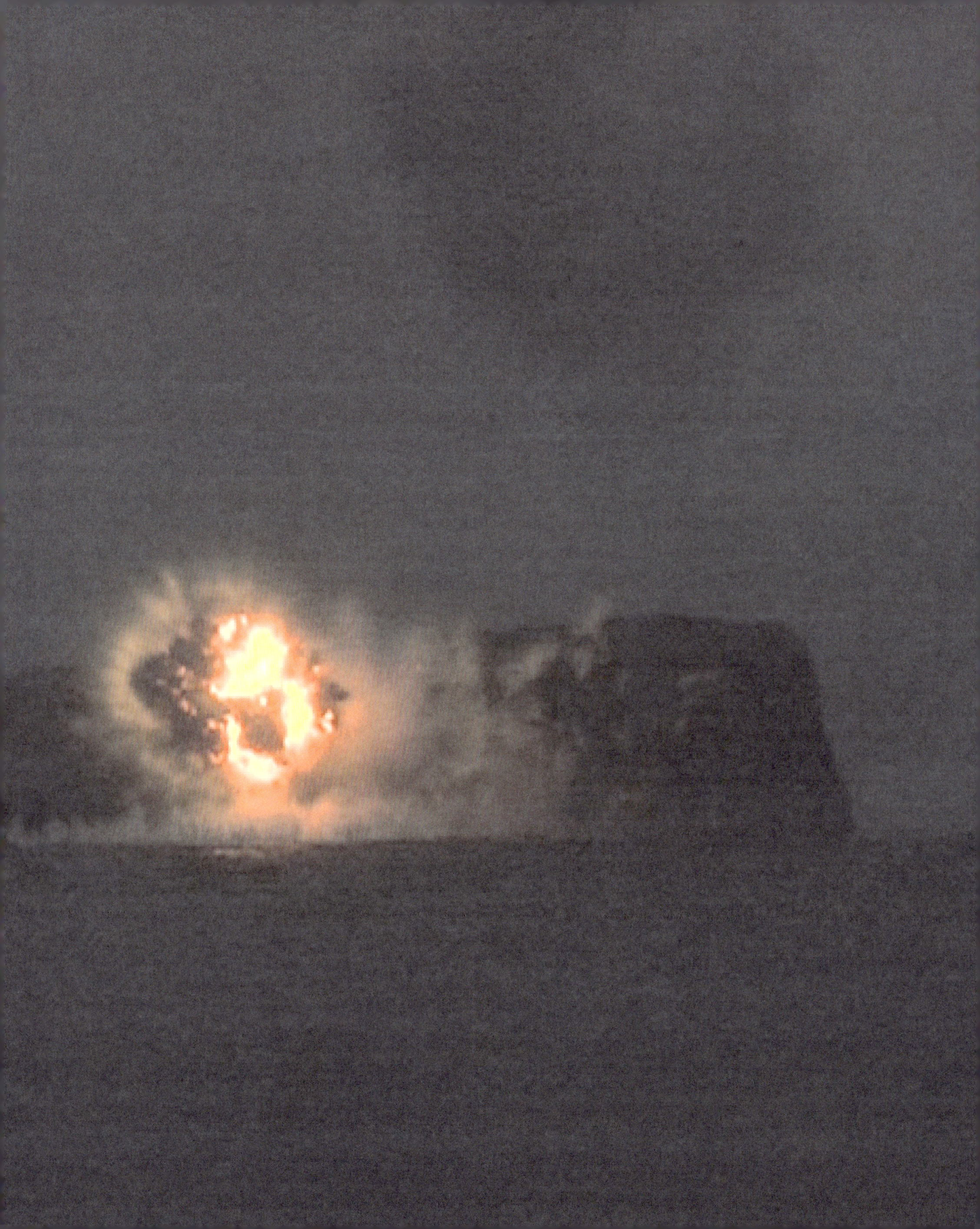

Jill Bennett

ATMOSPHERIC AFFECTS:
PAST EVENTS AND PRESENT FEELING

AIR

A man describes the panic aroused in him by the experience of walking through the village of Durness, a remote outpost in the north west Highlands of Scotland: pounding heart, breathlessness, a sickness like hunger, a silent hiss in the head; adrenaline taking possession of a body that feels 'so completely wired'. This man's voiceover is part of Shona Illingworth's *Balnakiel,* a video and sound installation, named for the village of Balnakiel, near Durness, both of which are seen from the aerial perspective of a plane in the opening sequence.

Prompted by memories of the local community's hostility to 'incomers', the man's anxiety is, it seems, common to many adults reviving childhood experiences of this isolated place, rendered inhospitable by geography and climate as well as by community division. Bounded by mountains, rock and bog, and pounded by continuous weather fronts during winter, the area has been shaped by a history of forced removal (Highland Clearances), and by its new populations: incomers from the South, escaping the pressures of urban living, and the military, who arrived during the Cold War to set up an Early Warning Station to guard the North Atlantic.

Threat – imminent or realised – has, at various moments, driven the inhabitation and organisation of this landscape, which has functioned as both retreat and frontline defence installation. If threat was the dominant sign of the Cold War, embodied in the Early Warning Station, the air of anticipated danger finds an echo not just in the affective tenor of remote village life but in the military manoeuvre underway as the man recounts his symptoms. His voice is counterpointed with that of an Air Traffic Controller rehearsing a show of force, a tactic of contemporary warfare in which planes fly as low as possible over a target area to 'buzz' the ground population, frightening civilians into hiding and exposing enemy combatants. Tornado fighter-bombers, armed with live bombs are guided in by features of the terrain; hence we hear the air traffic controller 'speaking' the landscape as the jets approach their target. In this explicit territorialising of threat, the Cape Wrath Bombardment Range stands in for the theatre of conflict and for the enemy insurgents: a virtual Afghanistan. Threat is materialised in the air, in this precise location, for transfer to the next event.

As far as the man remembers, nothing sinister happened to him on the village road. He does not recall an actual event or episode but a sensation, powerful enough to alter biochemistry and neurology. His memory is triggered by features of a landscape associated with childhood experience – with routine trips to the local shop or school. These landmarks, charged with affect, evoke a social experience. That is to say, they are not merely objects onto which inner anxieties are projected, repositories of the personal, but objects shaped by and perceived within a distinct environment. In *Balnakiel* the man experiences not just flashbacks of memory but environmental forces: atmosphere. The resurgence of his anxiety is not 'out of place' or misplaced. It is arguably mistimed, relating to a representation of the village at an earlier moment. But in attending to atmospherics *Balnakiel* opens up a different possibility, a way of seeing accumulated experience – memory – in terms of an encounter with something that endures in place, with affects that persist even in the absence of other people.

The metaphorics of atmosphere capture precisely this sense of lingering presence, figuring the enduring energies and affects that characterise an event or place as part of an environmental dynamics. People create atmosphere through the social communication of affect within a given environment. A good atmosphere may be generated by the connecting 'buzz' or 'vibe' of a group or crowd but the setting must be conducive; ambiance arises from the mix of social and environmental forces. The concept of an environment as the aggregate of surrounding things encompasses both the physical and atmospheric, though we rarely discuss the interdependence of social atmosphere and the biosphere that underpins it. In the most palpable sense, however, qualities of air (natural or artificially regulated) affect the way in which we see, hear, feel and smell in a given place, and hence condition social communications.

The question of how we sense what is in the air (a positive vibe or a foreboding atmosphere), itself a question of affective relations, is thus linked to the more distinctly environmental issue of how we understand and envisage air and climate. *Balnakiel* is a study of actual conditions of perception – of how Balnakiel the village and its environs are perceived from the air, from the sealed cockpit of an aircraft passing through cloud, from the ground immediately below an aircraft as it makes a deafening descent, from domestic structures battered by rain, and from the highland terrain during a weather front. It is a study of human communications in terms of what Peter Sloterdijk calls *a spherology*, focusing on taken-for-granted atmospheric knowledge.[1] Communication and sensing takes place within 'spheres' – areas of inhabitation characterised by specific atmospheric conditions. In *Balnakiel* spheres (which Sloterdijk argues may proliferate and connect as 'foam' or 'bubbles' bordered by membranes) are delineated within the film by air and noise regulating structures such as planes or buildings and in the gallery by the installation space.

The space of engagement, of 'viewing' is itself a sphere – an "inside-like, accessed, shared circle [*Runde*] that humans inhabit."[2] Inside-*like* because it is its own regulated atmosphere with its own air-conditions, a social space designed to enable the installation to promote certain means of connecting. *Balnakiel* presents the highland landscape as experience. But the vibrations of a plane sensed through a sub-woofer in the air-conditioned gallery space impact on the body of a viewer in quite a different way from the wind and turbulence of the air in *Balnakiel*, which appears in the film through various partitions. Glass windows are barriers to the battering wind and rain (which, we hear, can be like an 'attack', confining inhabitants for forty days at a time); a young girl climbs through a window and leads us out into the night; an air traffic controller guides in a Tornado from inside a tower with wrap-around windows.

At the same time, the effects of remote or radio controlled actions in these spheres (a plane's descent, an explosion, heather burning in its wake) are seen but not always heard, their sonic resonance muted in certain sequences as if to draw an atmospheric distinction. A silent explosion appears disconnected from our experience, and hence confined momentarily to a distinct sphere, discontinuous with the present: the virtual event of an explosion in Afghanistan or some future war, or a hint of the past when heather burned in the aftermath of Highland Clearance. By contrast, other sound effects penetrate the viewing sphere, folding into space and establishing continuity even as sounds distort and change.

Through this continuity of sound, inner mental space or body space is mapped onto external terrain; anxiety arises, as it were, from a pathway, a road, a rock, a low-flying Tornado. Memory is thereby extended topographically, the video and sound installation functioning as a cartographic process, registering the distribution of certain internal sensations across objects and landscape. In contrast to the more self-contained flashback, which confines memory to its own time, such a virtual mapping of actual living space folds into the present.[3]

As Sloterdijk has argued, atmospheric modeling is suppressed in much conventional cartographic representation. It is, however, the natural domain of immersive installation – a genre sometimes derided within art history for the inauthentic nature of the experience it purveys.[4] Sceptics contend that immersive video installation eradicates aesthetic distance, along with any capacity for judgment; being in media, as it were, obviates the possibility of thinking through media, purveying only a 'faux phenomenology' in Hal Foster's phrase.[5] Such a debased phenomenology delivers an experience with no perceivable link to actuality or 'outside' conditions; an experience beyond disorientation, the equivalent of 'being lost in space', Foster suggests. The shortfall of his exemplars is not a function of media or medium, however, but amounts to a lack of atmospheric awareness. Foster does not conceive a remedy in these terms, but a practical and conceptual engagement with atmosphere as a dimension of perception opens the possibility of mapping and navigating this space.

Conceived as an extension into space, a communication or an expression encounters degrees and qualities of resistance in air and environment. Hence, memory or thought that is externally mapped is transformed in its passage through the environment, which may be variously accommodating or resistant. It is possible in these terms to envisage place and atmosphere as modulating perception and affect, as intensifying or transforming anxiety rather than serving as its object.

ATMOSPHERE AND EVENT

'An atmosphere' – that quality, which an event may conspicuously generate or lack – is an effect of the transmission of affect, a process about which we still know surprisingly little. We theorise about expression and perception or reception – the twin poles of affect – which originate in an individual or social group. But, as Teresa Brennan noted, we know little about what happens in between these poles.[6] Yet, all of us know an atmosphere when we are in it: the tension and excitement of the streets, the sense that something is 'in the air', that we are part of something. Moreover, we often think and remember events in those terms; what happened may be less important than how we experienced the event, sense impressions, the detail of what were we doing when such and such happened. That we know where we were when President Kennedy or Princess Diana died is less a marker of the magnitude of the event than of the habit of returning the event – however distant – to experience. Such events precisely *don't matter* to us unless we can write them into our lives. As Christopher Bollas observes, we do not remember world events as historical sign-posts; the markers of history are rarely coordinates of our parochial lives.[7] Our connection to them is sometimes rendered palpable by direct consequences when an event literally touches 'our world' but more often it is their encompassing atmosphere – their mood – to which we connect or attune.[8]

Art is often casually credited with capturing the atmosphere of a time or place – the fulsomeness of its experience. An artwork can fill out an affective topology in a way that facilitates recognition and stimulates a feeling of being there, in the moment. Painting can do this – film perhaps more so – but immersive installation is the vehicle directly engaged with an investigation of transmission itself. At the intersection with experimental documentary, immersive video is now a means examining the experiential reach of an event as Adam Curtis's *It felt like a kiss* (2009) demonstrates. For this staged piece, Curtis transformed an abandoned Manchester office block into a 1950s house of fun/horrors, replete with the props of 50s domestic life and a video installation with pulsating sound, running throughout the building. Comprised of a mesmerising mash-up of media events from the America of the 1950s, interspersed with footage of 9/11, the video evokes the 'American Dream' and landmark political and cultural events of the 50s not as historical events or icons but as a potent atmospherics, literally 'felt' around the world. It is this 'feeling' – the means of its transmission as contagious affect – and the politics that it sustains that is the object of the work, which literally resonates and vibrates.

Such events and phenomena as the 'Cold War', the 'American Dream', 'Vietnam', are epochal signifiers, which is to say that they do not simply apply to actual events located in the theatres of war, politics or economics at their core but to a 'mood of the times'; to a set of anxieties, fears, hopes, dreams, investments that flowed more extensively, that touched, captured, mobilised people in their daily lives. Atmospherics in this regard are central to understanding the social and political reach of events, the boundaries of which are never fully definable.

In materialising the sensate processes that combine to engender atmosphere, art necessarily broaches the relationship of subjects to the world events: as Deleuze puts it, "Sensation has one face turned to the subject (the nervous system, vital movement, 'instinct', 'temperament'…) and one face turned toward the object (the 'fact', the place, the event)."[9] But this generation of sensation in the present – in the here and now event of an artwork – moves separately of its own accord and away from the 'past' event. Aesthetic sensation is characterised by immediacy. The impact of vibration in the body, and of an affectivity that precedes conscious recognition, it arises in the interaction of spectator and artwork. Affects find their own strength and intensity in the new configurations achieved in art, going "beyond the strength of those who undergo them."[10] Hence, art does not capture and replicate a given subject's experience of the event but draws bodies into sensations not yet experienced. It generates new experience *from* an event, moving outside the parameters of what is already known or habitual. How, then, is an affective aesthetic practice operating on its own terms (that is, by yielding sensory pleasures) made practical (capable of yielding new insight in relation to a real world event)? *Balnakiel* and

The Watch Man, enable us to frame this issue. Each is concerned with atmospherics and the mechanics of transmission, and with the manner in which a sensation connects to 'outside' events, both historical and anticipated, personal and communal.

The Watch Man is an immersive installation, focusing on an 80-year old watchmaker and the activities he performs in the interior of his home/workspace. These activities do not combine to present a narrative or portrait of a worker, but are framed as sequential actions – practical tasks, viewed in close proximity. Hence, this is less a study of the worker than of the substratum of daily life: the gestures and movements that comprise the material processes of making or mending. These include tactile processes: a steady hand manipulating tools, setting a ruby, buttering bread, lathering soap onto skin under the shower; and machinic processes, grinding and planing, polishing.

The watchmaker views the interior mechanism of a watch with the aid of various magnifying lenses – microscope, eyepiece, spectacles – optical devices that are echoed in the format of a circular screen. Viewers see his actions on this screen, as if this were itself a viewing aid, making visible the molecular detail within the normally visible world. But if this framing device is an ocular metaphor, hinting at the capture of the detail under a magnifying lens, it is offset by the surrounding elements of the installation – elements that render vision a profoundly bodily experience, mitigated by other kinds of sensing. The screen is the eye itself (bare trees in a forest in this circular format take on the association of capillaries in an iris) – the eye as physical organ, set in a room tinged blood-red by the luminous floor, which also emits vibrating sound.

To enter this room, to walk on the floor and feel its vibration, yields a particular experience of interiority. The spectator is not merely in this man's space, inside his home, his private world, his memory (all of which are evoked but somewhat circumscribed by the circular screen) but has the sensation of being inside a body, an indistinct, anonymous, collective body, an 'inside-like' experience of a shared space or sphere.

In reminiscences voiced in the soundtrack, the watch man describes his experience of entering the concentration camp at Belsen as a young soldier – the youngest in his troop – in 1945. In these momentary connections to the event of the Holocaust, intimacy takes on a weighty association. The work moves us inside experience; not, however, toward the privileged vantage point of the witness, but to an interior space where sight is altogether less consuming. Interiority is not *depicted* but felt at a point of contact; rather than peering at the subject through a viewing apparatus, we are, as viewers, in a place where vision is less clear, more tactile, synaesthetic.

A deep rhythm of very low frequency sound vibrates in the chest; nine other soundtracks are distributed across the floor and overhead.[11] The different planes of sound, emanating from various areas are synchronised to allow sound to sweep from ceiling to floor – or, conversely, to be contained and isolated. In this way, the sound of a pendulum moves across the floor; and the sound of the watchmaker's lathe, heard overhead, sharp and clear turns into the deep vibrating sound of a low-flying helicopter, sweeping the floor and rising back up overhead, so as to create a wave that enfolds the viewer. These fluid transitions perpetually open up interior spaces to outsides. The watch man's lathe becomes a military helicopter; his shower turns into forest rain, so that as we catch sight of his intimate ablutions we find ourselves back outdoors.

Sound, in other words, shifts the register of images, repeatedly giving rise to sensations that transform rather than reinforce the meaning of imagery on screen. If there is a narrative framing the action of the *The Watch Man*, its imagery is not 'read' in separation from the sensation generated by the immersive auditory component. This is not sensation that mimics representation or reproduces that felt by a character on screen, it is sensation drawn from the play of elements and energies that subsist beneath representation or the level of semantics and meaning. Deleuze describes this aesthetic operation in relation to Bacon's painting in which sensation emerges from the dynamic interplay of compositional forms.[12] Painting thereby disposes of any radical distinction between subjects and objects, figure and ground. Immersion, however, makes explicit its concern with qualities of environment and with the transition from one sphere to another.

AESTHETIC EXPERIENCE

Illingworth is not directly concerned with the meaning of images, nor with undermining meaning. Neither does she abandon the real for the realm of abstraction and formalism. She plays with shifting conditions of 'real' space that give affect, expression, noise and so on their character in a given sphere. Sound – the roar of a jet engine, the grinding lathe, rainfall – originates at a given point, travels through airspace, which has its own turbulence, humidity, density, to a given point in a new sphere (the highland landscape or ultimately, the art gallery). As it does so, it passes through and conjoins different spheres, sometimes rupturing or extending the membranes that delineate these spheres, which are permeable and extensive – like proliferating foam – at both macro and micro level. Space/place in this context does not equate to 'setting'. Air is not the backdrop against which events occur but a determinant of the quality of sound, seeping into the work at an elemental level.

This transposition of sound elements is the antithesis of an abstracting process that extracts a pure form or sound from its 'social' context. Sound connects to objects in Illingworth's work, playing on a certain habit of hearing. Unlike visual objects, aural objects have a peculiarly 'adjectival' quality, as Christian Metz noted: 'Lapping' is in and of itself an aural object, recognisable by sound alone, yet cultural and linguistic convention leads us to seek out its source, a lapping sea or river to which the onomatopoeic predicate belongs.[13] In film terms this habit tends to privilege the visual image, which serves to anchor the meaning of sound. But in both *The Watch Man* and *Balnakiel*, sound is relatively free ranging, attaching first to one event, then another. Ambient sounds build into rhythms: ticks, whirs, crackles, ringing, buzzing, splashing are heard as vibrations, often emanating from identifiable sources but then taking on different characteristics, transforming and translocating.

In some of the most mesmerising shots of endless rain in *Balnakiel*, we appear to be outside in the deluged highland landscape itself; that is, within or *inside* that landscape, attending to the sound of rain falling: the sharp pitter-patter of rain landing on hard surfaces, somewhere in audio range but out of shot, as well as on the absorbing earth. We watch rainfall in one place but the *sound* of rainfall is supervalent, coming not from the image but from multiple surrounding sources. Or sound might be absent, slow building in contrast to a violent event imaged on screen. This is not, then, a natural fusion, surround sound as 'ecomimesis' but a differential sense experience in which seeing and hearing are in a fluctuating accord.[14]

Dewey argues that we habitually undergo sensations as mechanical stimuli without fulfilling the interest of insight; we see without feeling, hear without vision and so forth.[15] From this we might infer that the virtual presentation of an ecosphere in surround sound does not guarantee the perfect, simultaneous engagement of all senses. A video installation offers not merely the illusion of reality, of being there, but reality filtered in ways that enhance, often simultaneously, discrete modes of perception. Accordingly, an intensification of sensory stimulation does not in itself engender greater knowledge. Aesthetic processes transform knowledge by achieving greater sensitivity to perceptual activity.

At stake here is how we understand information or meaning to be carried; that is, the issue of transmission. We readily assume that the meaning of a sound or an image is conveyed through signification. But sounds and images have their own qualities and intensities or valences. They may be social in origin but physical in impact, experienced as a matter of vibration, and hence, of intensity. Even where speech expresses meaning and agency, *prosody* – the rhythm, stress, and intonation of speech – is central to its 'message', or more precisely, to the effective transmission of a message. Hence, Brennan argues that we have failed to understand how "the social and physical transmission of the image are one and the same process," how sights and sounds are carriers of social matters, physical in their effects.[16] This being the case, however, prosody or the affective response to sound or image may outweigh and ultimately countermand a message, producing a cognitive dissonance that allows one to feel with or without believing. Hence, one may feel anxious on a given street even when one believes there is no just cause, no actual threat.

If the study of atmosphere in art is a study of communication and perception in a given sphere, each instance is a mapping of the axis of communication (the transmission of affect from one body or entity to another) in dense space, a modeling of intra-personal connection through an examination of the quality of space and air in between. The in-between space for Sloterdijk is not a gap between subject and object but a force field of turbulent tension in which human encounters are no longer merely 'intersubjective' but figure as 'interfacial greenhouse effects'.

Brennan is equally concrete in her attempt to model relational space, in this case by tracking mechanisms of transmission through air. The theories of entrainment utlised by Brennan prioritise two senses in particular, smell and hearing.[17] Smell is a key vehicle for chemical entrainment, which encompasses pheromonal transmission. Pheromones are externally secreted substances, which may communicate fear and anxiety, for example, when detected in the air. Nervous or electrical entrainment – "the driving effect one nervous system has on another" – is effected by touch, sight and sound, but particularly through the communication of rhythm, in regard to which auditory cues have priority.[18] Whereas chemical entrainment is largely unconscious, however, rhythmic or auditory entrainment may be both conscious and more readily manipulated (as, for example, in the case of dance parties or crowd chants that raise the intensity of an event).

In Illingworth's work rhythm plays a central role in effecting continuities and discon-tinuities, producing accord and discord through entrainment and dissonance, designed to disrupt habits of perception. The metaphorics of *The Watch Man* are explicitly concerned with the production of rhythm: with time and timing. It is the measurement of time – rather than the time of the historical event – that is thematised.

Clocks strike and tick, their metronomic function anchoring the acoustic rhythm of the piece but modified in places so that the marking of time becomes unstable, slightly out of synch, a struggle between competing forces. Where rhythm builds and connects, narrative remains inchoate.

The Watch Man – in spite of its arresting colour and visual sequences – might be deemed a sound installation first and foremost. Sound is the driving element, hearing the connecting sense, changing how things are perceived, and changing relations between sight and sound, sight and sensitivity. Yet the shrouded figures of Belsen, "slow moving…not reacting…not walking…just shuffling," and the "smell of decay" remain the most pronounced and striking images in the watchmaker's account of Belsen. Those images are not illustrated or replicated in any sense. Evoked simply in the words of 'The Watch Man', they are etched in memory as sights and smells, described but not transmitted.

The question of what is transmissible or accessible is an important one in this context. Acoustic rhythm achieves a 'deep' level of engagement in *The Watch Man*; sound is literally penetrating. At the same time, the projected imagery and radiating light is vibrant and textured in a way that offers a haptic engagement with surfaces, with details and processes, from tea making to watch mending. Yet none of this takes us into the narrative of Belsen. Neither abstract, nor an aesthetic detour, the sound installation makes only the vaguest gesture toward story-telling. The watch man's description frames this piece, making Belsen a kind of touchstone for everything that goes on, but his voice does not transport us there, its rhythms and prosody miring us in the space of the present.

The Watch Man is not a work *about trauma* in the sense of ordering images to evoke a traumatised subject. There are no flashbacks or images of Belsen. Traumatic memory of the horror of Belsen does not impinge on the here and now in a way that pathologises the former as out-of-its-time. Memory flows freely in the present, the watch man now able to describe the scenes of death and his own trauma (an "uncontrollable suffocating, frightening feeling") but both clocks and voice anchor the monologue in the here and now ("It's four o'clock, just past four," he reminds us). Trauma has been muted in the life of the watchmaker as he tells it ("people did not want to know; they did not want to hear") but it is neither suppressed nor enacted here. The Holocaust and the liberation of Belsen is an impetus for *The Watch Man* but, as with the life portrayed, not its leitmotif. The irruption of memory in the present follows a different logic, that of Deleuze's open, expansive cartography or of Dewey's rejection of representational and cognitive view-points that "isolate one strand in the total experience, a strand, moreover, that is what it is because of the entire pattern to which it contributes and in which it is absorbed." [19]

The 'total experience' is not the reconstructed past but the dense weave of everyday life. Insight through aesthetic engagement comes through making (creating, producing) connections, rather than through retrospective analysis.[20] In this vein, we might read *The Watch Man* as a study in aesthetic perception – a mode of perception enacted 'diagetically' in the watch man's transitions between everyday tasks and recollection – envisioning memory as inhabited experience, distributed across the terrain of everyday life, the world around him.

Practical activities are not left behind as memory takes hold; on the contrary, they sustain memory and promote its transformation. Memories are invested with meaning, affect and sensation; gestures, actions and objects enjoined into circuits of affect that carry thoughts, ideas and memories. In this sense, we can say that Illingworth's works are about remembering: processes of memory and processing memory rather than the memory image itself.

Most importantly, these works demonstrate the capacity of the aesthetic (aesthetic thought or practice) to redirect affect. The notion of the aesthetic defined in terms of its capacity to conduct, orchestrate, intensify, redistribute is the antithesis of the idea that an image generates intensity by virtue of what it represents. Certainly it is the case that shocking images of Belsen or other atrocities or violent acts incite anger simply because of what they are; on the other hand, there are many other kinds of images that take on a demonic status by virtue of an intense affective interest arising independently. The psychologist Silvan Tomkins explains this in terms of the propensity of affects such as fear to seek out objects. Hence, fear may precede the image and find its scapegoat, rather than the other way around. In this sense, affects travel benignly or otherwise in art or by aesthetic means, finding a place in the everyday.

Art is not about fixing the emotion to the event (in *The Watch Man* affect does not cling pathologically to its object; nor does it merely repeat or haunt the subject). Instead it offers the creative possibility of changing an emotional relationship to the event, gradually over time, suddenly, emphatically, radically. By contrast, some of the most controversial work on Holocaust imagery is that which holds to the possibility of representation and capture; to the conviction that a phenomenological trace of a subject might subsist within art, like a fragment of memory.[21] Such claims are always mired in arguments about their redemptive aspirations for art. For if art preserves a trace of a real life, it becomes a relic; and with the preservation of life in this form comes a duty of care. "We must remember" Auschwitz, "must imagine for ourselves," argues Georges Didi-Huberman.[22] This imperative is more than simply that of 'not forgetting' or marking the loss. It enjoins us to witness.

Herein lies the hubris in the representational position. Can art ever claim to capture profound trauma, the witnessing of which entails extreme horror? Its failure to do so is, of course, implied in the well-established argument that the Holocaust is *unrepresentable*. But often what is at stake more than representation is response; what we make of image and how we perform memory in relation to it. Believing in the claim of representation and capture, the secondary witness is compelled to mime, to produce a sadness that is clichéd: appropriate but inevitably inadequate to its subject, not by virtue of its insincerity but in its pallor and attenuation.

The necessity for art to refract the past, enabling viewers to experience its trace, diminishes as we attune to the ways in which aesthetic perception operates – always, already – along a continuum, connecting the past to the present. History and trauma are not merely subject matter to which art might gain access – or for that matter, pronounce off limits. Rather, the job of art and aesthetics is to trace aesthetic activity, following the strands that carry events forth, embedding it in the material world and transforming experience.

Sensation and affect is never novel as such but layered, thickened and accumulated; 'irreducibly synthetic', as Deleuze argues.[23] In art it arises from the newly connected with a degree of intensity, strengthened – not attenuated – by the aesthetic process, taking on new character. Likewise, the atmosphere of an event or place is "charged with accumulations of long-gathering energy,"[24] experienced in the present under ever changing circumstances. Art, then, concerns the lived – and living – event. Whatever it tells us of history – past events – does not come from presenting an image of that past but from the sensation that marks the very extension and reach of the 'past' event: history as accretion rather than history repeating. Aesthetic work follows the threads of a history of sensation that goes to the heart of what creates and energises the event, whether characterised by unrealised threat – a mood of the times – as in *Balnakiel*, or, as in *The Watch Man,* an all too real and inexpressible horror.

1
Peter Sloterdijk: *Sphären I – Blasen.* Frankfurt-am-Main: Suhrkamp, 1998; *Sphären II – Globen.* Frankfurt-am-Main: Suhrkamp, 1999; *Sphären III - Schäume.* Frankfurt-am-Main: Suhrkamp, 2004, Sloterdijk's trilogy on the spheres is not yet published in its entirety in English. See P. Sloterdijk, (2009) 'Something in the Air', *Frieze* magazine, 127, London: Central Books Ltd., Online. Available HTTP: <http://www.frieze.com/issue/print_article/something_in_the_air/>.

2
P. Sloterdijk, *Spharen 1: Blasen, Mikrospharologue,* Frankfurt-am-Main: Suhrkamp 1998, p.28.

3
On the inadequacy of the conventional flashback or 'recollection-image' see G. Deleuze, translated by Hugh Tomlinson and Robert Galeta, *Cinema Two: The Time Image,* Minneapolis: University of Minnesota Press, 1989.

4
H. Foster, 'Polemics, Postmodernism, Immersion, Militarized Space', *Journal of Visual Culture* 3, 2004, pp.320-335.

5
H. Foster, op.cit., p.327. See also F. Dyson, *Sounding New Media: Immersion and Embodiment in the Arts and Culture,* University of California Press, London, 2009, p.112. Dyson analyses an implicit assumption in the work of key theorists that inactive immersion undermines critical evaluation. She circumvents this objection by establishing the value of modes of embodied experience – the breath interface, for example.

6
T. Brennan, *The Transmission of Affect*, New York: Cornell University Press, 2004, p.1.

7
C. Bollas, *Cracking Up: The Work of Unconscious Experience,* New York: Hill and Wang, pp.116

8
Attunement is discussed by K. Stewart, 'Atmospheric Attunements', Transforming Cultures program, Sydney: University of Technology, August 20, 2009 [unpublished lecture].

9
G. Deleuze, *Francis Bacon: The Logic of Sensation,* Trans. D.W. Smith, Minneapolis: University of Minnesota Press, 2003, p.31.

10
G.Deleuze, and F. Guattari, *What Is Philosophy?* Trans. Hugh Tomlinson and Graham Burchill. London: Verso, p.164.

11
In addition to a subwoofer generating deeper sound, there are nine channels of sound: five running through the floor, four through overhead speakers. FeONIC 'actuators' attached to the underside of the specially constructed floor translate sound signals into vibrations, driving amplified sound through this floor. Unlike conventional speakers that generate sound from a single point, the actuators distribute sound across a horizontal plane.

12
G. Deleuze, *Francis Bacon: The Logic of Sensation.*

13
C. Metz, 'Aural Objects', *Cinema/Sound,* 60, 1980, 26. 'As soon as the source of the sound is recognized (jet plane), the taxonomies of the sound itself (buzzing, whispering etc.) can only provide, at least in our era and geographic location, supplementary precisions…of a basically adjectival nature.'

14
The term 'ecomimesis' is used by T. Morton, Ecology Without Nature, Cambridge, MA: Harvard University Press, 2007. See F. Dyson, *Sounding New Media: Immersion and Embodiment in the Arts and Culture,* p.132 for further discussion of ecomimesis in immersive art.

15
J. Dewey, *Art as Experience*, p.21.

16
T. Brennan, *The Transmission of Affect,* p.71.

17
T. Brennan, *The Transmission of Affect,* pp.68-73.

18
T. Brennan, *The Transmission of Affect,* pp.70. Cf G. Deleuze, *Francis Bacon: The Logic of Sensation*, pp.xv. Rhythm, like sensation, is a term Deleuze applies to the fundamental operation of art, a process distinguished from signification.

19
J. Dewey, *Art as Experience*, p.302.

20
J.Dewey, *Art as Experience*, p.24. 'Aesthetic experience' for Dewey is continuous with the processes of living, grounded in the same impetus to make for practical advantage. A certain 'anatomy of experience' divides and compartmentalises activities, bringing about the separation of 'practice' from insight, of imagination from executive doing, of emotion from thought. p.21.

21
J. Bennett, *Review of Georges Didi-Huberman 'Images in Spite of All: Four Photographs from Auschwitz',* caa.reviews, Online. http://www.caareviews.org/reviews/1380 (December 31, 2009).

22
Georges Didi-Huberman Images in Spite of All: Four Photographs from Auschwitz, Chicago: Chicago University Press, 2008.

23
G. Deleuze, *Francis Bacon: The Logic of Sensation*, p.33. 'Every sensation…is already an 'accumulated' or 'coagulated' sensation, as in a limestone figure. Hence the irreducibly synthetic character of sensation'.

24
J. Dewey, *Art as Experience*, p.24.

NOTES ON AUTHORS

Professor Martin A. Conway is a neuropsychologist and one of the foremost international experts in the field of autobiographical memory. His work explores the centrality of memory to our sense of self. He held the prestigious Economic and Social Research Council Professorial Fellowship at the University of Leeds, where he established the Memory Research Group. He has written extensively on autobiographical memory. He had a highly successful and personally rewarding nine-year SciArt collaboration with Shona Illingworth.

Dr Caterina Albano is a research fellow and curator for Artakt, Central Saint Martins College of Art and Design, University of the Arts London. Albano curates, lectures and publishes in the field of contemporary art, cultural theory, and the cultural history of emotion, and on the theory of curating. She is the author of *Fear and Art* (Reaktion, forthcoming).

Jill Bennett is founding director of the National Institute for Experimental Arts at the University of New South Wales. She has published widely on visual culture, contemporary art and new media. Her latest publication, *Practical Aesthetics*, explores the application of creative thinking and practice to world events. Her previous books include *Empathic Vision* (Stanford UP), a study of art and traumatic events.

Steven Bode is Director of Film and Video Umbrella. Alongside the various projects that the organisation commissions and produces, he has curated a number of large-scale exhibitions for galleries and institutions nationally and internationally. He writes regularly on artists' work with the moving image, and on visual culture, cinema and technology.

CREDITS AND ACKNOWLEDGMENTS

The Watch Man 2007
Shona Illingworth
Funded by Arts Council England.

Video and multi-channel sound installation
Video projected onto a circular screen suspended over
a luminous red floor.
17 minutes duration

Directed, Filmed and Edited by: Shona Illingworth

Sound Engineer: Charlie Dodd

Balnakiel 2009
Shona Illingworth

Co-commissioned by Film and Video Umbrella and
John Hansard Gallery, in association with Wolverhampton
Art Gallery. Funded by The Wellcome Trust with additional
support from The Highland Council and the Danish Embassy.
Supported by Arts Council England.

Video and multi-channel sound installation
Single screen video projection
30 minutes duration

Head of Production: Bevis Bowden

Project Co-ordinator: Nina Ernst

Young Girl: Sophie Anne MacLeod

Voices: Military personnel on live firing training exercises,
and current and former inhabitants of Balnakiel and Durness

Conceived, Directed and Edited by: Shona Illingworth

Director of Photography: Bevis Bowden

Sound Engineer: Charlie Dodd

Shona Illingworth would particularly like to thank Steven Bode
for his support and commitment to the realisation of *Balnakiel*
and this publication. Bevis Bowden for his skill, companionship
and focus on location shooting *Balnakiel*, Nina Ernst, Mike
Jones, Karen Murray, Brada Barassi and all at Film and Video
Umbrella. Ron Henocq and David Allen (CGP projects) for
their early support and for the first showing of *The Watch Man*
at Dilston Grove, London.

Thank you to Stephen Foster, Ros Carter, Adrian Hunt
(John Hansard Gallery); Kate Pryor Williams (Wolverhampton
Art Gallery); Rhonda Corvese; Kate Forde, James Peto,
Lucy Shanahan, Jane Holmes, Ken Arnold, Meroe Candy,
Shonagh Manson, Rosie Tooby (The Wellcome Trust); Brian
Smith (FeONIC plc); Stewart Crosbie (Gerriets Ltd); Graham
Campbell (RBS Screen Machine), David Adger, David Chandler,
Frances Coleman, Andree Cooke, Suzanne Cotter, Chris Darke,
Richard Deal, Catherine Elwes, Judith King, Claudia Losi,
Issie MacPhail, Roger McKinley, Simon Phipps, Doina Popescu,
Mark Segal, Verity Slater, Jeremy Theophilus, Angela Weight,
Jonathan Whitehall, Jamie Wyld and Luciano Zubillaga.

Thank you to the extended communities of Balnakeil Craft
Village and Durness for their generosity and support during
the research and production of *Balnakiel*, and to Sophie Anne
MacLeod for her considerable commitment and energy.
Thank you also to Brian and Nancy Foster, Hugh and Jennifer
Haggerty, and to the Range Staff and military personnel at
Cape Wrath Bombardment Range.

The artist would especially like to thank Martin A. Conway for
his intellectual generosity and for many years of inspirational
dialogue and exchange.

Special thanks to Jill Bennett, Caterina Albano, Jason Franks,
Anson Mackay, to Herman Lelie and Stefania Bonelli for the
pleasure, insight and clarity of thinking that they brought to
making this book, to Charlie and Tish Dodd, Ronnie Lansley,
Ishbel MacDonald, Nicola Philipson, Teri Harris, Maya Jarrett,
Suzy Karhani and Debbie Williams.

And very special thanks to Dave Illingworth, and Lotte Glob
for their trust, support and for living their lives according to
their ideals, to Alina and Sonny Sealy for their patience and
love, to Nickolai Globe, Rhuna Illingworth, Jemma Illingworth,
Anna Bowes and David Bowes, and especially to Mark Sealy,
for his inspired thinking, his encouragement and support.

Shona Illingworth *The Watch Man / Balnakiel*

Published by Film and Video Umbrella

Edited by Steven Bode, Nina Ernst and Shona Illingworth
Designed by Herman Lelie and Stefania Bonelli
Printed by die keure, Belgium

Publication supported by Arts Council England and The Wellcome Trust

Image credits: pp.48-49, gallery installation photograph by Simon Phipps. pp.8, 50, 51, 53, 54, 56, 70, 78-79, 85, 88, 90, 94, 97, 98, 101, 103, 106, photographic documentation of the artist's work by Alan Cook. p.88, memory drawing by Nickolai Globe. pp.104-105, gallery installation photograph by Adrian Hunt. All photographs and images by the artist unless otherwise stated.

Cover image: *Faraid Head*, former site of an early warning radar station and currently the Range Control Tower for Cape Wrath Bombardment Range, seen through heavy weather.

ISBN 978-1-904270-34-8
© 2011, Film and Video Umbrella, the artist and the authors

The Watch Man
14 March – 15 April 2007
Dilston Grove, Southwark Park, London

6 April – 12 May 2007
Interaccess Electronic Media Arts Centre, Toronto,
curated by Rhonda Corvese
presented in conjunction with the Images Festival of Film, Video and New Media

16 December 2008 – 11 January 2009
Wellcome Collection, London

Balnakiel
John Hansard Gallery, Southampton
17 February – 4 April 2009

Wolverhampton Art Gallery
6 February – 1 May 2010

Film and Video Umbrella
8, Vine Yard
London SE1 1QL
t (00 44) 20 7407 7755 e info@fvu.co.uk www.fvu.co.uk

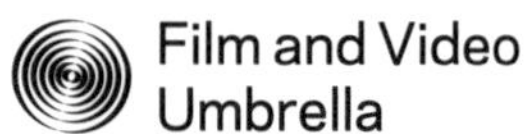
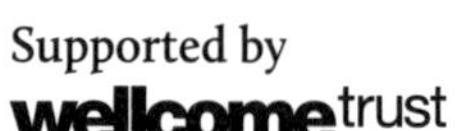
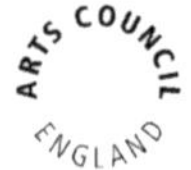